The Poetry Of Robert Browning...

Stopford Augustus Brooke

Nabu Public Domain Reprints:

You are holding a reproduction of an original work published before 1923 that is in the public domain in the United States of America, and possibly other countries. You may freely copy and distribute this work as no entity (individual or corporate) has a copyright on the body of the work. This book may contain prior copyright references, and library stamps (as most of these works were scanned from library copies). These have been scanned and retained as part of the historical artifact.

This book may have occasional imperfections such as missing or blurred pages, poor pictures, errant marks, etc. that were either part of the original artifact, or were introduced by the scanning process. We believe this work is culturally important, and despite the imperfections, have elected to bring it back into print as part of our continuing commitment to the preservation of printed works worldwide. We appreciate your understanding of the imperfections in the preservation process, and hope you enjoy this valuable book.

BY THE SAME AUTHOR
TENNYSON
HIS ART AND RELATION TO MODERN LIFE
By Stopford A. Brooke

"Will make a strong appeal to all lovers of our great laureate."—*Quarterly Review*.

"Comes within a measurable distance of being the perfect study of Tennyson's art."
Pall Mall Gazette.

"Always judicious, well balanced, and eminently suggestive."—*World*.

"Students of Tennyson's works will find here a most profitable guide."—*Liverpool Courier*.

In One Vol., cloth, Demy 8vo, price
SEVEN SHILLINGS AND SIXPENCE.

Pocket Edition, Two Vols., with Portrait Frontispiece to each Vol., Limp Lambskin, Fcap 8vo, price, each vol.,
TWO SHILLINGS AND SIXPENCE NET.

THE POETRY
OF
ROBERT BROWNING

BY

STOPFORD A. BROOKE

AUTHOR OF
"TENNYSON: HIS ART AND RELATION TO MODERN LIFE"

LONDON
ISBISTER AND COMPANY LIMITED
15 & 16 TAVISTOCK STREET COVENT GARDEN
1903

Printed by BALLANTYNE, HANSON & Co.
London & Edinburgh

THE POETRY
OF
ROBERT BROWNING

First Edition, September 1902
Reprinted, October 1902
Reprinted, January 1903.

CONTENTS

CHAP.		PAGE
I.	Browning and Tennyson	1
II.	The Treatment of Nature	57
III.	The Treatment of Nature	90
IV.	Browning's Theory of Human Life—Pauline and Paracelsus	115
V.	The Poet of Art	141
VI.	Sordello	177
VII.	Browning and Sordello	200
VIII.	The Dramas	219
IX.	Poems of the Passion of Love	242
X.	The Passions other than Love	264
XI.	Imaginative Representations	280
XII.	Imaginative Representations—Renaissance	301
XIII.	Womanhood in Browning	323
XIV.	Womanhood in Browning—(The Dramatic Lyrics and Pompilia)	344
XV.	Balaustion	365
XVI.	The Ring and the Book	391
XVII.	Later Poems	414
XVIII.	The Last Poems	431

The publishers are indebted to Messrs. Smith, Elder & Co. on behalf of the owner of the copyright for their permission to make extracts from copyright poems for use in this volume

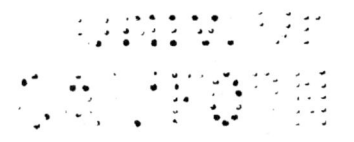

CHAPTER I

BROWNING AND TENNYSON

PARNASSUS, Apollo's mount, has two peaks, and on these, for sixty years, from 1830 to 1890,* two poets sat, till their right to these lofty peaks became unchallenged. Beneath them, during these years, on the lower knolls of the mount of song, many new poets sang; with diverse instruments, on various subjects, and in manifold ways. They had their listeners; the Muses were also their visitants; but none of them ventured seriously to dispute the royal summits where Browning and Tennyson sat, and smiled at one another across the vale between.

Both began together; and the impulses which came to them from the new and excited world which opened its fountains in and about 1832 continued to impel them till the close of their lives. While the poetic world altered around them, while two generations of poets made new schools of poetry, they remained, for the most part, unaffected

---

* I state it roughly. The *Poems of Two Brothers* appeared in 1826, Tennyson's first single volume in 1830, his second in 1833, his last in 1892. Browning's first poem was issued in 1833, his last in 1890. *Paracelsus*, in which his genius clearly disclosed itself, was published in 1835, while Tennyson, seven years later, proved his mastership in the two volumes of 1842.

by these schools. There is nothing of Arnold and Clough, of Swinburne, Rossetti or Morris, or of any of the others, in Browning or Tennyson. There is nothing even of Mrs. Browning in Browning. What changes took place in them were wrought, first, by the natural growth of their own character; secondly, by the natural development of their art-power; and thirdly, by the slow decaying of that power. They were, in comparison with the rest, curiously uninfluenced by the changes of the world around them. The main themes, with which they began, they retained to the end. Their methods, their instruments, their way of feeling into the world of man and of nature, their relation to the doctrines of God and of Man, did not, though on all these matters they held diverse views, alter with the alteration of the world. But this is more true of Browning than of Tennyson. The political and social events of those years touched Tennyson, as we see from *Maud* and the *Princess*, but his way of looking at them was not the way of a contemporary. It might have been predicted from his previous career and work. Then the new movements of Science and Criticism which disturbed Clough and Arnold so deeply, also troubled Tennyson, but not half so seriously. He staggered for a time under the attack on his old conceptions, but he never yielded to it. He was angry with himself for every doubt that beset him, and angry with the Science and Criticism which disturbed the ancient ideas he was determined not to change. Finally, he rested where he had been when he wrote *In Memoriam*, nay more, where he had been when he began to write.

There were no such intervals in Browning's thought. One could scarcely say from his poetry, except in a very few places, that he was aware of the social changes of his time, or of the scientific and critical movement which, while he lived, so profoundly modified both theology and religion.* *Asolando*, in 1890, strikes the same chords, but more feebly, which *Paracelsus* struck in 1835.

But though, in this lofty apartness and self-unity, Browning and Tennyson may fairly be said to be at one, in themselves and in their song they were different. There could scarcely be two characters, two musics, two minds, two methods in art, two imaginations, more distinct and contrasted than those which lodged in these men—and the object of this introduction is to bring out this contrast, with the purpose of placing in a clearer light some of the peculiar elements in the poetry of Browning, and in his position as a poet.

1. Their public fate was singularly different. In 1842 Tennyson, with his two volumes of Collected Poems, made his position. The *Princess*, in 1847, increased his reputation. In 1850, *In Memoriam*

---

* *A Death in the Desert* touches on the doubts which, when it was written, had gathered from historical criticism round the subject-matter of the Gospels, but the prophetic answer of St. John is not critical. It is Browning's personal reply to the critics, and is based on his own religious philosophy. The critical part of the argument is left untouched, and the answer is given from the poet's plane. It is the same when in the *Parleyings with certain People* Furini is made to embody Browning's belief in a personal God in contradistinction with the mere evolutionist. He does not argue the points. He places one doctrine over against the other and bids the reader choose. Moreover, he claims his view as his own alone. He seeks to impose it on no one.

raised him, it was said, above all the poets of his time, and the book was appreciated, read and loved by the greater part of the English-speaking world. The success and popular fame which now followed were well deserved and wisely borne. They have endured and will endure. A host of imitators, who caught his music and his manner, filled the groves and ledges which led up to the peak on which he lived. His side of Parnassus was thronged.

It was quite otherwise with his brother-poet. Only a few clear-eyed persons cared to read *Paracelsus*, which appeared in 1835. *Strafford*, Browning's first drama, had a little more vogue ; it was acted for a while. When *Sordello*, that strange child of genius, was born in 1840, those who tried to read its first pages declared they were incomprehensible. It seems that critics in those days had either less intelligence than we have, or were more impatient and less attentive, for not only *Sordello* but even *In Memoriam* was said to be exceedingly obscure.

Then, from 1841 to 1846, Browning published at intervals a series of varied poems and dramas, under the title of *Bells and Pomegranates*. These, one might imagine, would have grasped the heart of any public which had a care for poetry. Among them were such diverse poems as *Pippa Passes; A Blot in the 'Scutcheon; Saul; The Pied Piper of Hamelin; My Last Duchess; Waring*. I only mention a few (all different in note, subject and manner from one another), in order to mark the variety and range of imaginative power displayed in this wonderful set of little books. The

Bells of poetry's music, hung side by side with the golden Pomegranates of thought, made the fringe of the robe of this high priest of song. Rarely have imagination and intellect, ideal faith and the sense which handles daily life, passion and quietude, the impulse and self-mastery of an artist, the joy of nature and the fates of men, grave tragedy and noble grotesque, been mingled together more fully—bells for the pleasure and fruit for the food of man.

Yet, on the whole, they fell dead on the public. A few, however, loved them, and all the poems were collected in 1849. *In Memoriam* and this Collected Edition of Browning issued almost together; but with how different a fate and fame we see most plainly in the fact that Browning can scarcely be said to have had any imitators. The groves and ledges of his side of Apollo's mountain were empty, save for a few enchanted listeners, who said: "This is our music, and here we build our tent."

As the years went on, these readers increased in number, but even when the volumes entitled *Men and Women* were published in 1855, and the *Dramatis Personæ* in 1864, his followers were but a little company. For all this neglect Browning cared as a bird cares who sings for the love of singing, and who never muses in himself whether the wood is full or not of listeners. Being always a true artist, he could not stop versing and playing; and not one grain of villain envy touched his happy heart when he looked across the valley to Tennyson. He loved his mistress Art, and his love made him always joyful in creating.

At last his time came, but it was not till nearly twenty years after the Collected Poems of 1849 that *The Ring and the Book* astonished the reading public so much by its intellectual *tour de force* that it was felt to be unwise to ignore Browning any longer. His past work was now discovered, read and praised. It was not great success or worldwide fame that he attained, but it was pleasant to him, and those who already loved his poems rejoiced with him. Before he died he was widely read, never so much as Tennyson, but far more than he had ever expected. It had become clear to all the world that he sat on a rival height with Tennyson, above the rest of his fellow-poets.

Their public fate, then, was very different. Tennyson had fifty years of recognition, Browning barely ten. And to us who now know Browning this seems a strange thing. Had he been one of the smaller men, a modern specialist like Arnold or Rossetti, we could better understand it. But Browning's work was not limited to any particular or temporary phase of human nature. He set himself to represent, as far as he could, all types of human nature; and, more audacious still, types taken from many diverse ages, nations and climates. He told us of times and folk as far apart as Caliban and Cleon, as Karshish and Waring, as Balaustion and Fifine, as St. John and Bishop Blougram. The range and the contrasts of his subjects are equally great. And he did this work with a searching analysis, a humorous keenness, a joyous boldness, and an opulent imagination at once penetrative and passionate. When, then, we realise this as we realise it now, we are the more astonished that appreciation of him lingered so long. Why did it not come at first, and why did it come in the end?

The first answer to that question is a general one. During the years between 1860 and 1890, and especially during the latter half of these years, science and criticism were predominant. Their determination to penetrate to the roots of things made a change in the general direction of thought and feeling on the main subjects of life. Analysis became dearer to men than synthesis, reasoning than imagination. Doubtful questions were submitted to intellectual decision alone. The Understanding, to its great surprise, was employed on the investigation of the emotions, and even the artists were drawn in this direction. They, too, began to dissect the human heart. Poets and writers of fiction, students of human nature, were keenly interested, not so much in our thoughts and feelings as in exposing how and why we thought or felt in this or that fashion. In such analysis they seemed to touch the primal sources of life. They desired to dig about the tree of humanity and to describe all the windings of its roots and fibres—not much caring whether they withered the tree for a time—rather than to describe and sing its outward beauty, its varied foliage, and its ruddy fruit. And this liking to investigate the hidden inwardness of motives—which many persons, weary of self-contemplation, wisely prefer to keep hidden—ran through the practice of all the arts. They became, on the whole, less emotional, more intellectual. The close marriage between passion and thought, without whose cohabitation no work of genius is born in the arts, was dissolved; and the intellect of the artist often worked by itself, and his emotion by itself. Some of the parthenogenetic children of these divorced powers were curious products, freaks, even monsters of literature, in which the dry, cynical, or vivisecting temper had full play, or the naked, lustful, or cruel exposure of the emotions in ugly, unnatural, or morbid forms was glorified. They made an impudent claim to the name of Art, but they were nothing better than disagreeable Science. But this was an extreme deviation of the tendency. The main line it took was not so detestable. It was towards the ruthless analysis of life, and of the soul of man; a part, in fact, of the general scientific movement. The outward forms of things charmed writers less than the motives which led to their making. The description of the tangled emotions and thoughts of the inner life, before any action took place, was more pleasurable to the writer, and easier, than any description of their final result in act. This was borne to a wearisome extreme in fiction, and in these last days a comfortable reaction from it has arisen. In poetry it did not last so long. Morris carried us out of it. But long before it began, long before its entrance into the arts, Browning, who on another side of his genius delighted in the representation of action, anticipated in poetry, and from the beginning of his career, twenty, even thirty years before it became pronounced in literature, this tendency to the intellectual analysis of human nature. When he began it, no one cared for it; and *Paracelsus*, *Sordello* and the soul-dissecting poems in *Bells and*

Pomegranates fell on an unheeding world. But Browning did not heed the unheeding of the world. He had the courage of his aims in art, and while he frequently shaped in his verse the vigorous movement of life, even to its moments of fierce activity, he went on quietly, amid the silence of the world, to paint also the slowly interwoven and complex pattern of the inner life of men. And then, when the tendency of which I speak had collared the interest of society, society, with great and ludicrous amazement, found him out. "Here is a man," it said, "who has been doing in poetry for the last thirty years the very thing of which we are so fond, and who is doing it with delightful and varied subtlety. We will read him now." So Browning, anticipating by thirty years the drift of the world, was not read at first; but, afterwards, the world having reached him, he became a favoured poet.

However, fond as he was of metaphysical analysis, he did not fall into the extremes into which other writers carried it. *Paracelsus* is, indeed, entirely concerned with the inner history of a soul, but *Sordello* combines with a similar history a tale of political and warlike action in which men and women, like Salinguerra and Palma, who live in outward work rather than in inward thought, are described; while in poems like *Pippa Passes* and some of the Dramas, emotion and thought, intimately interwoven, are seen blazing, as it were, into a lightning of swift deeds. Nor are other poems wanting, in which, not long analysis, but short passion, fiery outbursts of thought, taking immediate form, are represented with astonishing intensity.

2. This second remarkable power of his touches the transition which has begun to carry us, in the last few years, from the subjective to the objective in art. The time came, and quite lately, when art, weary of intellectual and minute investigation, turned to realise, not the long inward life of a soul with all its motives laid bare, but sudden moments of human passion, swift and unoutlined impressions on the senses, the moody aspects of things, flared-out concentrations of critical hours of thought and feeling which years perhaps of action and emotion had brought to the point of eruption. Impressionism was born in painting, poetry, sculpture, and music.

It was curious that, when we sought for a master who had done this in the art of poetry, we found that Browning—who had in long poems done the very opposite of impressionism—had also, in a number of short poems, anticipated impressionist art by nearly forty years. *Porphyria's Lover*, many a scene in *Sordello, My Last Duchess, The Laboratory, Home Thoughts from Abroad,* are only a few out of many. It is pleasant to think of the ultimate appearance of Waring, flashed out for a moment on the sea, only to disappear. In method, swiftness and colour, but done in verse, it is an impressionist picture, as vivid in transient scenery as in colour. He did the same sort of work in poems of nature, of human life, of moments of passion, of states of the soul. That is another reason why he was not read at first, and why he is read now. He was impressionist long before Impressionism arrived. When it arrived he was found out. And he stood alone, for Tennyson is never impressionist, and never could have been. Neither was Swinburne nor Arnold, Morris nor Rossetti.

3. Again, in the leisured upper ranges of thought and emotion, and in the extraordinary complexity of human life which arose, first, out of the more intimate admixture of all classes in our society; and secondly, out of the wider and more varied world-life which increased means of travel and knowledge afforded to men, Tennyson's smooth, melodious, simple development of art-subjects did not represent the clashing complexity of human life, whether inward in the passions, the intellect or the soul, or in the active movement of the world. And the other poets were equally incapable of representing this complexity of which the world became clearly conscious. Arnold tried to express its beginnings, and failed, because he tried to explain instead of representing them. He wrote about them; he did not write them down. Nor did he really belong to this novel, quick, variegated, involved world which was so pleased with its own excitement and entanglement. He was the child of a world which was then passing away, out of which life was fading, which was tired like Obermann, and sought peace in reflective solitudes. Sometimes he felt, as in *The New Age*, the pleasure of the coming life of the world, but he was too weary to share in it, and he claimed quiet. But chiefly he saw the disturbance, the unregulated life; and, unable to realise that it was the trouble and wildness of youth, he mistook it for the trouble of decay. He painted it as such. But it was really young, and out of it broke all kinds of experiments in social,

religious, philosophical and political thought, such as we have seen and read of for the last thirty years. Art joined in the experiments of this youthful time. It opened a new fountain and sent forth from it another stream, to echo this attempting, clanging and complicated society; and this stream did not flow like a full river, making large or sweet melody, but like a mountain torrent thick with rocks, the thunderous whirlpools of whose surface were white with foam. Changing and sensational scenery haunted its lower banks where it became dangerously navigable. Strange boats, filled with outlandish figures, who played on unknown instruments, and sang of deeds and passions remote from common life, sailed by on its stormy waters. Few were the concords, many the discords, and some of the discords were never resolved. But in one case at least—in the case of Browning's poetry, and in very many cases in the art of music—out of the discords emerged at last a full melody of steady thought and controlled emotion as (to recapture my original metaphor) the rude, interrupted music of the mountain stream reaches full and concordant harmony when it flows in peace through the meadows of the valley.

These complex and intercleaving conditions of thought and passion into which society had grown Browning represented from almost the beginning of his work. When society became conscious of them—there it found him. And, amazed, it said, "Here is a man who forty years ago lived in the midst of our present life and wrote about it." They saw the wild, loud complexity of their world expressed in his verse; and yet were dimly conscious, to their consolation, that he was aware of a central peace where the noise was quieted and the tangle unravelled.

For Browning not only represented this discordant, varied hurly-burly of life, but also, out of all the discords which he described, and which, when he chose, even his rhythms and word-arrangements realised in sound, he drew a concordant melody at last, and gave to a world, troubled with itself, the hope of a great concent into which all the discords ran, and where they were resolved. And this hope for the individual and the race was one of the deepest elements in Browning's religion. It was also the hope of Tennyson, but Tennyson was often uncertain of it, and bewailed the uncertainty. Browning was certain of his hope, and for the most part resolved his discords. Even when he did not resolve them, he firmly believed that they would be resolved. This, his essential difference from the other poets of the last fifty years, marks not only his apartness from the self-ignorance of English society, and the self-sceptical scepticism which arises from that self-ignorance, but also how steadily assured was the foundation of his spiritual life. In the midst of the shifting storms of doubt and trouble, of mockery, contradiction, and assertion on religious matters, he stood unremoved. Whatever men may think of his faith and his certainties, they reveal the strength of his character, the enduring courage of his soul, and the inspiring joyousness that, born of his strength, characterised him to the last poem he wrote. While the other poets were tossing on the sea of unresolved Question, he rested, musing and creating, on a green island whose rocks were rooted on the ocean-bed, and wondered, with the smiling tolerance of his life-long charity, how his fellows were of so little faith, and why the sceptics made so much noise. He would have reversed the Psalmist's cry. He would have said, "Thou art not cast down, O my soul; thou art not disquieted within me. Thou hast hoped in God, who is the light of thy countenance, and thy God."

At first the world, enamoured of its own complex discords, and pleased, like boys in the street, with the alarms it made, only cared for that part of Browning which represented the tangle and the clash, and ignored his final melody. But of late it has begun, tired of the restless clatter of intellectual atoms, to desire to hear, if possible, the majestic harmonies in which the discords are resolved. And at this point many at present and many more in the future will find their poetic and religious satisfaction in Browning. At the very end, then, of the nineteenth century, in a movement which had only just begun, men said to themselves, "Browning felt beforehand what we are beginning to hope for, and wrote of it fifty, even sixty years ago. No one cared then for him, but we care now."

Again, though he thus anticipated the movements of the world, he did not, like the other poets, change his view about Nature, Man and God. He conceived that view when he was young, and he did not alter it. Hence, he did not follow or reflect from year to year the opinions of his time on these great matters. When *Paracelsus* was published in 1835 Browning had fully thought out, and in that poem fully expressed, his theory of God's relation to man, and of man's relation to the universe around him, to his fellow men, and to the world beyond. It was a theory which was original, if any theory can be so called. At least, its form, as he expressed it, was clearly original. Roughly sketched in *Pauline*, fully rounded in *Paracelsus*, it held and satisfied his mind till the day of his death. But Tennyson had no clear theory about Man or Nature or God when he began, nor was he afterwards, save perhaps when he wrote the last stanzas of *In Memoriam*, a fully satisfied citizen of the city that has foundations. He believed in that city, but he could not always live in it. He grew into this or that opinion about the relations of God and man, and then grew out of it. He held now this, now that view of nature, and of man in contact with nature. There was always battle in his soul; although he won his battle in the end, he had sixty years of war. Browning was at peace, firm-fixed. It is true the inward struggle of Tennyson enabled him to image from year to year his own time better than Browning did. It is true this struggle enabled him to have great variety in his art-work when it was engaged with the emotions which belong to doubt and faith; but it also made him unable to give to his readers that sense of things which cannot be shaken, of faith in God and in humanity wholly independent, in its depths, of storms on the surface of this mortal life, which was one of Browning's noblest legacies to that wavering, faithless, pessimistic, analysis-tormented world through which we have fought our way, and out of which we are emerging.

4. The danger in art, or for an artist, of so settled a theory is that in expression it tends to monotony; and sometimes, when we find almost every poem of Browning's running up into his theory, we arrive at the borders of the Land of Weary-men. But he seems to have been aware of this danger, and to have conquered it. He meets it by the immense variety of the subjects he chooses, and of the scenery in which he places them. I do not think he ever repeats any one of his examples, though he always repeats his theory. And the pleasant result is that we can either ignore the theory if we like, or rejoice over its universal application, or, beyond it altogether, be charmed and excited by the fresh examples alone. And they are likely to charm, at least by variety, for they are taken from all ages of history; from as many diverse phases of human act, character and passion as there are poems which concern them; from many periods of the arts; from most of the countries of Europe, from France, Germany, Spain, Italy, (rarely from England,) with their specialised types of race and of landscape; and from almost every class of educated modern society. Moreover, he had a guard within his own nature against the danger of this monotony. It was the youthful freshness with which, even in advanced age, he followed his rapid impulses to art-creation. No one was a greater child than he in the quickness with which he received a sudden call to poetry from passing events or scenes, and in the eagerness with which he seized them as subjects. He took the big subjects now and then which the world expects to be taken, and treated them with

elaborate thought and steadfast feeling, but he was more often like the girl in his half-dramatic poem, whom the transient occurrences and sights of the day touched into song. He picked up his subjects as a man culls flowers in a mountain walk, moved by an ever-recurring joy and fancy in them —a book on a stall, a bust in an Italian garden, a face seen at the opera, the market chatter of a Tuscan town, a story told by the roadside in Brittany, a picture in some Accademia—so that, though the ground-thought might incur the danger of dulness through repetition, the joy of the artist so filled the illustration, and his freshness of invention was so delighted with itself, that even to the reader the theory seemed like a new star.

In this way he kept the use of having an unwavering basis of thought which gave unity to his sixty years of work, and yet avoided the peril of monotony. An immense diversity animated his unity, filled it with gaiety and brightness, and secured impulsiveness of fancy. This also differentiates him from Tennyson, who often wanted freshness; who very rarely wrote on a sudden impulse, but after long and careful thought; to whose seriousness we cannot always climb with pleasure; who played so little with the world. These defects in Tennyson had the excellences which belong to them in art, just as these excellences in Browning had, in art, their own defects. We should be grateful for the excellences, and not trouble ourselves about the defects. However, neither the excellences nor the defects concern us in the present discussion. It is the contrast between the two men on which we dwell.

5. The next point of contrast, which will further illustrate why Browning was not read of old but is now read, has to do with historical criticism. There arose, some time ago, as part of the scientific and critical movement of the last forty years, a desire to know and record accurately the early life of peoples, pastoral, agricultural and in towns, and the beginning of their arts and knowledges; and not only their origins, but the whole history of their development. A close, critical investigation was made of the origins of each people; accurate knowledge, derived from contemporary documents, of their life, laws, customs and language was attained; the facts of their history were separated from their mythical and legendary elements; the dress, the looks of men, the climate of the time, the physical aspects of their country—all the skeleton of things was fitted together, bone to bone. And for a good while this merely critical school held the field. It did admirable and necessary work.

But when it was done, art claimed its place in this work. The desire sprang up among historians to conceive all this history in the imagination, to shape vividly its scenery, to animate and individualise its men and women, to paint the life of the human soul in it, to clothe it in flesh and blood, to make its feet move and its eyes flash—but to do all these things within the limits of the accurate knowledge which historical criticism had defined. "Let us saturate ourselves," said the historians, "with clear knowledge of the needful facts, and then, without violation of our knowledge, imagine the human life, the landscape, the thinking and feeling of a primæval man, of his early religion, of his passions; of Athens when the Persian came, of Rome when the Republic was passing into the Empire, of a Provincial in Spain or Britain, of a German town in the woods by the river. Let us see in imagination as well as in knowledge an English settlement on the Welsh border, an Italian mediæval town when its art was being born, a Jewish village when Christ wandered into its streets, a musician or a painter's life at a time when Greek art was decaying, or when a new impulse like the Renaissance or the French Revolution came upon the world." When that effort of the historians had established itself, and we have seen it from blossoming to fruitage, people began to wonder that no poet had ever tried to do this kind of work. It seemed eminently fitted for a poet's hand, full of subjects alluring to the penetrative imagination. It needed, of course, some scholarship, for it demanded accuracy in its grasp of the main ideas of the time to be represented; but that being given, immense opportunities remained for pictures of human life, full of colour, thought and passions; for subtle and brilliant representations of the eternal desires and thinkings of human nature as they were governed by the special circumstances of the time in which the poem was placed; and for the concentration into a single poem, gathered round one person, of the ideas whose new arrival formed a crisis in the history of art.

Men looked for this in Tennyson and did not find it. His Greek and mediæval poems were modernised. Their imaginative work was uncritical.

But when the historians and the critics of art and of religious movements happened at last to look into Browning, they discovered, to their delight and wonder, that he had been doing, with a curious knowledge, this kind of work for many years. He had anticipated the results of that movement of the imagination in historical work which did not exist when he began to write; he had worked that mine, and the discovery of this made another host of people readers of his poetry.

We need scarcely give examples of this. *Sordello*, in 1840 (long before the effort of which we speak began), was such a poem—the history of a specialised soul, with all its scenery and history vividly mediæval. Think of the *Spanish Cloister, The Laboratory, A Grammarian's Funeral,* the *Bishop orders his Tomb at Saint Praxed's Church*, poems, each of which paints an historical period or a vivid piece of its life. Think of *The Ring and the Book*, with all the world of Rome painted to the life, and all the soul of the time!

The same kind of work was done for phases and periods of the arts from Greek times to the Renaissance, I may even say, from the Renaissance to the present day. *Balaustion's Prologue* concentrates the passage of dramatic poetry from Sophocles to Euripides. *Aristophanes' Apology* realises the wild licence in which art and freedom died in Athens—their greatness in their ruin—and the passionate sorrow of those who loved what had been so beautiful. *Cleon* takes us into a later time when men had ceased to be original, and life and art had become darkened by the pain of the soul. We pass on to two different periods of the Renaissance in *Fra Lippo Lippi* and in *Andrea del Sarto*, and are carried further through the centuries of art when we read *Abt Vogler* and *A Toccata of Galuppi's*. Each of these poems is a concentrated, accurate piece of art-history, with the addition to it of the human soul.

Periods and phases of religious history are equally realised. *Caliban upon Setebos* begins the record— that philosophic savage who makes his God out of himself. Then follows study after study, from *A Death in the Desert* to *Bishop Blougram's Apology*. Some carry us from early Christianity through the mediæval faith; others lead us through the Paganism of the Renaissance and strange shows of Judaism to Browning's own conception of religion in the present day contrasted with those of the popular religion in *Christmas-Day and Easter-Day*.

Never, in poetry, was the desire of the historical critic for accuracy of fact and portraiture, combined with vivid presentation of life, so fully satisfied. No wonder Browning was not read of old; but it is no wonder, when the new History was made, when he was once found out, that he passed from a few to a multitude of readers.

6. Another contrast appears at the very beginning of their career. Tennyson, in his two earliest books in 1830 and 1833, though clearly original in some poems, had clinging round his singing robes some of the rags of the past. He wrote partly in the weak and sentimental strain of the poets between 1822 and 1832. Browning, on the contrary, sprang at once into an original poetic life of his own. *Pauline* was unfinished, irregular in form, harsh, abrupt, and overloaded, but it was

also entirely fresh and distinct. The influence of Shelley echoes in it, but much more in admiration than in imitation of him. The matter, the spirit of the poem were his own, and the verse-movement was his own. Had Browning been an imitator, the first thing he would have imitated would have been the sweet and rippling movement of Shelley's melodies. But the form of his verse, such as it was, arose directly out of his own nature and was as original as his matter. Tennyson grew into originality, Browning leaped into it; born, not of other poets, but of his own will. He begat himself. It had been better for his art, so far as technical excellence is concerned, had he studied and imitated at first the previous masters. But he did not; and his dominant individuality, whole in itself and creating its own powers, separates him at the very beginning from Tennyson.

7. Tennyson became fully original, but he always admitted, and sometimes encouraged in himself, a certain vein of conventionality. He kept the opinions of the past in the matter of caste. He clung to certain political and social maxims, and could not see beyond them. He sometimes expressed them as if they were freshly discovered truths or direct emanations from the Deity of England. He belonged to a certain type of English society, and he rarely got out of it in his poetry. He inhabited a certain Park of morals, and he had no sympathy with any self-ethical life beyond its palings. What had been, what was proper and recognised, somewhat enslaved in Tennyson that distinctiveness and freedom of personality which is of so much importance in poetry, and

which, had it had more liberty in Tennyson, would have made him a still greater poet than he was.

Browning, on the other hand—much more a person in society than Tennyson, much more a man of the world, and obeying in society its social conventions more than Tennyson—never allowed this to touch his poems. As the artist, he was quite free from the opinions, maxims, and class conventions of the past or the present. His poetry belongs to no special type of society, to no special nationality, to no separate creed or church, to no settled standard of social morality. What his own thought and emotion urged him to say, he said with an absolute carelessness of what the world would say. And in this freedom he preceded and prophesied the reaction of the last years of the nineteenth century against the tyranny of maxims and conventions in society, in morals, and in religion. That reaction has in many ways been carried beyond the proper limits of what is just and beautiful. But these excesses had to be, and the world is beginning to avoid them. What remains is the blessing of life set free, not altogether from the use of conventions, but from their tyranny and oppression, and lifted to a higher level, where the test of what is right and fitting in act, and just in thought, is not the opinion of society, but that Law of Love which gives us full liberty to develop our own nature and lead our own life in the way we think best independent of all conventions, provided we do not injure the life of others, or violate any of the great moral and spiritual truths by obedience to which the progress of mankind is promoted and secured. Into that high and free region of thought and action Browning brought us long ago. Tennyson did not, save at intervals when the poet over-rode the man. This differentiates the men. But it also tells us why Browning was not read fifty years ago, when social conventions were tyrannous and respectability a despot, and why he has been read for the last fifteen years and is read now.

8. There is another contrast between these poets. It is quite clear that Tennyson was a distinctively English poet and a patriotic poet; at times too much of a patriot to judge tolerantly, or to write fairly, about other countries. He had, at least, a touch of national contempts, even of national hatreds. His position towards France was much that of the British sailor of Nelson's time. His position towards Ireland was that of the bishop, who has been a schoolmaster, to the naughty curate who has a will of his own. His position towards Scotland was that of one who was aware that it had a geographical existence, and that a regiment in the English army which had a genius for fighting was drawn from its Highlands. He condescends to write a poem at Edinburgh, but then Edinburgh was of English origin and name. Even with that help he cannot be patient of the place. The poem is a recollection of an Italian journey, and he forgets in memories of the South—though surely Edinburgh might have awakened some romantic associations—

> the clouded Forth,
> The gloom which saddens Heaven and Earth,
> The bitter East, the misty summer
> And gray metropolis of the North.

Edinburgh is English in origin, but Tennyson did not feel England beyond the Border. There the

Celt intruded, and he looked askance upon the Celt. The Celtic spirit smiled, and took its vengeance on him in its own way. It imposed on him, as his chief subject, a Celtic tale and a Celtic hero; and though he did his best to de-celticise the story, the vengeance lasts, for the more he did this the more he injured his work. However, being always a noble artist, he made a good fight for his insularity, and the expression of it harmonised with the pride of England in herself, alike with that which is just and noble in it, and with that which is neither the one nor the other.

Then, too, his scenery (with some exceptions, and those invented) was of his own land, and chiefly of the places where he lived. It was quite excellent, but it was limited. But, within the limit of England, it was steeped in the love of England; and so sweet and full is this love, and so lovely are its results in song, that every Englishman has, for this reason if for no other, a deep and just affection for Tennyson. Nevertheless, in that point also his poetry was insular. A fault in the poet, not in the poetry. Perhaps, from this passionate concentration, the poetry was all the lovelier.

Again, when Tennyson took a great gest of war as his subject, he took it exclusively from the history of his own land. No one would know from his writings that high deeds of sacrifice in battle had been done by other nations. He knew of them, but he did not care to write about them. Nor can we trace in his work any care for national struggles or national life beyond this island—except in a few sonnets and short pieces concerning Poland and Montenegro—an isolation of interests which cannot be imputed to any other great poet of the first part of the nineteenth century, excepting Keats, who had no British or foreign interests. Keats had no country save the country of Beauty.

At all these points Browning differed from Tennyson. He never displayed a special patriotism. On the contrary, he is more Italian than English, and he is more quick to see and sympathise with the national characteristics of Spain or France or Germany, than he is with those of England. No insular feeling prevented him from being just to foreigners, or from having a keen pleasure in writing about them. *Strafford* is the only play he wrote on an English subject, and it is rather a study of a character which might find its place in any aristocracy than of an English character. Even Pym and Hampden fail to be truly English, and it would have been difficult for any one but Browning to take their eminent English elements out of them. *Paracelsus* and *Sordello* belong to Germany and Italy, and there are scarcely three poems in the whole of the seven numbers of the *Bells and Pomegranates* which even refer to England. Italy is there, and chiefly Italy. In *De Gustibus* he contrasts himself with his friend who loves England:

> Your ghost will walk, you lover of trees,
>   (If our loves remain)
>   In an English lane
> By a cornfield-side a-flutter with poppies.
>   *   *   *   *
> What I love best in all the world
> Is a castle, precipice-encurled,
> In a gash of the wind-grieved Apennine.

"Look for me, old fellow of mine, if I get out of the

grave, in a seaside house in South Italy," and he describes the place and folk he loves, and ends:

> Open my heart and you will see
> Graved inside of it, "Italy."
> Such lovers old are I and she:
> So it always was, so shall ever be!

It is a poem written out of his very heart.

And then, the scenery? It is not of our country at all. It is of many lands, but, above all, it is vividly Italian. There is no more minute and subtly-felt description of the scenery of a piece of village country between the mountains and the sea, with all its life, than in the poem called *The Englishman in Italy*. The very title is an outline of Browning's position in this matter. We find this English poet in France, in Syria, in Greece, in Spain, but not in England. We find Rome, Florence, Venice, Mantua, Verona, and forgotten towns among the Apennines painted with happy love in verse, but not an English town nor an English village. The flowers, the hills, the ways of the streams, the talk of the woods, the doings of the sea and the clouds in tempest and in peace, the aspects of the sky at noon, at sunrise and sunset, are all foreign, not English. The one little poem which is of English landscape is written by him in Italy (in a momentary weariness with his daily adoration), and under a green impulse. Delightful as it is, he would not have remained faithful to it for a day. Every one knows it, but that we may realise how quick he was to remember and to touch a corner of early Spring in England, on a soft and windy day—for all the blossoms are scattered—I quote it here. It is well to read his sole contribution (except in *Pauline* and a few scattered illustrations) to the scenery of his own country:

> Oh, to be in England
> Now that April's there,
> And whoever wakes in England
> Sees, some morning, unaware,
> That the lowest boughs and the brushwood sheaf
> Round the elm-tree bole are in tiny leaf,
> While the chaffinch sings on the orchard bough
> In England—now!
>
> And after April, when May follows,
> And the whitethroat builds, and all the swallows!
> Hark! where my blossomed pear-tree in the hedge
> Leans to the field and scatters on the clover
> Blossoms and dewdrops—at the bent spray's edge—
> That's the wise thrush; he sings each song twice over,
> Lest you should think he never could recapture
> The first fine careless rapture!
> And though the fields look rough with hoary dew,
> All will be gay, when noontide wakes anew
> The buttercups, the little children's dower;
> —Far brighter than this gaudy melon-flower!

So it runs; but it is only a momentary memory; and he knew, when he had done it, and to his great comfort, that he was far away from England. But when Tennyson writes of Italy—as, for instance, in *Mariana in the South*—how apart he is! How great is his joy when he gets back to England!

Then, again, when Browning was touched by the impulse to write about a great deed in war, he does not choose, like Tennyson, English subjects. The *Cavalier Tunes* have no importance as patriot songs. They are mere experiments. The poem, *How They brought the Good News from Ghent to Aix*, has twice their vigour. His most intense war-incident is taken from the history of the French wars under Napoleon. The most ringing and swiftest poem of personal dash and daring—and at sea, as if he was tired of England's mistress-ship of the waves—a poem one may set side by side with the fight of *The Revenge*, is *Hervé Riel*. It is a tale of a Breton sailor saving the French fleet from the English, with the sailor's mockery of England embedded in it; and Browning sent the hundred pounds he got for it to the French, after the siege of Paris.

It was not that he did not honour his country, but that, as an artist, he loved more the foreign lands; and that in his deepest life he belonged less to England than to the world of man. The great deeds of England did not prevent him from feeling, with as much keenness as Tennyson felt those of England, the great deeds of France and Italy. National self-sacrifice in critical hours, splendid courage in love and war, belonged, he thought, to all peoples. Perhaps he felt, with Tennyson's insularity dominating his ears, that it was as well to put the other side. I think he might have done a little more for England. There is only one poem, out of all his huge production, which recognises the great deeds of our Empire in war; and this did not come of a life-long feeling, such as he had for Italy, but from a sudden impulse which arose in him, as sailing by, he saw Trafalgar and Gibraltar, glorified and incarnadined by a battle-sunset:

> Nobly, nobly Cape Saint Vincent to the North-west died away;
> Sunset ran, one glorious blood-red, reeking into Cadiz Bay;
> Bluish 'mid the burning water, full in face Trafalgar lay;
> In the dimmest North-east distance dawned Gibraltar grand and gray;

> "Here and here did England help me: how can I help England?"—say.
> Whoso turns as I, this evening, turn to God to praise and pray,
> While Jove's planet rises yonder, silent over Africa.

It is a little thing, and when it leaves the sunset it is poor. And there is twice the fervour of its sunset in the description of the sunrise at Asolo in *Pippa Passes*.

Again, there is scarcely a trace in his work of any vital interest in the changes of thought and feeling in England during the sixty years of his life, such as appear everywhere in Tennyson. No one would know from his poetry (at least until the very end of his life, when he wrote *Francis Furini*) that the science of life and its origins had been revolutionised in the midst of his career, or, save in *A Death in the Desert*, that the whole aspect of theology had been altered, or that the democratic movement had taken so many new forms. He showed to these English struggles neither attraction nor repulsion. They scarcely existed for him—transient elements of the world, merely national, not universal. Nor did the literature or art of his own country engage him half so much as the literature and art of Italy. He loved both. Few were better acquainted with English poetry, or reverenced it more; but he loved it, not because it was English, but of that world of imagination which has no special country. He cared also for English art, but he gave all his personal love to the art of Italy. Nor does he write, as Tennyson loved to do, of the daily life of the English farmer, squire, miller and sailor, and of English sweethearting, nor of the English park and brook and village-green and their indwellers, but of the work-girl at Asolo, and the Spanish monk in his garden, and the Arab riding through the desert, and of the Duchess and her servant flying through the mountains of Moldavia, and of the poor painters at Fano and Florence, and of the threadbare poet at Valladolid, and of the peasant-girl who fed the Tuscan outlaw, and of the poor grammarian who died somewhere in Germany (as I think Browning meant it), and of the Jews at Rome, and of the girl at Pornic with the gold hair and the peasant's hand, and of a hundred others, none of whom are English. All his common life, all his love-making, sorrow and joy among the poor, are outside this country, with perhaps two exceptions; and neither of these has the English note which sounds so soft and clear in Tennyson. This is curious enough, and it is probably one of the reasons why English people for a long time would have so little to do with him. All the same, he was himself woven of England even more than of Italy. The English elements in his character and work are more than the Italian. His intellect was English, and had the English faults as well as the English excellences. His optimism was English; his steadfast fighting quality, his unyielding energy, his directness, his desire to get to the root of things, were English. His religion was the excellent English compromise or rather balance of dogma, practice and spirituality which laymen make for their own life. His bold sense of personal freedom was English. His constancy to his theories, whether of faith or art, was English; his roughness of form was positively early Teutonic.

Then his wit, his *esprit*,* his capacity for induing the skin and the soul of other persons at remote times of history; his amazing inventiveness and the ease of it, at which point he beats Tennyson out of the field; his play, so high fantastical, with his subjects, and the way in which the pleasure he took in this play overmastered his literary self-control; his fantastic games with metre and with rhyme, his want of reverence for the rules of his art; his general lawlessness, belong to one side, but to one one side only, of the Celtic nature. But the ardour of the man, the pathos of his passion and the passion of his pathos, his impulse towards the infinite and the constant rush he made into its indefinite realms; the special set of his imagination towards the fulfilment of perfection in Love; his vision of Nature as in colour, rather than in light and shade; his love of beauty and the kind of beauty that he loved; his extraordinary delight in all kinds of art as the passionate shaping of part of the unapproachable Beauty—these were all old Italian.

---

* Much has been said of the humour of Browning. But it is rather wit than humour which we perceive. The gentle pathos which belongs to humour, the pitiful turn of the humourist upon himself, his smile at his own follies and those of mankind, the half light, like that of evening, in which humour dwells, are wanting in Browning. It is true he has the charity of humour, though not its pathetic power. Pity for the follies and sins of men does fill Browning's poetry. But, all the same, he is too keen, too brilliant, too fierce at times for a humourist. The light in which we see the foolish, fantastic, amusing or contemptible things of life is too bright for humour. He is a Wit—with charity—not a humourist. As for Tennyson, save in his Lincolnshire poems and *Will Waterproof's Soliloquy*, he was strangely devoid either of humour or of wit.

Then I do not know whether Browning had any Jewish blood in his body by descent, but he certainly had Jewish elements in his intellect, spirit and character. His sense of an ever-victorious Righteousness at the centre of the universe, whom one might always trust and be untroubled, was Jewish, but he carried it forward with the New Testament and made the Righteousness identical with absolute Love. Yet, even in this, the Old Testament elements were more plainly seen than is usual among Christians. The appearance of Christ as all-conquering love in *Easter-Day* and the scenery which surrounds him are such as Ezekiel might have conceived and written. Then his intellectual subtlety, the metaphysical minuteness of his arguments, his fondness for parenthesis, the way in which he pursued the absolute while he loaded it with a host of relatives, and conceived the universal through a multitude of particulars, the love he had for remote and unexpected analogies, the craft with which his intellect persuaded him that he could insert into his poems thoughts, illustrations, legends, and twisted knots of reasoning which a fine artistic sense would have omitted, were all as Jewish as the Talmud. There was also a Jewish quality in his natural description, in the way he invented diverse phrases to express different aspects of the same phenomenon, a thing for which the Jews were famous; and in the way in which he peopled what he described with animal life of all kinds, another remarkable habit of the Jewish poets. Moreover, his pleasure in intense colour, in splashes and blots of scarlet and crimson and deep blue and glowing green; in precious stones for the sake of their colour—sapphire, ruby, emerald, chrysolite, pearl, onyx, chalcedony (he does not care for the diamond); in the flame of gold, in the crimson of blood, is Jewish. So also is his love of music, of music especially as bringing us nearest to what is ineffable in God, of music with human aspiration in its heart and sounding in its phrases. It was this Jewish element in Browning, in all its many forms, which caused him to feel with and to write so much about the Jews in his poetry. The two poems in which he most fully enshrines his view of human life, as it may be in the thought of God and as it ought to be conceived by us, are both in the mouth of Jews, of *Rabbi Ben Ezra* and *Jochanan Hakkadosh*. In *Filippo Baldinucci* the Jew has the best of the battle; his courtesy, intelligence and physical power are contrasted with the coarseness, feeble brains and body of the Christians. In *Holy-Cross Day*, the Jew, forced to listen to a Christian sermon, begins with coarse and angry mockery, but passes into solemn thought and dignified phrase. No English poet, save perhaps Shakespeare, whose exquisite sympathy could not leave even Shylock unpitied, has spoken of the Jew with compassion, knowledge and admiration, till Browning wrote of him. The Jew lay deep in Browning. He was a complex creature; and who would understand or rather feel him rightly, must be able to feel something of the nature of all these races in himself. But Tennyson was not complex. He was English and only English.

But to return from this digression. Browning does not stand alone among the poets in the apartness from his own land of which I have written. Byron is partly with him. Where Byron differs from him is, first, in this—that Byron had no poetic love for any special country as Browning had for Italy; and, secondly, that his country was, alas, himself, until at the end, sick of his self-patriotism, he gave himself to Greece. Keats, on the other hand, had no country except, as I have said, the country of Loveliness. Wordsworth, Coleridge and Shelley were not exclusively English. Shelley belonged partly to Italy, but chiefly to that future of mankind in which separate nationalities and divided patriotisms are absorbed. Wordsworth and Coleridge, in their early days, were patriots of humanity; they actually for a time abjured their country. Even in his later days Wordsworth's sympathies reach far beyond England. But none of these were so distinctively English as Tennyson, and none of them were so outside of England as Browning. Interesting as it is, the *completeness* of this isolation from England was a misfortune, not a strength, in his poetry.

There is another thing to say in this connection. The expansion of the interests of the English poets beyond England was due in Wordsworth, Coleridge, Shelley, and partly in Byron, to the great tidal-wave of feeling for man as man, which, rising long before the French Revolution, was lifted into twice its height and dashed on the shore of the world with overwhelming volume, by the earthquake in France of 1789. Special national sentiments were drowned in its waters. Patriotism was the duty of man, not to any one nation but to the whole of humanity, conceived of as the only nation.

In 1832 there was little left of that influence in England among the educated classes, and Tennyson's insular patriotism represented their feeling for many years, and partly represents it now. But the ideas of the Revolution were at the same time taking a wiser and more practical form among the English democracy than they even had at their first outburst in France, and this emerged, on one side of it, in the idea of internationalism. It grew among the propertied classes from the greater facilities of travel, from the wide extension of commercial, and especially of literary, intercommunication. Literature, even more than commerce, diminishes the oppositions and increases the amalgamation of nations. On her lofty plane nations breathe an air in which their quarrels die. The same idea grew up of itself among the working classes, not only in England, but in Germany, Italy, France, America. They began, and have continued, to lose their old belief in distinct and warring nationalities. To denationalise the nations into one nation only—the nation of mankind—is too vast an idea to grow quickly, but in all classes, and perhaps most in the working class, there are an increasing number of thinking men who say to the varied nations, " We are all one ; our interests, duties, rights, nature and aims are one." And, for my part, I believe that in the full development of that conception the progress of mankind is most deeply concerned, and will be best secured.

Now, when all these classes in England, brought to much the same point by different paths, seek for a poetry which is international rather than national, and which recognises no special country as its own, they do not find it in Tennyson, but they do find Browning writing, and quite naturally, as if he belonged to other peoples as much as to his own, even more than to his own. And they also find that he had been doing this for many years before their own international interests had been awakened. That, then, differentiates him completely from Tennyson, and is another reason why he was not read in the past but is read in the present.

9. Again, with regard to politics and social questions, Tennyson made us know what his general politics were, and he has always pleased or displeased men by his political position. The British Constitution appears throughout his work seated like Zeus on Olympus, with all the world awaiting its nod. Then, also, social problems raise their storm-awakening heads in his poetry: the Woman's Question; War; Competition; the State of the Poor; Education; a State without Religion; the Marriage Question; where Freedom lies; and others. These are brought by Tennyson, though tentatively, into the palace of poetry and given rooms in it.

At both these points Browning differed from Tennyson. He was not the politician, not the sociologist, only the poet. No trace of the British Constitution is to be found in his poetry; no one could tell from it that he had any social views or politics at all. Sixty years in close contact with this country and its movements, and not a line about them!

He records the politics of the place and people of whom or of which he is for the moment writing, but he takes no side. We know what they thought at Rome or among the Druses of these matters, but we do not know what Browning thought. The art-representation, the *Vorstellung* of the thing, is all; the personal view of the poet is nothing. It is the same in social matters. What he says as a poet concerning the ideas which should rule the temper of the soul and human life in relation to our fellow men may be applied to our social questions, and usefully; but Browning is not on that plane. There are no poems directly applied to them. This means that he kept himself outside the realm of political and social discussions and in the realm of those high emotions and ideas out of which imagination in lonely creation draws her work to light. With steady purpose he refused to make his poetry the servant of the transient, of the changing elements of the world. He avoided the contemporary. For this high reserve we and the future of art will owe him gratitude.

On the contrast between the theology we find in Tennyson and Browning, and on the contrast between their ethical positions, it will be wiser not to speak in this introduction. These two contrasts would lead me too far afield, and they have little or nothing to do with poetry. Moreover, Browning's theology and ethics, as they are called, have been discussed at wearying length for the last ten years, and especially by persons who use his poetry to illustrate from it their own systems of theology, philosophy and ethics.

10. I will pass, therefore, to another contrast—the contrast between them as Artists.

A great number of persons who write about the poets think, when they have said the sort of things I have been saying, that they have said either enough, or the most important things. The things are, indeed, useful to say; they enable us to realise the poet and his character, and the elements of which his poetry is made. They place him in a clear relation to his time; they distinguish him from other poets, and, taken all together, they throw light upon his work. But they are not half enough, nor are they the most important. They leave out the essence of the whole matter; they leave out the poetry. They illuminate the surface of his poetry, but they do not penetrate into his interpretation, by means of his special art, and under the influence of high emotion, of the beautiful and sublime Matter of thought and feeling which arises out of Nature and Human Nature, the two great subjects of song; which Matter the poets represent in a form so noble and so lovely in itself that, when it is received into a heart prepared for it, it kindles in the receiver a love of beauty and sublimity similar to that which the poet felt before he formed, and while he formed, his poem. Such a receiver, reading the poem, makes the poem, with an individual difference, in himself. And this is the main thing; the eternal, not the temporary thing.

Almost all I have already discussed with regard to Tennyson and Browning belongs to the temporary; and the varying judgments which their public have formed of them, chiefly based on their appeal to the tendencies of the time, do not at all predict what the final judgment on these men as poets is likely to be. That will depend, not on feelings which belong to the temporary elements of the passing day, but on how far the eternal and unchanging elements of art appear in their work. The things which fitted the poetry of Tennyson to the years between 1840 and 1870 have already passed away; the things which, as I have explained, fitted the poetry of Browning to the tendencies of the years after 1870 will also disappear, and are already disappearing. Indeed, the excessive transiency of nearly all the interests of cultivated society during the last ten years is that in them which most deeply impresses any man who sits somewhat apart from them. And, at any rate, none of these merely contemporary elements, which often seem to men the most important, will count a hundred years hence in the estimate of the poetry either of Tennyson or Browning. They will be of historical interest, and no more. Matters in their poetry, now the subjects of warm discussion among their critics, will be laid aside as materials for judgment; and justly, for they are of quite impermanent value.

Whenever, then, we try to judge them as poets, we must do our best to discharge these temporary things, and consider their poetry as it will seem a hundred years hence to men who will think seriously and feel sensitively, even passionately, towards great and noble Matter of imaginative thought and emotion concerning human life and the natural world, and towards lovely creation of such matter into Form. Their judgment will be made apart from the natural prejudices that arise from contemporary movements. They will not be wiser in their judgment of their own poets than we are about ours, but they will be wiser in their judgment of our poets, because, though they will have their own prejudices, they will not have ours. Moreover, the long, growing, and incessantly corrected judgment of those best fitted to feel what is most beautiful in shaping and most enduring in thought and feeling penetrated and made infinite by imagination, will, by that time, have separated the permanent from the impermanent in the work of Browning and Tennyson.

That judgment will partly depend on the answers, slowly, as it were unconsciously, given by the world to two questions. First, how far does their poetry represent truly and passionately what is natural and most widely felt in loving human nature, whether terrible or joyful, simple or complex, tragic or humorous? Secondly, how far is the representation beautiful and noble in form, and true to the laws of their art. That poetry which is nearest to the most natural, the most universal elements of human life when they are suffused with love—in some at least of its various moods—and at the same time the most beautiful in form, is the best. It wins most affection from mankind, for it is about noble matters of thought which the greater number of men and women desire to contemplate, and about noble matters of passion which the greater number love and therefore enjoy. This poetry lasts from generation to generation, is independent of differences made by climate, by caste, by nationality, by religion, by politics, by knowledge, custom, tradition or morals. These universal, natural elements of human nature are, in all their infinite variety and striving, beloved by men, of undying interest in action, and of immortal pleasure in thought. The nearer a poet is to them, especially to what is lovable, and therefore beautiful in them, the greater and the more enduring is his work. It follows that this greater work will also be simple, that is, easy to feel with the heart though it may be difficult to grasp by the intelligence. Were it not simple in feeling, the general answer of mankind to the call of love, in all its forms, for sympathy would be unheard. And if it be simple in feeling, it does not much matter if the deep waters of its thought are difficult for the understanding to fathom.

It would be ridiculous to dogmatise on a matter which can only be fully answered a century hence, but this much is plain. Of these two poets, taking into consideration the whole of their work, Tennyson is the closest to human nature in its noble, common and loving forms, as Browning is the closest to what is complex, subtle and uncommon in human nature. The representation both of the simple and of the complex is a good thing, and both poets have their place and honour. But the representation of the complex is plainly the more limited in range of influence, and appeals to a special class of minds rather than to mankind at large. There are some, indeed, who think that the appeal to the few, to thinkers alone or high-wrought specialists in various forms of culture, marks out the greater poet. It is the tendency of literary castes to think that specialised work is the greatest. "This man," they say, "is our poet, not the mob's. He stands apart, and his apartness marks his greatness." These are amusing persons, who practically say, "We alone understand him, therefore he is great."

Yet a phrase like "apartness makes greatness," when justly applied to a poet, marks, not his superiority of rank, but his inferiority. It relegates him at once to a lower place. The greatest poets are loved by all, and understood by all who think and feel naturally. Homer was loved by Pericles and by the sausage-seller. Vergil was read with joy by Mæcenas and Augustus, and by the vine-dressers of Mantua. Dante drew after him the greatest minds in Italy, and yet is sung to-day by the shepherds and peasants of the hill-villages of Tuscany. Shakespeare pleases the most selected spirits of the world and the galleries of the strolling theatres.

And though Tennyson and Browning are far below these mightier poets, yet when we apply to them this rule, drawn from what we know to be true of the greatest, Tennyson answers its demand more closely than Browning. The highest work which poetry can do is to glorify what is most natural and simple in the whole of loving human nature, and to show the excelling beauty, not so much of the stranger and wilder doings of the natural world, but of its everyday doings and their common changes. In doing these two things with simplicity, passion and beauty is the finest work of the arts, the eternal youth, the illimitable material of poetry, and it will endure while humanity endures in this world, and in that which is to come. Among all our cultivated love of the uncommon, the remote, the subtle, the involved, the metaphysical and the terrible—the representation of which things has its due place, even its necessity—it is well to think of that quiet truth, and to keep it as a first principle in the judgment of the arts. Indeed, the recovery of the natural, simple and universal ways of acting and feeling in men and women who love as the finest subjects of the arts has always regenerated them whenever, in pursuit of the unnatural, the complicated, the analytic, and the sensational, they have fallen into decay.

Browning did not like this view, being conscious that his poetry did not answer its demand. Not only in early but also in later poems, he pictured his critics stating it, and his picture is scornful enough. There is an entertaining sketch of Naddo, the Philistine critic, in the second book of *Sordello*; and the view I speak of is expressed by him among a huddle of criticisms—

> "Would you have your songs endure?
> Build on the human heart!—why, to be sure
> Yours is one sort of heart.—But I mean theirs,
> Ours, every one's, the healthy heart one cares
> To build on! Central peace, mother of strength,
> That's father of . . . ."

This is good fooling, and Naddo is an ass. Nevertheless, though Naddo makes nonsense of the truth, he was right in the main, and Browning as well as Sordello suffered when they forgot or ignored that truth. And, of course, Browning did not forget or ignore it in more than half his work. Even in *Sordello* he tells us how he gave himself up to recording with pity and love the doings of the universal soul. He strove to paint the whole. It was a bold ambition. Few have fulfilled it so well. None, since Shakespeare, have had a wider range. His portraiture of life was so much more varied than that of Tennyson, so much more extensive and detailed, that on this side he excels Tennyson; but such portraiture is not necessarily poetic, and when it is fond of the complex, it is always in danger of tending to prose. And

Browning, picturing human life, deviated too much into the delineation of its more obscure and complex forms. It was in his nature to do and love this kind of work; and indeed it has to be done, if human life is to be painted fully. Only, it is not to be done too much, if one desires to be always the poet. For the representation of the complex and obscure is chiefly done by the analysing understanding, and its work and pleasure in it lures the poet away from art. He loses the poetic turn of the thing of which he writes, and what he produces is not better than rhythmical prose. Again and again Browning fell into that misfortune; and it is a strange problem how a man, who was in one part of his nature a great poet, could, under the sway of another, cease to be a poet. At this point his inferiority to Tennyson as a poet is plain. Tennyson scarcely ever wrote a line which was not unmistakably poetry, while Browning could write pages which were unmistakably not poetry.

I do not mean, in saying all this, that Browning did not appeal to that which is deepest and universal in nature and human nature, but only that he did not appeal to it as much as Tennyson. Browning is often simple, lovely and universal. And when he speaks out of that emotional imagination wherein is the hiding of a poet's power, and which is the legitimate sovereign of his intellectual work, he will win and keep the delight and love of the centuries to come. By work of this type he will be finally judged and finally endure; and, even now, every one who loves great poetry knows what these master-poems are. As to the others, the merely subtle, analytic poems in which intellect, not imagination, is supreme, especially those into which he drifted in his later life when the ardour of his poetic youth glowed less warmly—they will always appeal to a certain class of persons who would like to persuade themselves that they like poetry but to whom its book is sealed; and who, in finding out what Browning means, imagine to their great surprise that they find out that they care for poetry. What they really care for is their own cleverness in discovering riddles, and they are as far away from poetry as Sirius is from the Sun.

There are, however, many true lovers of poetry who are enthusiastic about these poems. And parts of them deserve this enthusiasm, for they have been conceived and made in a wild borderland between analysis and imagination. They occupy a place apart, a backwater in the noble stream of English poetry, filled with strange plants; and the final judgment of Browning's rank as an artist will not depend on them but on the earlier poems, which, being more " simple, sensuous and passionate," are nearer to the common love and life of man. When, then, we apply this test, the difference of rank between him and Tennyson is not great, but it is plain. Yet comparison, on this point, is difficult. Both drew mankind. Tennyson is closer to that which is most universal in the human heart, Browning to the vast variety within it; and men in the future will find their poetic wants best satisfied by reading the work of both these poets. Let us say then that in this matter they are equal. Each has done a different part of that portraiture of human nature which is the chief work of a poet.

But this is not the only test we may apply to these men as poets. The second question which tries the endurance and greatness of poetic work is this: "How far is any poet's representation of what is true and loving in itself lovely?" Their stuff may be equally good. Is their form equally good? Is it as beautiful as an artist, whose first duty is to be true to beauty as the shape of love and truth, ought to make it? The judgment of the future will also be formed on that ground, and inevitably.

What we call form in poetry may be said to consist of, or to depend on, three things: (1) on a noble style; (2) on a harmonious composition, varied but at unity; (3) on a clear, sweet melody of lawful movement in verse. These are not everything in poetry, but they are the half of its whole. The other half is that the "matter"—that is, the deep substance of amalgamated Thought and Emotion—should be great, vital and fair. But both halves are necessary, and when the half which regards form is weak or unbeautiful, the judgment of the future drops the poems which are faulty in form out of memory, just as it drops out of its affections poems which are excellent in form, but of ignoble, unimpassioned, feeble or thoughtless matter. There was, for example, a whole set of poets towards the end of the Elizabethan period who were close and weighty thinkers, whose poetry is full of intellectual surprises and difficulties, who were capable of subtlety of expression and even of lovely turns and phantasies of feeling; whom students read to-day, but whom the poetical world does not read at all. And the reason is that their style, their melody, and their composition do not match in excellence their matter. Their stuff is good, their form is bad. The judgment of the future gives them no high rank. They do not answer well to the test of which I speak.

I do not mean to apply that analogy altogether, only partly, to Browning. He rises far above these poets in style, composition and melody, but he skirts their faults. And if we are asked to compare him to Tennyson, he is inferior to Tennyson at all these points of Form.

(1) His composition was rarely sufficiently careful. It was broken up, overcrowded; minor objects of thought or feeling are made too remarkable for the whole; there is far too little of poetical perspective; the variety of the poem does not always grow out of the subject itself, but out of the external play of Browning's mind upon things remotely connected with the subject; too many side-issues are introduced; everything he imagined is cast upon the canvas, too little is laid aside, so that the poems run to a length which weakens instead of strengthening the main impression. A number of the poems have, that is, the faults of a composer whose fancy runs away with him, who does not ride it as a master; and in whom therefore, for a time, imagination has gone to sleep. Moreover, only too often, they have those faults of composition which naturally belong to a poet when he writes as if intellect rather than passion were the ultimate umpire of the work of his art. Of course, there are many exceptions; and the study of those exceptions, as exceptions, would make an interesting essay. On the other hand, Tennyson's

composition was for the most part excellent, and always careful.

(2) Then as to style. Browning had a style of his own, wholly devoid of imitation, perfectly individual, and this is one of the marks of a good artist. It was the outcome of his poetic character, and represented it. At this point his style is more interesting than Tennyson's. Tennyson's style was often too much worked, too consciously subjected to the rules of his art, too worn down to smoothness of texture. Moreover, the natural surprises of an unchartered individuality do not sufficiently appear in it (Tennyson repressed the fantastic), though the whole weight of his character does magnificently appear. But if Tennyson was too conscious of his style—a great misfortune especially in passionate song—Browning did not take any deliberate pains with his style, and that is a greater misfortune. His freedom ran into undue licence; and he seems to be over-conscious, even proud, of his fantastical way of writing. His individuality runs riot in his style. He paid little attention to the well-established rules of his art, in a revulsion, perhaps, from any imitation of the great models. He had not enough reverence for his art, and little for the public. He flung his diction at our heads and said: "This is myself; take it or leave it."

None of the greater artists of the world have ever done this. They have not cared for what the world said, but they have cared for their art. There are certain limits to individual capriciousness in style, long since laid down, as it were, by Beauty herself; which, transgressed, lessen, injure or lose beauty; and Browning continually transgressed those limits.

Again, clearness is one of the first elements in style, and on poetry attaining clearness, depends, in great measure, its enduringness in the future. So far as clearness carries him, Tennyson's poetry is sure to last. So far as Browning's obscurity goes, his poetry will not last like Tennyson's. It is all very well for his students to say that he is not obscure; he is. Nor is it by any exceptional depth of thought or by any specially profound analysis of the soul that Browning is obscure. It is by his style. By that he makes what is easy difficult. The reader does not get at what he means as he gets at what Homer, Dante, and Shakespeare mean. Dante and Shakespeare are often difficult through the depth and difficulty of their matter; they are not difficult, except Shakespeare when he was learning his art, by obscurity or carelessness of style. But Browning is difficult, not by his thoughts, but by his expression of them. A poet has no right to be so indifferent, so careless of clearness in his art, I might almost say, so lazy. Browning is negligent to a fault, almost to impertinence. The great poets put the right words in the right places, and Tennyson is with them in that. Browning continually puts his words into the wrong places. He leaves out words necessary for the easy understanding of the passage, and for no reason except his fancy. He leaves his sentences half-finished and his meaning half-expressed. He begins a sentence, and having begun it, three or four thoughts connected with it slide into his mind, and instead of putting them aside or using them in another place, he jerks them into the middle of his sentence in a series of parentheses, and then inserts the end of the original sentence, or does not insert it at all.

This is irritating except to folk who like discovery of the twisted rather than poetry; and it is quite needless. It is worse than needless, for it lowers the charm and the dignity of the poetry.

Yet, there is something to say on the other side. It is said, and with a certain justice, that " the style is the man. Strip his style away, and where is the man? Where is the real Browning if we get him to change a way of writing in which he naturally shaped his thought?" Well, no one would ask him to impose on himself a style which did not fit his nature. That would be fatal. When he has sometimes tried to do so, as in a few of the dramas, we scarcely recognise our poet, and we lose half of his intellectual and poetic charm. Just as Carlyle when he wrote away from his natural style, as in the life of Sterling and Schiller, is not the great writer he is elsewhere, so was it with Browning. Were we savage satirists, blinded by our savagery, we might then say both of Browning and Carlyle that half their power lay in their fantastic, rocky style. We should be quite wrong. Their style was the exact clothing of their thought. They wrote exactly as they thought; and when they put their thought into other clothing, when they doctored their style, they did not represent what they really thought. No sensible person then would have asked Browning to change his style, but would have asked him not to exaggerate it into its defects. It is plain he could have kept it within bounds. He has done so frequently. But as frequently he has allowed it to leap about as wildly as a young colt. He should have submitted it to the *manège*, and ridden it then where he pleased. A very little trouble on his part, a very little sacrifice of his unbridled fancifulness, would have spared us a great deal of unnecessary trouble, and made his poetry better and more enduring.

Another excuse may be made for his faults of style. It may be said that in one sense the faults are excellences. When a poet has to represent excessively subtle phases of thought and feeling, with a crowd of side-thoughts and side-feelings intruding on them; when he has to describe the excessive oddities, the curious turns of human emotion in strange inward conditions or outward circumstances or when he has to deal with rugged or even savage characters under the sway of the passions; he cannot, we are told, do it otherwise than Browning did it, and, instead of being lazy, he used these quips and cranks of style deliberately.

The excuse has something in it. But, all the same, an artist should have managed it otherwise. Shakespeare was far more subtle in thought than Browning, and he had to deal with every kind of strange circumstance and characters; but his composition and his style illuminate the characters, order the circumstances, and render clear, as, for example, in the Sonnets, the subtleties of his thought. A great artist, by his comprehensive grasp of the main issue of his work, even in a short lyric or a small picture, and by his luminous representation of it, suggests, without direct expression of them, all the strange psychology, and the play of character in the situations. And such an artist does this excellent thing by his noble composition, and by his lofty, clear, and melodious style. The excuse is, then, of some weight, but it does not relieve Browning of the charge. Had he been a greater artist, he would have been a greater master of the right way of saying things and a greater pleasurer of the future. Had he taken more pains with his style, but without losing its individual elements, he might have had as high a poetic place as Tennyson in the judgment of posterity.

(3) In one thing more—in this matter of form—the beauty of poetry lies. It is in sweetness of melody and its charm; in exquisite fitness of its music to its thought and its emotion; in lawful change of harmony making enchanting variety to the ear; in the obedience of the melodies to the laws of the different kinds of poetry; and in the lovely conduct of the harmonies, through all their changes, to that finished close which throws back its own beauty on all that has preceded it. This part of the loveliness of form in poetry, along with composition and style—for without these and without noble matter of thought poetry is nothing but pleasant noise—secures also the continuous delight of men and the approving judgment of the future; and in this also Tennyson, who gave to it the steady work of a lifetime, stands above his brother-poet. Browning was far too careless of his melody. He frequently sacrificed it, and needlessly, to his thought. He may have imagined that he strengthened the thing he thought by breaking the melody. He did not, he injured it. He injured the melody also by casting into the middle of it, like stones into a clear water, rough parenthetic sounds to suit his parenthetic phrases. He breaks it sometimes into two with violent clanging words, with discords which he

does not resolve, but forgets. And in the pleasure he took in quaint oddities of sound, in jarring tricks with his metre, in fantastic and difficult arrangements of rhyme, in scientific displays of double rhymes, he, only too often, immolates melody on the altar of his own cleverness.

A great many of the poems in which the natural loveliness of melody is thus sacrificed or maimed will last, on account of the closely-woven work of the intellect in them, and on account of their vivid presentation of the travail of the soul; that is, they will last for qualities which might belong to prose; but they will not last as poetry. And other poems, in which the melody is only interrupted here and there, will lose a great deal of the continuity of pleasure they would have given to man had they been more careful to obey those laws of fine melody which Tennyson never disobeys.

It is fortunate that neither of these injuries can be attributed to the whole of his work; and I am equally far from saying that his faults of style and composition belong to all his poetry.

There are a number of poems the melody of which is beautiful, in which, if there are discords, they are resolved into a happy concord at their close. There are others the melody of which is so strange, brilliant, and capturing that their sound is never forgotten. There are others the subtle, minor harmonies of which belong to and represent remote pathetic phases of human passion, and they, too, are heard by us in lonely hours of pitiful feeling, and enchant the ear and heart. And these will endure for the noble pleasure of man.

There are also poems the style of which is fitted

most happily to the subject, like the Letter of Karshish to his Friend, in which Browning has been so seized by his subject, and yet has so mastered it, that he has forgotten to intercalate his own fancies; and in which, if the style is broken, it is broken in full harmony with the situation, and in obedience to the unity of impression he desired to make. There are others, like *Abt Vogler*, in which the style is extraordinarily noble, clear, and uplifted; and there are long passages in the more important poems, like *Paracelsus*, where the joy and glory of the thought and passion of Browning inform the verse with dignity, and make its march stately with solemn and beautiful music. Where the style and melody are thus fine the composition is also good. The parts, in their variety, belong to one another and to the unity of the whole. Style, melody and composition are always in the closest relation. And this nobleness of composition, style, and melody is chiefly found in those poems of his which have to do with the great matter of poetry —the representation of the universal and simple passions of human nature with their attendant and necessary thoughts. And there, in that part of his work, not in that other part for which he is unduly praised, and which belongs to the over-subtilised and over-intellectual time in which our self-conscious culture now is striving to resist its decay, and to prove that its disease is health, is the lasting power of Browning.

And then, beyond all these matters of form, there is the poet himself, alone among his fellows in his unique and individual power, who has fastened himself into our hearts, added a new world to our perceptions, developed our lives and enlarged our interests. And there are the separate and distinguished excellences of his work—the virtues which have no defects, the virtues, too, of his defects, all the new wonders of his realm—the many originalities which have justly earned for him that high and lonely seat on Parnassus on which his noble Shadow sits to-day, unchallenged in our time save by that other Shadow with whom, in reverence and love, we have been perhaps too bold to contrast him.

CHAPTER II

THE TREATMENT OF NATURE

IT is a difficult task to explain or analyse the treatment of Nature by Browning. It is easy enough to point out his remarkable love of her colour, his vivid painting of brief landscapes, his minute observation, his flashing way of description, his feeling for the breadth and freshness of Nature, his love of flowers and animals, and the way he has of hitting and emphasising the central point or light of a landscape. This is easy work, but it is not so easy to capture and define the way in which his soul, when he was alone, felt with regard to the heavens, and the earth and all that therein is. Others, like Wordsworth, have stated this plainly: Browning has nowhere defined his way. What his intellect held the Natural World to be, in itself; what it meant for man; the relation in which it stood to God and God to it—these things are partly plain. They have their attraction for us. It is always interesting to know what an imaginative genius thinks about such matters. But it is only a biographical or a half-scientific interest. But what we want to discover is how Browning, as a poet, felt the world of Nature. We have to try and catch the unconscious attitude of his soul when the

Universe was at work around him, and he was for the time its centre—and this is the real difficulty.

Sometimes we imagine we have caught and fixed this elusive thing, but we finally give up the quest. The best we can do is to try to find the two or three general thoughts, the most frequently recurring emotions Browning had when Nature at sundry hours and in diverse manners displayed before him her beauty, splendour and fire, and seemed to ask his worship; or again, when she stood apart from him, with the mocking smile she often wears, and whispered in his ear, "Thou shalt pursue me always, but never find my secret, never grasp my streaming hair." And both these experiences are to be found in Browning. Nature and he are sometimes at one, and sometimes at two; but seldom the first, and generally the second.

The natural world Tennyson describes is for the greater part of it a reflection of man, or used to heighten man's feeling, or to illustrate his action, or sentimentalised by memorial associations of humanity, or, finally, invented as a background for a human subject, and with a distinct direction towards that subject. Browning, with a few exceptions, does the exact opposite. His natural world is not made by our thought, nor does it reflect our passions. His illustrations, drawn from it, of our actions, break down at certain points, as if the illustrating material were alien from our nature. Nature, it is true, he thinks, leads up to man, and therefore has elements in her which are dim prophecies and prognostics of us; but she is only connected with us as the road is with the goal it reaches in the end. She exists independently of us, but yet she exists to suggest to us what we may become, to awaken in us dim longings and desires, to surprise us into confession of our inadequacy, to startle us with perceptions of an infinitude we do not possess as yet but may possess; to make us feel our ignorance, weakness, want of finish; and by partly exhibiting the variety, knowledge, love, power and finish of God, to urge us forward in humble pursuit to the infinite in him. The day Browning climbs Mont Salève, at the beginning of his poem *La Saisiaz*, after a description of his climb in which he notes a host of minute quaintnesses in rock and flower, and especially little flares of colour, all of them unsentimentalised, he suddenly stands on the mountain-top, and is smitten with the glory of the view. What does he see? Himself in Nature? or Nature herself, like a living being? Not at all. He sees what he thinks Nature is there to teach us—not herself, but what is beyond herself. "I was stationed," he cries, deliberately making this point, "face to face with—Nature?—rather with Infinitude." We are not in Nature: a part of God aspiring to the whole is there, but not the all of God. And Nature shows forth her glory, not to keep us with herself, but to send us on to her Source, of whom the universe is but a shred.

The universe of what we call matter in all its forms, which is the definition of Nature as I speak of it here, is one form to Browning of the creative joy of God: we are another form of the same joy. Nor does Browning conceive, as Wordsworth conceived, of any pre-established harmony between us and the natural world, so that Humanity and Nature can easily converse and live together; so that we can express our thoughts and emotions in terms of Nature; or so that Nature can have, as it were, a human soul. This is not Browning's conception. If he had such a conception he would frequently use in his descriptions what Ruskin calls the "pathetic fallacy," the use of which is excessively common in Tennyson. I can scarcely recall more than a very few instances of this in all the poetry of Browning. Even where it seems to occur, where Nature is spoken of in human terms, it does not really occur. Take this passage from *James Lee's Wife*:

> Oh, good gigantic smile o' the brown old earth,
>   This autumn morning! How he sets his bones
> To bask i' the sun, and thrusts out knees and feet
> For the ripple to run over in its mirth;
>   Listening the while, where on the heap of stones
> The white breast of the sea-lark twitters sweet.

The smile, the mirth, the listening, might be said to impute humanity to Nature: but the Earth and the Sea are plainly quite distinct from us. These are great giant creatures who are not ourselves: Titans who live with one another and not with us; and the terms of our humanity are used to make us aware of their separate existence from us, not of their being images only of our mind.

Another passage will illustrate the same habit of Browning's mind with nature. He describes, for the purpose of his general thought, in *Fifine at the Fair*, the course of a stormy sunset. The clouds, the sun, the night, act like men, and are written of in terms of humanity. But this is only to explain matters to us; the mighty creatures themselves have nothing to do with us. They live their own vast, indifferent life; and we see, like spectators, what they are doing, and do not understand what we see. The sunset seems to him the last act of an ever-recurring drama, in which the clouds barricade the Sun against his rest, and he plays with their opposition like the huge giant he is; till Night, with her terrific mace, angry with them for preventing the Sun from repose, repose which will make her Queen of the world, beats them into ruin. This is the passage:

> For as on edifice of cloud i' the grey and green
> Of evening,—built about some glory of the west,
> To barricade the sun's departure,—manifest,
> He plays, pre-eminently gold, gilds vapour, crag and crest
> Which bend in rapt suspense above the act and deed
> They cluster round and keep their very own, nor heed
> The world at watch; while we, breathlessly at the base
> O' the castellated bulk, note momently the mace
> Of night fall here, fall there, bring change with every blow,
> Alike to sharpened shaft and broadened portico
> I' the structure; heights and depths, beneath the leaden stress
> Crumble and melt and mix together, coalesce,
> Reform, but sadder still, subdued yet more and more
> By every fresh defeat, till wearied eyes need pore
> No longer on the dull impoverished decadence
> Of all that pomp of pile in towering evidence
> So lately. *Fifine, cvi.*

It is plain that Browning separates us altogether from the elemental life of these gigantic beings. And what is true of these passages is true, with one or two exceptions, of all the natural descriptions of Browning in which the pathetic fallacy seems to be used by him. I need not say how extraordinarily apart this method of his is from that of Tennyson.

Then Tennyson, like Coleridge—only Tennyson

is as vague and wavering in this belief as Coleridge is firm and clear in it—sometimes speaks as if Nature did not exist at all apart from our thought:

> Her life the eddying of our living soul—

a possible, even a probable explanation. But it is not Browning's view. There is a celebrated passage in *Paracelsus* which is quite inconsistent with it. All Nature, from the beginning, is made to issue forth from the joy God has in making, in embodying his thought in form; and when one form has been made and rejoiced in, in making another still more lovely on the foundation of the last. So, joy after joy, the world was built, till, in the life of all he has made, God sees his ancient rapture of movement and power, and feels his delight renewed. I will not quote it here, but only mark that we and the " eddying of our living soul " have nothing to do with the making of this Nature. It is not even the thoughts of God in us. God and Nature are alone, and were alone together countless years before we were born. But man was the close of all. Nature was built up, through every stage, that man might know himself to be its close—its seal—but not it. It is a separate, unhuman form of God. Existing thus apart, it does a certain work on us, impressing us from without. The God in it speaks to the God in us. It may sometimes be said to be interested in us, but not like a man in a man. He even goes so far as to impute to Nature, but rarely, such an interest in us; but in reality he rather thinks that we, being Nature's end, have at such times touched for a moment some of those elements in her which have come down to us—elements apart from the soul. And Browning takes care, even when he represents Nature as suddenly at one with us, to keep up the separateness. The interest spoken of is not a human interest, nor resembles it. It is like the interest Ariel takes in Prospero and Miranda—an elemental interest, that of a creature whose nature knows its radical difference from human nature. If Nature sees us in sorrow or in joy, she knows, in these few passages of Browning's poetry, or seems to know, that we mourn or rejoice, and if she could feel with us she would; but she cannot quite do so. Like Ariel, she would be grieved with the grief of Gonzalo, were her affections human. She has then a wild, unhuman, unmoral, unspiritual interest in us, like a being who has an elemental life, but no soul. But sometimes she is made to go farther, and has the same kind of interest in us which Oberon has in the loves of Helena and Hermia. When we are loving, and on the verge of such untroubled joy as Nature has always in her being, then she seems able, in Browning's poetry, actually to work for us, and help us into the fulness of our joy. In his poem, *By the Fireside*, he tells how he and the woman he loved were brought to know their love. It is a passage full of his peculiar view of Nature. The place where the two lovers stay their footsteps on the hill knows all about them. "It is silent and aware." But it is apart from them also:

> It has had its scenes, its joys and crimes,
> But that is its own affair.

And its silence also is its own. Those who linger there think that the place longs to speak; its bosom seems to heave with all it knows; but the desire is its own, not ours transferred to it. But when the two lovers were there, Nature, of her own accord, made up a spell for them and troubled them into speech:

> A moment after, and hands unseen
>   Were hanging the night around us fast;
> But we knew that a bar was broken between
>   Life and life: we were mixed at last
> In spite of the mortal screen.
>
> The forests had done it; there they stood;
>   We caught for a moment the powers at play:
> They had mingled us so, for once and good,
>   Their work was done—we might go or stay,
> They relapsed to their ancient mood.

Not one of the poets of this century would have thought in that fashion concerning Nature. Only for a second, man happened to be in harmony with the Powers at play in Nature. They took the two lovers up for a moment, made them one, and dropped them. "They relapsed to their ancient mood." The line is a whole lesson in Browning's view of Nature. But this special interest in us is rare, for we are seldom in the blessed mood of unself-conscious joy and love. When we are, on the other hand, self-conscious, or in doubt, or out of harmony with love and joy, or anxious for the transient things of the world—Nature, unsympathetic wholly, mocks and plays with us like a faun. When Sordello climbs the ravine, thinking of himself as Apollo, the wood, "proud of its observer," a mocking phrase, "tried surprises on him, stratagems and games."

Or, our life is too small for her greatness. When

we are unworthy our high lineage, noisy or mean, then we

> quail before a quiet sky
> Or sea, too little for their quietude.

That is a phrase which might fall in with Wordsworth's theory of Nature, but this which follows from *The Englishman in Italy*, is only Browning's. The man has climbed to the top of Calvano,

> And God's own profound
> Was above me, and round me the mountains,
> And under, the sea,
> And within me, my heart to bear witness
> What was and shall be.

He is worthy of the glorious sight; full of eternal thoughts. Wordsworth would then have made the soul of Nature sympathise with his soul. But Browning makes Nature manifest her apartness from the man. The mountains know nothing of his soul: they amuse themselves with him; they are even half angry with him for his intrusion—a foreigner who dares an entrance into their untrespassed world. Tennyson could not have thought that way. It is true the mountains are alive in the poet's thought, but not with the poet's life: nor does he touch them with his sentiment.

> Oh, those mountains, their infinite movement
> Still moving with you;
> For, ever some new head and heart of them
> Thrusts into view
> To observe the intruder; you see it
> If quickly you turn
> And, before they escape you surprise them.
> They grudge you should learn
> How the soft plains they look on, lean over
> And love (they pretend)—
> Cower beneath them.

Total apartness from us! Nature mocking, surprising us; watching us from a distance, even pleased to see us going to our destruction. We may remember how the hills look grimly on Childe Roland when he comes to the tower. The very sunset comes back to see him die:

> before it left,
> The dying sunset kindled through a cleft:
> The hills, like giants at a hunting, lay,
> Chin upon hand, to see the game at bay.—

Then, as if they loved to see the death of their quarry, cried, without one touch of sympathy:

> "Now stab and end the creature—to the heft!"

And once, so divided from our life is her life, she pities her own case and refuses our pity. Man cannot help her. The starved, ignoble country in *Childe Roland*, one of the finest pieces of description in Browning, wicked, waste and leprous land, makes Nature herself sick with peevish wrath. "I cannot help my case," she cries. "Nothing but the Judgment's fire can cure the place."

On the whole, then, for these instances might be supported by many more, Nature is alive in Browning, but she is not humanised at all, nor at all at one with us. Tennyson does not make her alive, but he does humanise her. The other poets of the century do make her alive, but they harmonise her in one way or another with us. Browning is distinct from them all in keeping her quite divided from man.

But then he has observed that Nature is expressed in terms of man, and he naturally, for this conflicts with his general view, desires to explain this. He does explain it in a passage in *Paracelsus*. Man once descried, imprints for ever

> His presence on all lifeless things; the winds
> Are henceforth voices, wailing or a shout,
> A querulous mutter or a quick gay laugh,
> Never a senseless gust now man is born.
> The herded pines commune and have deep thoughts
> A secret they assemble to discuss
> When the sun drops behind their trunks which glare
> Like grates of hell: the peerless cup afloat
> Of the lake-lily is an urn, some nymph
> Swims bearing high above her head: no bird
> Whistles unseen, but through the gaps above
> That let light in upon the gloomy woods,
> A shape peeps from the breezy forest-top,
> Arch with small puckered mouth and mocking eye.
> The morn has enterprise, deep quiet droops
> With evening, triumph takes the sunset hour,
> Voluptuous transport ripens with the corn
> Beneath a warm moon like a happy face:
> —And this to fill us with regard for Man.

He does not say, as the other poets do, that the pines really commune, or that the morn has enterprise, or that nymphs and satyrs live in the woods, but that this *seems* to be, because man, as the crown of the natural world, throws back his soul and his soul's life on all the grades of inferior life which preceded him. It is Browning's contradiction of any one who thinks that the pathetic fallacy exists in his poetry.

Nature has then a life of her own, her own joys and sorrows, or rather, only joy. Browning, indeed, with his intensity of imagination and his ineradicable desire of life, was not the man to conceive Nature as dead, as having no conscious being of any kind. He did not impute a personality like ours to Nature, but he saw joy and rapture and play, even love, moving in everything; and sometimes he added to this delight she has in herself—and just because the creature was not human—a touch of elemental unmoral malice, a tricksome sportiveness like that of Puck in *Midsummer Night's Dream*. The life, then, of Nature had no relation of its own to our life; but we had some relation to it because we were conscious that we were its close and its completion.

It follows from this idea of Browning's that he was capable of describing Nature as she is, without adding any deceiving mist of human sentiment to his descriptions; and of describing her as accurately and as vividly as Tennyson, even more vividly, because of his extraordinary eye for colour. And Nature, so described, is of great interest in Browning's poetry.

But, then, in any description of Nature, we desire the entrance into such description of some human feeling so that it may be a more complete theme for poetry. Browning does this in a different way from Tennyson, who gives human feelings and thoughts to Nature, or steeps it in human memories. Browning catches Nature up into himself, and the human element is not in Nature but in him, in what *he* thinks and feels, in all that Nature, quite apart from him, awakens in him. Sometimes he even goes so far as to toss Nature aside altogether, as unworthy to be thought of in comparison with humanity. That joy in Nature herself, for her own sake, which was so distinguishing a mark of Wordsworth, Coleridge, Shelley, Byron and Keats, is rarely, if ever, found in Browning. This places him apart. What he loved was man; and save at those times of which I have spoken, when he conceives Nature as the life and play and wrath and fancy of huge elemental powers like gods and goddesses, he uses her as a background only for human life. She is of little importance unless man be present, and then she is no more than the scenery in a drama. Take the first two verses of *A Lovers' Quarrel,*

> Oh, what a dawn of day!
> How the March sun feels like May!
>   All is blue again
>   After last night's rain,
> And the South dries the hawthorn-spray.

That is well done—he has liked what he saw. But what is it all, he thinks; what do I care about it? And he ends the verse:

> Only, my Love's away!
> I'd as lief that the blue were grey.

Then take the next verse:

> Runnels, which rillets swell,
> Must be dancing down the dell,
>   With a foaming head
>   On the beryl bed
> Paven smooth as a hermit's cell.

It is excellent description, but it is only scenery for the real passion in Browning's mind.

> Each with a tale to tell—
> Could my Love but attend as well.

By the Fireside illustrates the same point. No description can be better, more close, more observed, than of the whole walk over the hill; but it is mere scenery for the lovers. The real passion lies in their hearts.

We have then direct description of Nature; direct description of man sometimes as influenced by Nature; sometimes Nature used as the scenery of human passion; but no intermingling of them both. Each is for ever distinct. The only thing that unites them in idea, and in the end, is that both have proceeded from the creative joy of God.

Of course this way of thinking permits of the things of Nature being used to illustrate the doings, thinkings and character of man; and in none of his poems is such illustration better used than in *Sordello*. There is a famous passage, in itself a noble description of the opulent generativeness of a warm land like Italy, in which he compares the rich, poetic soul of Sordello to such a land, and the lovely line in it,

> And still more labyrinthine buds the rose,

holds in its symbolism the whole essence of a great artist's nature. I quote the passage. It describes Sordello, and it could not better describe Italy:

> Sordello foremost in the regal class
> Nature has broadly severed from the mass
> Of men, and framed for pleasure, as she frames
> Some happy lands, that have luxurious names,
> For loose fertility; a footfall there
> Suffices to upturn to the warm air
> Half-germinating spices; mere decay
> Produces richer life; and day by day
> New pollen on the lily-petal grows,
> And still more labyrinthine buds the rose.

That compares to the character of a whole country the character of a whole type of humanity. I take another of such comparisons, and it is as minute as this is broad, and done with as great skill and charm. Sordello is full of poetic fancies, touched and glimmering with the dew of youth, and he has woven them around the old castle where he lives. Browning compares the young man's imaginative play to the airy and audacious labour of the spider. He, that is, Sordello,

> O'er-festooning every interval,
> As the adventurous spider, making light
> Of distance, shoots her threads from depth to height,
> From barbican to battlement: so flung
> Fantasies forth and in their centre swung
> Our architect,—the breezy morning fresh
> Above, and merry,—all his waving mesa
> Laughing with lucid dew-drops rainbow-edged.

It could not be better done. The description might stand alone, but better than it is the image it gives of the joy, fancifulness and creativeness of a young poet, making his web of thoughts and imaginations, swinging in their centre like the spider; all of them subtle as the spider's threads, obeying every passing wind of impulse, and gemmed with the dew and sunlight of youth.

Again, in *A Bean-stripe: also Apple-Eating*, Ferishtah is asked—Is life a good or bad thing, white or black? "Good," says Ferishtah, "if one keeps moving. I only move. When I stop, I may stop in a black place or a white. But everything around me is motionless as regards me, and is nothing more than stuff which tests my power of throwing light and colour on them as I move. It is I who make life good or bad, black or white. I am like the moon going through vapour"—and this is the illustration:

>   Mark the flying orb
> Think'st thou the halo, painted still afresh
> At each new cloud-fleece pierced and passaged through
> This was and is and will be evermore
> Coloured in permanence?   The glory swims
> Girdling the glory-giver, swallowed straight
> By night's abysmal gloom, unglorified
> Behind as erst before the advancer : gloom?
> Faced by the onward-faring, see, succeeds
> From the abandoned heaven a next surprise,
> And where's the gloom now?—silver-smitten straight,
> One glow and variegation!   So, with me,
> Who move and make,—myself,—the black, the white,
> The good, the bad, of life's environment.

Fine as these illustrations are, intimate and minute, they are only a few out of a multitude of those comparisons which in Browning image what is in man from that which is within Nature—hints, prognostics, prophecies, as he would call them, of humanity, but not human.

There is, however, one human passion which Browning conceives as existing in Nature—the passion of joy. But it is a different joy from ours. It is not dashed by any sorrow, and it is very rarely that we are so freed from pain or from self-contemplation as to be able to enter even for a brief hour into the rapture of Nature. That rapture, in Browning's thought, was derived from the creative thought of God exercising itself with delight in the incessant making of Nature. And its manifestation was life, that joyful rush of life in all things into fuller and fuller being. No poet felt this ecstasy of mere living in Nature more deeply than Browning. His own rapture (the word is not too strong) in it appears again and again in his poetry, and when it does, Browning is not a man sympathising from without with Nature. He is then a part of Nature herself, a living piece of the great organism, having his own rejoicing life in the mightier life which includes him; and feeling, with the rest, the abounding pleasure of continuous life reaching upwards through growth to higher forms of being, swifter powers of living. I might give many examples, but one will suffice, and it is the more important because it belongs not to his ardent youth, but to his mature manhood. It is part of the song of Thamyris in *Aristophanes' Apology*. Thamyris, going to meet the Muses in rivalry, sings as he walks in the splendid morning the song of the rapture of the life of Earth, and is himself part of the rejoicing movement.

>
> Thamuris, marching, laughed " Each flake of foam "
> (As sparklingly the ripple raced him by)
> " Mocks slower clouds adrift in the blue dome ! "
>
> For Autumn was the season; red the sky
> Held morn's conclusive signet of the sun
> To break the mists up, bid them blaze and die.
>
> Morn had the mastery as, one by one
> All pomps produced themselves along the tract
> From earth's far ending to near heaven begun.
>
> Was there a ravaged tree ? it laughed compact
> With gold, a leaf-ball crisp, high brandished now,
> Tempting to onset frost which late attacked.
>
> Was there a wizened shrub, a starveling bough,
> A fleecy thistle filched from by the wind,
> A weed, Pan's trampling hoof would disallow ?
>
> Each, with a glory and a rapture twined
> About it, joined the rush of air and light
> And force: the world was of one joyous mind.

> Say not the birds flew! they forebore their right—
> Swam, revelling onward in the roll of things.
> Say not the beasts' mirth bounded! that was flight—
>
> How could the creatures leap, no lift of wings?
> Such earth's community of purpose, such
> The ease of earth's fulfilled imaginings,—
>
> So did the near and far appear to touch
> I' the moment's transport,—that an interchange
> Of function, far with near, seemed scarce too much;
>
> And had the rooted plant aspired to range
> With the snake's licence, while the insect yearned
> To glow fixed as the flower, it were not strange—
>
> No more than if the fluttery tree-top turned
> To actual music, sang itself aloft;
> Or if the wind, impassioned chantress, earned
>
> The right to soar embodied in some soft
> Fine form all fit for cloud companionship,
> And, blissful, once touch beauty chased so oft.
>
> Thamuris, marching, let no fancy slip
> Born of the fiery transport; lyre and song
> Were his, to smite with hand and launch from lip—

The next thing to touch on is his drawing of landscape, not now of separate pieces of Nature, but of the whole view of a land seen under a certain aspect of the heavens. All the poets ought to be able to do this well, and I drew attention to the brief, condensed, yet fan-opening fashion in which Tennyson has done it. Sometimes the poets describe what they see before them, or have seen; drawing directly from Nature. Sometimes they invent a wide or varied landscape as a background for a human subject, and arrange and tone it for that purpose. Shelley did this with great stateliness and subtlety. Browning does not do it, except, perhaps, in *Christmas-Eve*, when he prepares the night for the appearance of Christ. Nevertheless, even in *Christmas-Eve*, the description of the lunar rainbow is of a thing he has seen, of a not-invented thing, and it is as clear, vivid and natural as it can be; only it is heightened and thrilled through by the expectancy and the thrill in Browning's soul which the reader feels and which the poet, through his emotion, makes the reader comprehend. But there is no suggestion that any of this feeling exists in Nature. The rainbow has no consciousness of the vision to come or of the passion in the poet (as it would have had in Wordsworth), and therefore is painted with an accuracy undimmed by any transference to Nature of the soul of the poet.

I quote the piece; it is a noble specimen of his landscape work:

> But lo, what think you? suddenly
> The rain and the wind ceased, and the sky
> Received at once the full fruition
> Of the moon's consummate apparition.
> The black cloud barricade was riven,
> Ruined beneath her feet, and driven
> Deep in the West; while, bare and breathless,
>   North and South and East lay ready
> For a glorious thing that, dauntless, deathless,
>   Sprang across them and stood steady.
>
> 'Twas a moon-rainbow, vast and perfect,
> From heaven to heaven extending, perfect
> As the mother-moon's self, full in face.
> It rose, distinctly at the base
>   With its severe proper colours chorded
> Which still, in the rising, were compressed,
> Until at last they coalesced,
>   And supreme the spectral creature lorded

> In a triumph of whitest white,—
> Above which intervened the night.
> But above night too, like only the next,
>   The second of a wondrous sequence,
>   Reaching in rare and rarer frequence,
> Till the heaven of heavens were circumflexed,
> Another rainbow rose, a mightier,
> Fainter, flushier and flightier,—
> Rapture dying along its verge.
> Oh, whose foot shall I see emerge,
> Whose, from the straining topmost dark,
> On to the key-stone of that arc?

This is only a piece of sky, though I have called it landscape work. But then the sky is frequently treated alone by Browning; and is always present in power over his landscapes—it, and the winds in it. This is natural enough for one who lived so much in Italy, where the scenery of the sky is more superb than that of the earth—so various, noble and surprising that when Nature plays there, as a poet, her tragedy and comedy, one scarcely takes the trouble of considering the earth.

However, we find an abundance of true landscapes in Browning. They are, with a few exceptions, Italian; and they have that grandeur and breadth, that intensity given by blazing colour, that peculiar tint either of labyrinthine or of tragic sentiment which belong to Italy. I select a few of them:

>   The morn when first it thunders in March
>   The eel in the pond gives a leap, they say;
>   As I leaned and looked over the aloed arch
>   Of the villa-gate this warm March day,
>   No flash snapped, no dumb thunder rolled
>   In the valley beneath where, white and wide
>   Washed by the morning water-gold,
>   Florence lay out on the mountain side

> River and bridge and street and square
>   Lay mine, as much at my beck and call,
> Through the live translucent bath of air,
>   As the sights in a magic crystal ball.

Here is the Roman Campagna and its very sentiment:

> The champaign with its endless fleece
>   Of feathery grasses everywhere!
> Silence and passion, joy and peace,
>   An everlasting wash of air—
> Rome's ghost since her decease.

And this might be in the same place:

> Where the quiet-coloured end of evening smiles,
>   Miles and miles
> On the solitary pastures where our sheep
>   Half-asleep
> Tinkle homeward through the twilight—

This is a crimson sunset over dark and distant woods in autumn:

> That autumn eve was stilled:
> A last remains of sunset dimly burned
> O'er the far forests, like a torch-flame turned
> By the wind back upon its bearer's hand
> In one long flare of crimson; as a brand
> The woods beneath lay black. A single eye
> From all Verona cared for the soft sky.

And if we desire a sunrise, there is the triumphant beginning of *Pippa Passes*—a glorious outburst of light, colour and splendour, impassioned and rushing, the very upsoaring of Apollo's head behind his furious steeds. It begins with one word, like a single stroke on the gong of Nature: it continues till the whole of the overarching vault, and the world below, in vast disclosure, is flooded with an ocean of gold.

> Day!
> Faster and more fast,
> O'er night's brim, day boils at last;
> Boils, pure gold, o'er the cloud-cup's brim
> Where spurting and suppressed it lay,
> For not a froth-flake touched the rim
> Of yonder gap in the solid gray
> Of the eastern cloud, an hour away;
> But forth one wavelet, then another, curled,
> Till the whole sunrise, not to be suppressed,
> Rose, reddened, and its seething breast
> Flickered in bounds, grew gold, then overflowed the world.

This is chiefly of the sky, but the description in that gipsy-hearted poem, *The Flight of the Duchess*, brings before us, at great length, league after league of wide-spreading landscape. It is, first, of the great wild country, cornfield, vineyards, sheep-ranges, open chase, till we arrive at last at the mountains; and climbing up among their pines, dip down into a yet vaster and wilder country, a red, drear, burnt-up plain, over which we are carried for miles:

> Till at the last, for a bounding belt,
> Comes the salt sand hoar of the great sea-shore.

Or we may read the *Grammarian's Funeral*, where we leave the city walls and climb the peak on whose topmost ledge he is to be buried. As we ascend the landscape widens; we see it expanding in the verse. Moreover, with a wonderful power, Browning makes us feel the air grow keener, fresher, brighter, more soundless and lonelier. That, too, is given by the verse; it is a triumph in Nature-poetry.

Nor is he less effective in narrow landscape, in the description of small shut-in spaces of

Nature. There is the garden at the beginning of *Paracelsus;* the ravine, step by step, in *Pauline;* the sea-beach, and its little cabinet landscapes, in *James Lee's Wife;* the exquisite pictures of the path over the Col di Colma in *By the Fireside*—for though the whole of the landscape is given, yet each verse almost might stand as a small picture by itself. It is one of Browning's favourite ways of description, to walk slowly through the landscape, describing step by step those parts of it which strike him, and leaving to us to combine the parts into the whole. But *his* way of combination is to touch the last thing he describes with human love, and to throw back this atmosphere of feeling over all the pictures he has made. The verses I quote do this.

> Oh moment, one and infinite!
>   The water slips o'er stock and stone;
> The West is tender, hardly bright:
>   How grey at once is the evening grown—
> One star, its chrysolite!
>
> We two stood there with never a third,
>   But each by each, as each knew well:
> The sights we saw and the sounds we heard,
>   The lights and the shades made up a spell
> Till the trouble grew and stirred.
>
> Oh, the little more, and how much it is!
>   And the little less, and what worlds away!
> How a sound shall quicken content to bliss,
>   Or a breath suspend the blood's best play,
> And life be a proof of this!

There are many such miniatures of Nature in Browning's poetry. Sometimes, however, the pictures are larger and nobler, when the natural thing described is in itself charged with power, terror or dignity. I give one instance of this, where the fierce Italian thunderstorm is enhanced by being the messenger of God's vengeance on guilt. It is from *Pippa Passes*. The heaven's pillars are overbowed with heat. The black-blue canopy descends close on Ottima and Sebald.

> Buried in woods we lay, you recollect;
> Swift ran the searching tempest overhead;
> And ever and anon some bright white shaft
> Burned thro' the pine-tree roof, here burned and there,
> As if God's messenger thro' the close wood-screen
> Plunged and replunged his weapon at a venture,
> Feeling for guilty thee and me; then broke
> The thunder like a whole sea overhead—

That is as splendid as the thing itself.

Again, no one can help observing in all these quotations the extraordinary love of colour, a love Tennyson has in far fainter measure, but which Browning seems to possess more than any other English poet. Only Sir Walter Scott approaches him in this. Scott, knowing the Highlands, knew dark magnificence of colour. But Browning's love of colour arose from his having lived so long in Italy, where the light is so pure, clear, and brilliant that colour is more intense, and at dawn and sunset more deep, delicate, and various than it is in our land. Sometimes, as Ruskin says, "it is not colour, it is conflagration"; but wherever it is, in the bell of a flower, on the edge of a cloud, on the back of a lizard, on the veins of a lichen, it strikes in Browning's verse at our eyes, and he only, in English poetry, has joy enough in it to be its full interpreter.

He sees the wild tulip blow out its great red

bell; he sees the thin clear bubble of blood at its tip; he sees the spike of gold which burns deep in the bluebell's womb; the corals that, like lamps, disperse thick red flame through the dusk green universe of the ocean; the lakes which, when the morn breaks,

> Blaze like a wyvern flying round the sun;

the woodland brake whose withered fern Dawn feeds with gold; the moon carried off at sunrise in purple fire; the larch-blooms crisp and pink; the sanguine heart of the pomegranate; the filberts russet-sheathed and velvet-capped; the poppies crimson to blackness; the red fans of the butterfly falling on the rock like a drop of fire from a brandished torch; the star-fish, rose-jacynth to the finger-tips; and a hundred other passionate seizures of colour. And, for the last of these colour remembrances, in quieter tints—almost in black and white—I quote this lovely verse from *James Lee's Wife*:

> The swallow has set her six young on the rail,
>   And looks seaward:
> The water's in stripes like a snake, olive pale
>   To the leeward,—
> On the weather-side, black, spotted white with the wind.
>   "Good fortune departs, and disaster's behind"—
> Hark, the wind with its wants and its infinite wail!

So, not only do we possess all these landscapes but we possess them in colour. They are painted as well as drawn. It is his love of colour which made at least half of the impulse that drove him at times into Impressionism. Good drawing is little to the impressionist painters. It is the sudden glow, splash or flicker of colour that moves them, which makes on them the swift, the momentary impression they wish to record.

And colour acted on Browning in the same way. I said he had been impressionist, when he liked, for forty years before Impressionism was born in modern art. He was so, because from the beginning he saw things in colour, more than in light and shade. It is well worth a reader's while to search him for colour-impressions. I take one, for example, with the black horse flung in at the end exactly in the way an artist would do it who loved a flash of black life midst of a dead expanse of gold and green:

> Fancy the Pampas' sheen!
> Miles and miles of gold and green
>   Where the sunflowers blow
>   In a solid glow,
> And—to break now and then the screen—
>   Black neck and eyeballs keen,
> Up a wild horse leaps between!

Having, then, this extraordinary power of sight, needing no carefulness of observation or study, but capable of catching and holding without trouble all that his eye rested or glanced upon, it is no wonder that sometimes it amused him to put into verse the doings of a whole day: the work done in it by men of all classes and the natural objects that encompassed them; not cataloguing them dryly, but shooting through them, like rays of light, either his own fancies and thoughts, or the fancies and thoughts of some typical character whom he invented. This he has done specially in two poems: *The Englishman in Italy*, where the vast shell of the Sorrento plain, its sea and mountains, and all the doings of the peasantry, are detailed with the most intimate delight and truth. The second of these poems is *Up at a Villa—Down in the City*, where a farm of the Casentino with its surroundings is contrasted with the street-life of Florence; and both are described through the delightful character whom he invents to see them. These poems are astonishing pieces of intimate, joyful observation of scenery.

Again, there is no poet whose love of animals is greater than Browning's, and none who has so frequently, so carefully, so vividly described them. It is amazing, as we go through his work, to realise the largeness of his range in this matter, from the river-horse to the lizard, from the eagle to the wren, from the loud singing bee to the filmy insect in the sunshine. I give a few examples. Mortal man could not see a lynx more clearly than Karshish—

> A black lynx snarled and pricked a tufted ear;
> Lust of my blood inflamed his yellow balls.

And the very soul of the Eagle is in this question—

> Ask the geier-eagle why she stoops at once
> Into the vast and unexplored abyss,
> What full-grown power informs her from the first,
> Why she not marvels, strenuously beating
> The silent boundless regions of the sky!

He has watched the heavy-winged osprey in its haunts, fain to fly,

> but forced the earth his couch to make
> Far inland, till his friend the tempest wake,

on whose fiercer wings he can flap his own into activity.

In *Caliban upon Setebos*, as would naturally be the

case, animal life is everywhere; and how close to truth, how keenly observed it is, how the right points for description are chosen to make us feel the beast and bird in a single line; how full of colour, how flashed into words which seem like colours, the descriptions are, any animal-lover may hear in the few lines I quote:

> Yon otter, sleek-wet, black, lithe as a leech;
> Yon auk, one fire-eye in a ball of foam,
> That floats and feeds; a certain badger brown
> He hath watched hunt with that slant white-wedge eye,
> By moonlight.

That is enough to prove his power. And the animals are seen, not as a cultured person sees them, but as a savage, with his eyes untroubled by thoughts, sees them; for Browning, with his curious self-transmuting power, has put himself into the skin of Caliban. Then again, in that lovely lyric in *Paracelsus*,

> Thus the Mayne glideth,

the banks and waves are full of all the bird and beast life of a river. Elsewhere, he sees the falcon spread his wings like a banner, the stork clapping his bill in the marsh, the coot dipping his blue breast in the water, the swallow flying to Venice—"that stout sea-farer"—the lark shivering for joy, and a hundred other birds; and lastly, even the great bird of the Imagination, the Phœnix, flying home; and in a splendid verse records the sight:

> As the King-bird with ages on his plumes
> Travels to die in his ancestral glooms.

Not less wonderful, and more unique in English poetry, is his painting of insects. He describes the hermit-bee, the soft, small, unfrighted thing, lighting on the dead vine-leaf, and twirling and filing all day. He strikes out the grasshopper at a touch—

> Chirrups the contumacious grasshopper.

He has a swift vision of the azure damsel-fly flittering in the wood:

> Child of the simmering quiet, there to die.

He sees all the insect population of an old green wall; fancies the fancies of the crickets and the flies, and the carousing of the cicala in the trees, and the bee swinging in the chalice of the campanula, and the wasps pricking the papers round the peaches, and the gnats and early moths craving their food from God when dawn awakes them, and the fireflies crawling like lamps through the moss, and the spider, sprinkled with mottles on an ash-grey back, and building his web on the edge of tombs. These are but a few things out of this treasure-house of animal observation and love. It is a love which animates and populates with life his landscapes.

Many of the points I have attempted here to make are illustrated in *Saul*. In verse v. the sheep are pictured, with all a shepherd's delightful affection, coming back at evening to the folding; and, with David's poetic imagination, compared to the stars following one another into the meadows of night—

> And now one after one seeks his lodging, as star follows star
> Into eve and the blue far above us,—so blue and so far!—

In verse vi. the quails, and the crickets, and the

jerboa at the door of his sand house, are thrilled into quicker life by David's music. In verse ix. the full joy of living in beasts and men is painted in the midst of landscape after landscape, struck out in single lines,—till all nature seems crowded and simmering with the intense life whose rapture Browning loved so well. These fully reveal his poetic communion with animals. Then, there is a fine passage in verse x. where he describes the loosening of a thick bed of snow from the mountain-side*—an occurrence which also drew the interest of Shelley in the *Prometheus*—which illustrates what I have said of Browning's conception of the separate life, as of giant Titans, of the vaster things in Nature. The mountain is alive and lives his life with his own grim joy, and wears his snow like a breastplate, and discharges it when it pleases him. It is only David who thinks that the great creature lives to guard us from the tempests. And Hebron, high on its crested hill, lifts itself out of the morning mist in the same giant fashion,

> For I wake in the grey dewy covert, while Hebron upheaves
> The dawn struggling with night on his shoulder, and Kidron retrieves
> Slow the damage of yesterday's sunshine.

Then, at the end of the poem, Browning represents all Nature as full of emotion, as gathered into a fuller life, by David's prophecy of the coming of

---

* David could only have seen this on the upper slopes of Hermon. But at the time of the poem, when he is the shepherd-youth, he could scarcely have visited the north of Palestine. Indeed, he does not seem all his life long to have been near Hermon. Browning has transferred to David what he himself had seen in Switzerland.

immortal Love in Christ to man. This sympathy of Nature with humanity is so rare a thought in Browning, and so apart from his view of her, that I think he felt its strangeness here; so that he has taken some pains to make us understand that it is not Nature herself who does this, but David, in his uplifted inspiration, who imputes it to her. If that is not the case, it is at least interesting to find the poet, impassioned by his imagination of the situation, driven beyond his usual view into another land of thought.

There is one more thing to say in closing this chapter. Browning, unlike Tennyson, did not invent his landscapes. He drew directly from nature. The landscapes in *Pauline* and *Sordello*, and in the lyrical poems are plainly recollections of what he has seen and noted in his memory, from the sweep of the mountainous or oceanic horizon to the lichen on the rock and the painted shell on the seashore. Even the imaginative landscape of *Childe Roland* is a memory, not an invention. I do not say he would have been incapable of such invented landscape as we find in *Œnone* and the *Lotos-Eaters*, but it was not his way to do this. However, he does it once; but he takes care to show that it is not real landscape he is drawing, but landscape in a picture. In *Gerard de Lairesse*, one of the poems in *Parleyings with Certain People*, he sets himself to rival the "Walk" in Lairesse's *Art of Painting*, and he invents as a background to mythological or historic scenes, five landscapes, of dawn, morning, and noon, evening and falling night. They may be compared with the walk in *Pauline*, and indeed one of them with its deep pool watched over by the trees recalls his description of a similar pool in *Pauline*—a lasting impression of his youth, for it is again used in *Sordello*. These landscapes are some of his most careful natural description. They begin with the great thunderstorm of dawn in which Prometheus is seen riveted to his rock and the eagle-hound of Zeus beside him. Then the morning is described and the awakening of the earth and Artemis going forth, the huntress-queen and the queen of death; then noon with Lyda and the Satyr—that sad story; then evening charged with the fate of empires; and then the night, and in it a vast ghost, the ghost of departing glory and beauty. The descriptions are too long to quote, but far too short to read. I would that Browning had done more of this excellent work; but that these were created when he was an old man proves that the fire of imagination burnt in him to the end. They are full of those keen picture-words in which he smites into expression the central point of a landscape. They realise the glory of light, the force, fierceness, even the quiet of Nature, but they have lost a great deal of the colour of which once he was so lavish. Nevertheless, the whole scheme of colour in these pictures, with their figures, recalls the pictures of Tintoret. They have his *furia*, his black, gold, and sombre purple, his white mist and barred clouds and the thunder-roar in his skies. Nor are Prometheus and Artemis, and Lyda on her heap of skins in the deep woods, unworthy of the daring hand of the great Venetian. They seem to stand forth from his canvas.

The poem closes with a charming lyric, half-sad, half-joyful, in which he hails the spring, and which in itself is full of his heart when it was close to the hopefulness he drew from natural beauty. I quote it to close this chapter :

> Dance, yellows and whites and reds,
> Lead your gay orgy, leaves, stalks, heads
> Astir with the wind in the tulip-beds
>
> There's sunshine ; scarcely a wind at all
> Disturbs starved grass and daisies small
> On a certain mound by a churchyard wall.
>
> Daisies and grass be my heart's bed-fellows,
> On the mound wind spares and sunshine mellows:
> Dance you, reds and whites and yellows

CHAPTER III

THE TREATMENT OF NATURE

IN the previous chapter, some of the statements made on Browning as a poet of Nature were not sufficiently illustrated; and there are other elements in his natural description which demand attention. The best way to repair these deficiencies will be to take chronologically the natural descriptions in his poems and to comment upon them, leaving out those on which we have already touched. New points of interest will thus arise; and, moreover, taking his natural description as it occurs from volume to volume, we may be able—within this phase of his poetic nature—to place his poetic development in a clearer light.

I begin, therefore, with *Pauline*. The descriptions of nature in that poem are more deliberate, more for their own sake, than elsewhere in Browning's poetry. The first of them faintly recalls the manner of Shelley in the *Alastor*, and I have no doubt was influenced by him. The two others, and the more finished, have already escaped from Shelley, and are almost pre-Raphaelite, as much so as Keats, in their detail. Yet all the three are original, not imitative. They suggest Shelley and Keats, and no more, and it is only the manner and not the matter of these poets that they suggest. Browning became instantly original in this as in other modes of poetry. It was characteristic of him from the beginning to the end of his career, to possess within himself his own methods, to draw out of himself new matter and new shapings.

From one point of view this was full of treasureable matter for us. It is not often the gods give us so opulent an originality. From another point of view it was unfortunate. If he had begun by imitating a little; if he had studied the excellences of his predecessors more; if he had curbed his individuality sufficiently to mark, learn and inwardly digest the noble style of others in natural description, and in all other matters of poetry as well, his work would have been much better than it is; his original excellences would have found fitter and finer expression; his faults would have been enfeebled instead of being developed; his style would have been more concise on one side, less abrupt on another, and we should not have been wrongly disturbed by obscurities of diction and angularities of expression. He would have reached more continuously the splendid level he often attained. This is plentifully illustrated by his work on external nature, but less perhaps than by his work on humanity.

The first natural description he published is in the beginning of *Pauline:*

> Thou wilt remember one warm morn when winter
> Crept agèd from the earth, and spring's first breath
> Blew soft from the moist hills; the blackthorn boughs,
> So dark in the bare wood, when glistening
> In the sunshine were white with coming buds,
> Like the bright side of a sorrow, and the banks
> Had violets opening from sleep like eyes.

That is fairly good; he describes what he has seen; but it might have been better. We know what he means, but his words do not accurately or imaginatively convey this meaning. The best lines are the first three, but the peculiar note of Shelley sighs so fully in them that they do not represent Browning. What is special in them is his peculiar delight not only in the morning which here he celebrates, but in the spring. It was in his nature, even in old age, to love with passion the beginnings of things; dawn, morning, spring and youth, and their quick blood; their changes, impulses, their unpremeditated rush into fresh experiment. Unlike Tennyson, who was old when he was old, Browning was young when he was old. Only once in *Asolando*, in one poem, can we trace that he felt winter in his heart. And the lines in *Pauline* which I now quote, spoken by a young man who had dramatised himself into momentary age, are no ill description of his temper at times when he was really old:

> As life wanes, all its care and strife and toil
> Seem strangely valueless, while the old trees
> Which grew by our youth's home, the waving mass
> Of climbing plants heavy with bloom and dew,
> The morning swallows with their songs like words,
> All these seem clear and only worth our thoughts:
> So, aught connected with my early life,
> My rude songs or my wild imaginings,
> How I look on them—most distinct amid
> The fever and the stir of after years!

The next description in *Pauline* is that in which he describes—to illustrate what Shelley was to him—the woodland spring which became a mighty river. Shelley, as first conceived by Browning, seemed to him like a sacred spring:

> Scarce worth a moth's flitting, which long grasses cross,
> And one small tree embowers droopingly—
> Joying to see some wandering insect won
> To live in its few rushes, or some locust
> To pasture on its boughs, or some wild bird
> Stoop for its freshness from the trackless air.

A piece of careful detail, close to nature, but not close enough; needing to be more detailed or less detailed, but the first instance in his work of his deliberate use of Nature, not for love of herself only, (Wordsworth, Coleridge or Byron would have described the spring in the woods for its own sake), but for illustration of humanity. It is Shelley—Shelley in his lonely withdrawn character, Shelley hidden in the wood of his own thoughts, and, like a spring in that wood, bubbling upwards into personal poetry—of whom Browning is now thinking. The image is good, but a better poet would have dwelt more on the fountain and left the insects and birds alone. It is Shelley also of whom he thinks—Shelley breaking away from personal poetry to write of the fates of men, of liberty and love and overthrow of wrong, of the future of mankind—when he expands his tree-shaded fountain into the river and follows it to the sea:

> And then should find it but the fountain head,
> Long lost, of some great river washing towns
> And towers, and seeing old woods which will live
> But by its banks untrod of human foot,
> Which, when the great sun sinks, lie quivering
> In light as some thing lieth half of life
> Before God's foot, waiting a wondrous change;
> Then girt with rocks which seek to turn or stay
> Its course in vain, for it does ever spread
> Like a sea's arm as it goes rolling on,
> Being the pulse of some great country—so
> Wast thou to me, and art thou to the world!

How good some of that is; how bad it is elsewhere! How much it needs thought, concentration, and yet how vivid also and original! And the faults of it, of grammar, of want of clearness, of irritating parenthesis, of broken threads of thought, of inability to leave out the needless, are faults of which Browning never quite cleared his work. I do not think he ever cared to rid himself of them.

The next description is not an illustration of man by means of Nature. It is almost the only set description of Nature, without reference to man, which occurs in the whole of Browning's work. It is introduced by his declaration (for in this I think he speaks from himself) of his power of living in the life of all living things. He does not think of himself as living in the whole Being of Nature, as Wordsworth or Shelley might have done. There was a certain matter of factness in him which prevented his belief in any theory of that kind. But he does transfer himself into the rejoicing life of the animals and plants, a life which he knows is akin to his own. And this distinction is true of all his poetry of Nature. "I can mount with the bird," he says,

> Leaping airily his pyramid of leaves
> And twisted boughs of some tall mountain tree,
> Or like a fish breathe deep the morning air
> In the misty sun-warm water.

This introduces the description of a walk of twenty-four hours through various scenes of natural beauty. It is long and elaborate—the scenery he conceives round the home where he and Pauline are to live. And it is so close, and so much of it is repeated in other forms in his later poetry, that I think it is drawn direct from Nature; that it is here done of set purpose to show his hand in natural description. It begins with night, but soon leaves night for the morning and the noon. Here is a piece of it:

> Morning, the rocks and valleys and old woods.
> How the sun brightens in the mist, and here,
> Half in the air, like * creatures of the place,
> Trusting the elements, living on high boughs
> That sway in the wind—look at the silver spray
> Flung from the foam-sheet of the cataract
> Amid the broken rocks! Shall we stay here
> With the wild hawks? No, ere the hot noon come
> Dive we down—safe! See, this is our new retreat
> Walled in with a sloped mound of matted shrubs,
> Dark, tangled, old and green, still sloping down
> To a small pool whose waters lie asleep,
> Amid the trailing boughs turned water-plants:
> And tall trees overarch to keep us in,
> Breaking the sunbeams into emerald shafts,
> And in the dreamy water one small group
> Of two or three strange trees are got together
> Wondering at all around—

This is nerveless work, tentative, talkative, no clear expression of the whole; and as he tries to expand it further in lines we may study with interest, for the very failures of genius are interesting, he becomes even more feeble. Yet the feebleness is traversed by verses of power, like lightning flashing through a mist upon the sea. The chief thing to say about this direct, detailed work is that he got out of its manner as fast as he could. He never tried it again, but passed on to suggest the landscape by a few sharp, high-coloured words; choosing out one or two of its elements and

* Creatures accordant with the place?

flashing them into prominence. The rest was left to the imagination of the reader.

He is better when he comes forth from the shadowy woodland-pool into the clear air and open landscape :

> Up for the glowing day, leave the old woods!
> See, they part like a ruined arch : the sky!
> Blue sunny air, where a great cloud floats laden
> With light, like a dead whale that white birds pick,
> Floating away in the sun in some north sea.
> Air, air, fresh life-blood, thin and searching air,
> The clear, dear breath of God that loveth us,
> Where small birds reel and winds take their delight!

The last three lines are excellent, but nothing could be worse than the sensational image of the dead whale. It does not fit the thing he desires to illustrate, and it violates the sentiment of the scene he is describing, but its strangeness pleased his imagination, and he put it in without a question. Alas, in after times, he only too often, both in the poetry of nature and of the human soul, hurried into his verse illustrations which had no natural relation to the matter in hand, just because it amused him to indulge his fancy. The finished artist could not do this; he would hear, as it were, the false note, and reject it. But Browning, a natural artist, never became a perfect one. Nevertheless, as his poetry went on, he reached, by natural power, splendid description, as indeed I have fully confessed; but, on the other hand, one is never sure of him. He is never quite "inevitable."

The attempt at deliberate natural description in *Pauline*, of which I have now spoken, is not renewed in *Paracelsus*. By the time he wrote that poem the movement and problem of the spirit of man had all but quenched his interest in natural scenery. Nature is only introduced as a background, almost a scenic background for the players, who are the passions, thoughts, and aspirations of the intellectual life of Paracelsus. It is only at the beginning of Part II. that we touch a landscape:

> Over the waters in the vaporous West
> The sun goes down as in a sphere of gold
> Behind the arm of the city, which between;
> With all the length of domes and minarets,
> Athwart the splendour, black and crooked runs
> Like a Turk verse along a scimitar.

That is all; nothing but an introduction. Paracelsus turns in a moment from the sight, and absorbs himself in himself, just as Browning was then doing in his own soul. Nearly two thousand lines are then written before Nature is again touched upon, and then Festus and Paracelsus are looking at the dawn; and it is worth saying how in this description Browning's work on Nature has so greatly improved that one can scarcely believe he is the same poet who wrote the wavering descriptions of *Pauline*. This is close and clear:

> Morn must be near.
>   FESTUS.   Best ope the casement: see,
> The night, late strewn with clouds and flying stars,
> Is blank and motionless: how peaceful sleep
> The tree-tops all together! Like an asp *
> The wind slips whispering from bough to bough.
>   *   *   *   *   *

* Browning, even more than Shelley, was fond of using the snake in his poetry. Italy is in that habit.

> PARACELSUS. See, morn at length. The heavy darkness seems
> Diluted, grey and clear without the stars;
> The shrubs bestir and rouse themselves as if
> Some snake, that weighed them down all night, let go
> His hold; and from the East, fuller and fuller,
> Day, like a mighty river, flowing in;
> But clouded, wintry, desolate and cold.

That is good, clear, and sufficient; and there the description should end. But Browning, driven by some small demon, adds to it three lines of mere observant fancy.

> Yet see how that broad prickly star-shaped plant,
> Half-down in the crevice, spreads its woolly leaves,
> All thick and glistening with diamond dew.

What is that for? To give local colour or reality? It does neither. It is mere childish artistry. Tennyson could not have done it. He knew when to stay his hand.*

The finest piece of natural description in *Para-*

---

* There is a fine picture of the passing of a hurricane in *Paracelsus* (p. 67, vol i.) which illustrates this inability to stop when he has done all he needs. Paracelsus speaks:

> The hurricane is spent,
> And the good boat speeds through the brightening weather;
> But is it earth or sea that heaves below?
> The gulf rolls like a meadow-swell, o'erstrewn
> With ravaged boughs and remnants of the shore;
> And now, some islet, loosened from the land,
> Swims past with all its trees, sailing to ocean:
> *And now the air is full of uptorn canes,*
> *Light strippings from the fan-trees, tamarisks*
> *Unrooted, with their birds still clinging to them,*
> *All high in the wind.* Even so my varied life
> Drifts by me.

I think that the lines I have italicised should have been left out. They weaken what he has well done.

celsus is of the coming of Spring. It is full of the joy of life; it is inspired by a passionate thought, lying behind it, concerning man. It is still more inspired by his belief that God himself was eternal joy and filled the universe with rapture. Nowhere did Browning reach a greater height in his Nature poetry than in these lines, yet they are more a description, as usual, of animal life than of the beauty of the earth and sea:

> Then all is still; earth is a wintry clod:
> But spring-wind, like a dancing psaltress, passes
> Over its breast to waken it, rare verdure
> Buds tenderly upon rough banks, between
> The withered tree-roots and the cracks of frost,
> Like a smile striving with a wrinkled face;
> The grass grows bright, the boughs are swoln with blooms
> Like chrysalids impatient for the air,
> The shining dorrs are busy, beetles run
> Along the furrows, ants make their ado;
> Above, birds fly in merry flocks, the lark
> Soars up and up, shivering for very joy;
> Afar the ocean sleeps; white fishing-gulls
> Flit where the strand is purple with its tribe
> Of nested limpets; savage creatures seek
> Their loves in wood and plain—and God renews
> His ancient rapture.

Once more, in *Paracelsus*, there is the lovely lyric about the flowing of the Mayne. I have driven through that gracious country of low hill and dale and wide water-meadows, where under flowered banks only a foot high the slow river winds in gentleness; and this poem is steeped in the sentiment of the scenery. But, as before, Browning quickly slides away from the beauty of inanimate nature into a record of the animals that haunt the stream. He could not get on long with mountains and rivers alone. He must people them with breathing, feeling things; anything for life!

> Thus the Mayne glideth
> Where my Love abideth.
> Sleep's no softer; it proceeds
> On through lawns, on through meads,
> On and on, whate'er befall,
> Meandering and musical,
> Though the niggard pasturage
> Bears not on its shaven ledge
> Aught but weeds and waving grasses
> To view the river as it passes,
> Save here and there a scanty patch
> Of primroses too faint to catch
> A weary bee.
>   And scarce it pushes
> Its gentle way through strangling rushes
> Where the glossy kingfisher
> Flutters when noon-heats are near,
> Glad the shelving banks to shun
> Red and steaming in the sun,
> Where the shrew-mouse with pale throat
> Burrows, and the speckled stoat;
> Where the quick sandpipers flit
> In and out the marl and grit
> That seems to breed them, brown as they:
> Naught disturbs its quiet way,
> Save some lazy stork that springs,
> Trailing it with legs and wings,
> Whom the shy fox from the hill
> Rouses, creep he ne'er so still.

"My heart, they loose my heart, those simple words," cries Paracelsus, and he was right. They tell of that which to see and love is better, wiser, than to probe and know all the problems of knowledge. But that is a truth not understood, not believed. And few there be who find it. And if Browning had found the secret of how to live more outside of his understanding than he did, or having found it, had not forgotten it, he would not perhaps have spoken more wisely for the good of man, but he would have more continuously written better poetry.

The next poem in which he may be said to touch Nature is *Sordello*. *Strafford* does not count, save for the charming song of the boat in music and moonlight, which the children sing. In *Sordello*, the problem of life, as in *Paracelsus*, is still the chief matter, but outward life, as not in *Paracelsus*, takes an equal place with inward life. And naturally, Nature, its changes and beauty, being outward, are more fully treated than in *Paracelsus*. But it is never treated for itself alone. It is made to image or reflect the sentiment of the man who sees it, or to illustrate a phase of his passion or his thought. But there is a closer grip upon it than before, a clearer definition, a greater power of concentrated expression of it, and especially, a fuller use of colour. Browning paints Nature now like a Venetian; the very shadows of objects are in colour. This new power was a kind of revelation to him, and he frequently uses it with a personal joy in its exercise. Things in Nature blaze in his poetry now and afterwards in gold, purple, the crimson of blood, in sunlit green and topaz, in radiant blue, in dyes of earthquake and eclipse. Then, when he has done his landscape thus in colour, he adds more; he places in its foreground one drop, one eye of still more flaming colour, to vivify and inflame the whole.

The main landscape of *Sordello* is the plain and the low pine-clad hills around Mantua; the half-circle of the deep lagoon which enarms the battlemented town; and the river Mincio, seen by Sordello when he comes out of the forest on the hill, as it enters and leaves the lagoon, and winds, a silver ribbon, through the plain. It is the landscape Vergil must have loved. A long bridge of more than a hundred arches, with towers of defence, crosses the marsh from the towered gateway of the walls to the mainland, and in the midst of the lagoon the deep river flows fresh and clear with a steady swiftness. Scarcely anywhere in North Italy is the upper sky more pure at dawn and even, and there is no view now so mystic in its desolation. Over the lagoon, and puffing from it, the mists, daily encrimsoned by sunrise and sunset, continually rise and disperse.

The character and the peculiarities of this landscape Browning has seized and enshrined in verse. But his descriptions are so arranged as to reflect certain moments of crisis in the soul of Sordello. He does not describe this striking landscape for its own sake, but for the sake of his human subject. The lines I quote below describe noon-day on the lagoon, seen from the golden woods and black pines; and the vision of the plain, city and river, suddenly opening out from the wood, symbolises the soul of Sordello opening out from solitude "into the veritable business of mankind."

> Then wide
> Opened the great morass, shot every side
> With flashing water through and through; a-shine,
> Thick-steaming, all-alive. Whose shape divine
> Quivered i' the farthest rainbow-vapour, glanced
> Athwart the flying herons? He advanced,
> But warily; though Mincio leaped no more,
> Each footfall burst up in the marish-floor
> A diamond jet.

And then he somewhat spoils this excellent thing by a piece of detail too minute for the largeness of the impression. But how clear and how full of true sentiment it is; and how the image of Palma rainbowed in the mist, and of Sordello seeing her, fills the landscape with youthful passion!

Here is the same view in the morning, when Mincio has come down in flood and filled the marsh:

> Mincio, in its place,
> Laughed, a broad water, in next morning's face,
> And, where the mists broke up immense and white
> I' the steady wind, burned like a spilth of light
> Out of the crashing of a million stars.

It were well to compare that brilliant piece of light with the grey water-sunset at Ferrara in the beginning of Book VI.

> While eve slow sank
> Down the near terrace to the farther bank,
> And only one spot left from out the night
> Glimmered upon the river opposite—
> A breadth of watery heaven like a bay,
> A sky-like space of water, ray for ray,
> And star for star, one richness where they mixed
> As this and that wing of an angel, fixed,
> Tumultuary splendours folded in
> To die.

As usual, Spring enchants him. The second book begins with her coming, and predicates the coming change in Sordello's soul.

> The woods were long austere with snow; at last
> Pink leaflets budded on the beech, and fast
> Larches, scattered through pine-tree solitudes,
> Brightened, as in the slumbrous heart of the woods
> Our buried year, a witch, grew young again
> To placid incantations, and that stain
> About were from her cauldron, green smoke blent
> With those black pines.

Nor does he omit in *Sordello* to recall two other favourite aspects of nature, long since recorded in *Pauline*, the ravine and the woodland spring. Just as Turner repeated in many pictures of the same place what he had first observed in it, so Browning recalled in various poems the first impressions of his youth. He had a curious love for a ravine with overhanging trees and a thin thread of water, looping itself round rocks. It occurs in the *Fireside*, it is taken up in his later poems, and up such a ravine Sordello climbs among the pines of Goito:

> He climbed with (June at deep) some close ravine
> Mid clatter of its million pebbles sheen,
> Over which, singing soft, the runnel slipped
> Elate with rains.

Then, in *Sordello*, we come again across the fountain in the grove he draws in *Pauline*, now greatly improved in clearness and word-brightness—a real vision. Fate has given him here a fount

> Of pure loquacious pearl, the soft tree-tent
> Guards, with its face of reate and sedge, nor fail
> The silver globules and gold-sparkling grail
> At bottom—

where the impulse of the water sends up the sand in a cone—a solitary loveliness of Nature that Coleridge and Tennyson have both drawn with a finer pencil than Browning. The other examples of natural description in *Sordello*, as well as those in *Balaustion* I shall reserve till I speak of those poems. As to the dramas, they are wholly employed with humanity. In them man's soul has so overmastered Browning that they are scarcely diversified half a dozen times by any illustrations derived from Nature.

We now come, with *The Ring and the Book*, to a clear division in his poetry of Nature. From this time forth Nature decays in his verse. Man masters it and drives it out. In *The Ring and the Book*, huge as it is, Nature rarely intrudes; the human passion of the matter is so great that it swallows up all Browning's interest. There is a little forky flashing description of the entrance to the Val d'Ema in Guido's first statement. Caponsacchi is too intensely gathered round the tragedy to use a single illustration from Nature. The only person who does use illustrations from Nature is the only one who is by age, by his life, by the apartness of his high place, capable of sufficient quiet and contemplation to think of Nature at all. This is the Pope.

He illustrates with great vigour the way in which Guido destroyed all the home life which clung about him and himself remained dark and vile, by the burning of a nest-like hut in the Campagna, with all its vines and ivy and flowers; till nothing remains but the blackened walls of the malicious tower round which the hut had been built.

He illustrates the sudden event which, breaking in on Caponsacchi's life, drew out of him his latent power and his inward good, by this vigorous description:

> As when a thundrous midnight, with black air
> That burns, rain-drops that blister, breaks a spell,
> Draws out the excessive virtue of some sheathed
> Shut unsuspected flower that hoards and hides
> Immensity of sweetness.

And the last illustration, in which the Pope hopes that Guido's soul may yet be sayed by the suddenness of his death, is one of the finest pieces of natural description in Browning, and reads like one of his own memories:

> I stood at Naples once, a night so dark
> I could have scarce conjectured there was earth
> Anywhere, sky or sea or world at all:
> But the night's black was burst through by a blaze—
> Thunder struck blow on blow, earth groaned and bore,
> Through her whole length of mountain visible:
> There lay the city thick and plain with spires,
> And, like a ghost disshrouded, white the sea.
> So may the truth be flashed out by one blow,
> And Guido see, one instant, and be saved.

After *The Ring and the Book*, poor Nature, as one of Browning's mistresses, was somewhat neglected for a time, and he gave himself up to ugly representations of what was odd or twisted in humanity, to its smaller problems, like that contained in *Fifine at the Fair*, to its fantastic impulses, its strange madnesses, its basenesses, even its commonplace crimes. These subjects were redeemed by his steady effort to show that underneath these evil developments of human nature lay immortal good; and that a wise tolerance, based on this underlying godlikeness in man, was the true attitude of the soul towards the false and the stupid in mankind. This had been his attitude from the beginning. It differentiates him from Tennyson, who did not maintain that view; and at that point he is a nobler poet than Tennyson.

But he became too much absorbed in the intellectual treatment of these side-issues in human nature. And I think that he was left unprotected from this or not held back from it by his having almost given up Nature in her relation to man as a subject for his poetry. To love that great, solemn and beautiful Creature, who even when she seems most merciless retains her glory and loveliness, keeps us from thinking too much on the lower problems of humanity, on its ignobler movements; holds before us infinite grandeur, infinite beauty, infinite order, and suggests and confirms within us eternal aspiration. Those intimations of the ideal and endless perfectness which are dimmed within us by the meaner aspects of human life, or by the sordid difficulties of thought which a sensual and wealth-seeking society present to us, are restored to us by her quiet, order and beauty. When he wrote *Prince Hohenstiel-Schwangau*, *Red Cotton Night-cap Country*, and *The Inn Album*, Nature had ceased to awaken the poetic passion in him, and his poetry suffered from the loss. Its interest lies in the narrow realm of intellectual analysis, not in the large realm of tragic or joyous passion. He became the dissector of corrupt bodies, not the creator of living beings.

Nevertheless, in *Fifine at the Fair* there are several intercalated illustrations from Nature, all of which are interesting and some beautiful. The sunset over Sainte-Marie and the Île Noirmoutier, with the birds who sing to the dead, and the coming of the nightwind and the tide, is as largely wrought as the description of the mountain rill—the "infant of mist and dew," and its voyage to the sea is minute and delicate. There is also that magnificent description of a sunset which I have already quoted. It is drawn to illustrate some remote point in the argument, and is far too magnificent for the thing it illustrates. Yet how few in this long poem, how remote from Browning's heart, are these touches of Nature.

Again, in *The Inn Album* there is a description of an English elm-tree, as an image of a woman who makes marriage life seem perfect, which is interesting because it is the third, and only the third, reference to English scenery in the multitude of Browning's verses. The first is in *Pauline*, the second in that poem, "Oh, to be in England," and this is the third. The woman has never ceased to gaze

> On the great elm-tree in the open, posed
> Placidly full in front, smooth bole, broad branch,
> And leafage, one green plenitude of May.
> . . . bosomful
> Of lights and shades, murmurs and silences,
> Sun-warmth, dew-coolness, squirrel, bee, bird,
> High, higher, highest, till the blue proclaims
> " Leave Earth, there's nothing better till next step
> Heavenward!"

This, save in one line, is not felt or expressed with any of that passion which makes what a poet says completely right.

Browning could not stay altogether in this condition, in which, moreover, his humour was also in abeyance; and in his next book, *Pacchiarotto, &c.*, he broke away from these morbid subjects, and, with that recovery, recovered also some of his old love of Nature. The prologue to that book is poetry; and Nature (though he only describes an old stone wall in Italy covered with straying plants) is interwoven with his sorrow and his love. Then, all through the book, even in its most fantastic humour, Nature is not altogether neglected for humanity; and the poetry, which Browning seemed to have lost the power to create, has partly returned to him. That is also the case in *La Saisiaz*, and I have already spoken of the peculiar elements of the nature-poetry in that work. In the *Dramatic Idyls*, of which he was himself fond; and in *Jocoseria*, there is very little natural description. The subjects did not allow of it, but yet Nature sometimes glides in, and when she does, thrills the verse into a higher humanity. In *Ferishtah's Fancies*, a book full of flying charm, Nature has her proper place, and in the lyrics which close the stories she is not forgotten; but still there is not the care for her which once ran like a full river of delight through his landscape of human nature. He loved, indeed, that landscape of mankind the most, the plains and hills and woods of human life; but when he watered it with the great river of Nature his best work was done. Now, as life grew to a close, that river had too much dried up in his poetry.

It was not that he had not the power to describe Nature if he cared. But he did not care. I have spoken of the invented descriptions of morn and noon and sunset in Gerard de Lairesse in the book which preceded *Asolando*. They have his trenchant power, words that beat out the scene like strokes on an anvil, but, curiously enough, they are quite unsuffused with human feeling; as if, having once divorced Nature from humanity, he never could bring them together again. Nor is this a mere theory. The Prologue to *Asolando* supports it.

That sorrowful poem, written, it seems, in the year he died (1889), reveals his position towards Nature when he had lost the power of youth to pour fire on the world. It is full of his last thinking. "The poet's age is sad," he says. "In youth his eye lent to everything in the natural world the colours of his own soul, the rainbow glory of imagination:

> And now a flower is just a flower:
>   Man, bird, beast are but beast, bird, man—
> Simply themselves, uncinct by dower
>   Of dyes which, when life's day began,
> Round each in glory ran."

"Ah! what would you have?" he says. "What is the best: things draped in colour, as by a lens, or the naked things themselves? truth ablaze, or falsehood's fancy haze? I choose the first."

It is an old man's effort to make the best of age. For my part, I do not see that the things are the better for losing the colour the soul gives them. The things themselves are indifferent. But as seen by the soul, they are seen in God, and the colour and light which imagination gives them are themselves divine. Nor is their colour or light only in our imagination, but in themselves also, part of the glory and beauty of God. A flower is never only a flower, or a beast a beast. And so Browning would have said in the days when he was still a lover of Nature as well as of man, when he was still a faithful soldier in the army of imagination, a poet more than a philosopher at play. It is a sad business. He has not lost his eagerness to advance, to climb beyond the flaming walls, to find God in his heaven. He has not lost the great hopes with which he began, nor the ideals he nursed of old. He has not lost his fighting power, nor his cheerful cry that life is before him in the fulness of the world to come. The *Rêverie* and the *Epilogue* to *Asolando* are noble statements of his courage, faith, and joy. There is nothing sad there, nothing to make us beat the breast. But there is sadness in this abandonment of the imaginative glory with which once he clothed the world of Nature; and he ought to have retained it. He would have done so had he not forgotten Nature in anatomising man.

However, he goes on with his undying effort to make the best of things, and though he has lost his rapture in Nature, he has not lost his main theory of man's life and of the use of the universe. The end of this *Prologue* puts it as clearly as it was put in *Paracelsus*. Nothing is changed in that.

"At Asolo," he continues, "my Asolo, when I was young, all natural objects were palpably clothed with fire. They mastered me, not I them. Terror was in their beauty. I was like Moses before the Bush that burned. I adored the splendour I saw. Then I was in danger of being content with it; of mistaking the finite for the infinite beauty. To be satisfied—that was the peril. Now I see the natural world as it is, without the rainbow hues the soul bestowed upon it. Is that well? In one sense yes.

> And now? The lambent flame is—where?
>   Lost from the naked world: earth, sky,
> Hill, vale, tree, flower—Italia's rare
>   O'er-running beauty crowds the eye—
> But flame?—The Bush is bare.

All is distinct, naked, clear, Nature and nothing else. Have I lost anything in getting down to fact instead of to fancy? Have I shut my eyes in pain—pain for disillusion? No—now I know that my home is not in Nature; there is no awe and splendour in her which can keep me with her. Oh, far beyond is the true splendour, the infinite source of awe and love which transcends her:

> No, for the purged ear apprehends
>   Earth's import, not the eye late dazed:
> The Voice said "Call my works thy friends!
>   At Nature dost thou shrink amazed?
> God is it who transcends."

All Browning is in that way of seeing the matter; but he forgets that he could see it in the same fashion while he still retained the imaginative outlook on the world of Nature. And the fact is that he did do so in *Paracelsus*, in *Easter-Day*, in a host of other poems. There was then no need for him to reduce to naked fact the glory with which young imagination clothed the world, in order to realise that God transcended Nature. He had conceived that truth and believed it long ago. And this explanation, placed here, only tells us that he had lost his ancient love of Nature, and it is sorrowful to understand it of him.

Finally, the main contentions of this chapter, which are drawn from a chronological view of Browning's treatment of Nature, are perhaps worth a summary. The first is that, though the love of Nature was always less in him than his love of human nature, yet for the first half of his work it was so interwoven with his human poetry that Nature suggested to him humanity and humanity Nature. And these two, as subjects for thought and feeling, were each uplifted and impassioned, illustrated and developed, by this intercommunion.

That was a true and high position. Humanity was first, Nature second in Browning's poetry, but both were linked together in a noble marriage; and at that time he wrote his best poetry.

The second thing this chronological treatment of his Nature-poetry shows, is that his interest in human nature pushed out his love of Nature, gradually at first, but afterwards more swiftly, till Nature became almost non-existent in his poetry. With that his work sank down into intellectual or ethical exercises, in which poetry decayed.

It shows, thirdly, how the love of Nature, returning, but returning with diminished power, entered again into his love of human nature, and renewed the passion of his poetry, its singing, and its health. But reconciliations of this kind do not bring back all the ancient affection and happiness. Nature and humanity never lived together in his poetry in as vital a harmony as before, nor was the work done on them as good as it was of old. A broken marriage is not repaired by an apparent condonation. Nature and humanity, though both now dwelt in him, kept separate rooms. Their home-life was destroyed. Browning had been drawn away by a Fifine of humanity. He never succeeded in living happily again with Elvire; and while our intellectual interest in his work remained, our poetic interest in it lessened. We read it for mental and ethical entertainment, not for ideal joy.

No; if poetry is to be perfectly written; if the art is to be brought to its noblest height; if it is to continue to lift the hearts of men into the realm where perfection lives; if it is to glow, an unwearied fire, in the world; the love of Nature must be justly mingled in it with the love of humanity. The love of humanity must be first, the love of Nature second, but they must not be divorced. When they are, when the love of Nature forms the only subject, or when the love of Man forms the only subject, poetry decays and dies.

CHAPTER IV

BROWNING'S THEORY OF HUMAN LIFE
PAULINE AND PARACELSUS

TO isolate Browning's view of Nature, and to leave it behind us, seemed advisable before speaking of his work as a poet of mankind. We can now enter freely on that which is most distinctive, most excellent in his work—his human poetry; and the first thing that meets us and in his very first poems, is his special view of human nature, and of human life, and of the relation of both to God. It marks his originality that this view was entirely his own. Ancient thoughts of course are to be found in it, but his combination of them is original amongst the English poets. It marks his genius that he wrought out this conception while he was yet so young. It is partly shaped in *Pauline;* it is fully set forth in *Paracelsus*. And it marks his consistency of mind that he never changed it. I do not think he ever added to it or developed it. It satisfied him when he was a youth, and when he was an old man. We have already seen it clearly expressed in the *Prologue* to *Asolando*.

That theory needs to be outlined, for till it is understood Browning's poetry cannot be understood or loved as fully as we should desire to love it. It exists in *Pauline*, but all its elements are in solution; uncombined, but waiting the electric flash which will mix them, in due proportions, into a composite substance, having a lucid form, and capable of being used. That flash was sent through the confused elements of *Pauline*, and the result was *Paracelsus*.

I will state the theory first, and then, lightly passing through *Pauline* and *Paracelsus*, re-tell it. It is fitting to apologise for the repetition which this method of treatment will naturally cause; but, considering that the theory underlies every drama and poem that he wrote during sixty years, such repetition does not seem unnecessary. There are many who do not easily grasp it, or do not grasp it at all, and they may be grateful. As to those who do understand it, they will be happy in their anger with any explanation of what they know so well.

He asks what is the secret of the world: "of man and man's true purpose, path and fate." He proposes to understand "God and his works and all God's intercourse with the human soul."

We are here, he thinks, to grow enough to be able to take our part in another life or lives. But we are surrounded by limitations which baffle and retard our growth. That is miserable, but not so much as we think; for the failures these limitations cause prevent us—and this is a main point in Browning's view—from being content with our condition on the earth. There is that within us which is always endeavouring to transcend those limitations, and which believes in their final dispersal. This aspiration rises to something higher than any possible actual on earth. It is never worn out; it is the divine in us; and when it seems to decay, God renews it by spiritual influences from without and within, coming to us from nature as seen by us, from humanity as felt by us, and from himself who dwells in us.

But then, unless we find out and submit to those limitations, and work within them, life is useless, so far as any life is useless. But while we work within them, we see beyond them an illimitable land, and thirst for it. This battle between the dire necessity of working in chains and longing for freedom, between the infinite destiny of the soul and the baffling of its effort to realise its infinitude on earth, makes the storm and misery of life. We may try to escape that tempest and sorrow by determining to think, feel, and act only within our limitations, to be content with them as Goethe said; but if we do, we are worse off than before. We have thrown away our divine destiny. If we take this world and are satisfied with it, cease to aspire, beyond our limits, to full perfection in God; if our soul should ever say, "I want no more; what I have here—the pleasure, fame, knowledge, beauty or love of this world—is all I need or care for," then we are indeed lost. That is the last damnation. The worst failure, the deepest misery, is better than contentment with the success of earth; and seen in this light, the failures and misery of earth are actually good things, the cause of a chastened joy. They open to us the larger light. They suggest, and in Browning's belief they proved, that this life is but the threshold of an infinite life, that our true life is beyond, that there is an infinite of happiness, of knowledge, of love, of beauty which we shall attain. Our failures are prophecies of eternal successes. To choose the finite life is to miss the infinite Life! O fool, to claim the little cup of water earth's knowledge offers to thy thirst, or the beauty or love of earth, when the immeasurable waters of the Knowledge, Beauty and Love of the Eternal Paradise are thine beyond the earth.

Two things are then clear: (1) The attainment of our desires for perfection, the satisfaction of our passion for the infinite, is forbidden to us on earth by the limitations of life. We are made imperfect; we are kept imperfect here; and we must do all our work within the limits this natural imperfection makes. (2) We must, nevertheless, not cease to strive towards the perfection unattainable on earth, but which shall be attained hereafter. Our destiny, the God within us, demands that. And we lose it, if we are content with our earthly life, even with its highest things, with knowledge, beauty, or with love.

Hence, the foundation of Browning's theory is a kind of Original Sin in us, a natural defectiveness deliberately imposed on us by God, which prevents us attaining any absolute success on earth. And this defectiveness of nature is met by the truth, which, while we aspire, we know—that God will fulfil all noble desire in a life to come.

We must aspire then, but at the same time all aspiring is to be conterminous with steady work within our limits. Aspiration to the perfect is not to make us idle, indifferent to the present, but to drive us on. Its passion teaches us, as it urges into action all our powers, what we can and what we cannot do. That is, it teaches us, through the action it engenders, what our limits are; and when we know them, the main duties of life rise clear. The first of these is, to work patiently within our limits; and the second is the apparent contradiction of the first, never to be satisfied with our limits, or with the results we attain within them. Then, having worked within them, but always looked beyond them, we, as life closes, learn the secret. The failures of earth prove the victory beyond: " For—

> what is our failure here but a triumph's evidence
> For the fulness of the days? Have we withered or agonised?
> Why else was the pause prolonged but that singing might issue
>   thence?
> Why rushed the discords in but that harmony should be
>   prized?
> Sorrow is hard to bear, and doubt is slow to clear,
>   Each sufferer says his say, his scheme of the weal and the
>   woe:
> But God has a few of us whom he whispers in the ear;
>   The rest may reason, and welcome: 'tis we musicians know.
>   *Abt Vogler.*

Finally, the root and flower of this patient but uncontented work is Love for man because of his being in God, because of his high and immortal destiny. All that we do, whether failure or not, builds up the perfect humanity to come, and flows into the perfection of God in whom is the perfection of man. This love, grounded on this faith, brings joy into life; and, in this joy of love, we enter into the eternal temple of the Life to come. Love opens Heaven while Earth closes us round. At last limitations cease to trouble us.

They are lost in the vision, they bring no more sorrow, doubt or baffling. Therefore, in this confused chaotic time on earth—

> Earn the means first. God surely will contrive
>   Use for our earning.
> Others mistrust, and say: "But time escapes;
>   Live now or never!"
> He said, "What's time? Leave Now for dogs and apes!
>   Man has Forever."
>
> *A Grammarian's Funeral.*

This is a sketch of his explanation of life. The expression of it began in *Pauline*. Had that poem been as imitative, as poor as the first efforts of poets usually are, we might leave it aside. But though, as he said, "good draughtsmanship and right handling were far beyond the artist at that time," though "with repugnance and purely of necessity" he republished it, he did republish it; and he was right. It was crude and confused, but the stuff in it was original and poetic; wonderful stuff for a young man.

The first design of it was huge. *Pauline* is but a fragment of a poem which was to represent, not one but various types of human life. It became only the presentation of the type of the poet, the first sketch of the youth of Sordello. The other types conceived were worked up into other poems.

The hero in *Pauline* hides in his love for Pauline from a past he longed to forget. He had aspired to the absolute beauty and goodness, and the end was vanity and vexation. The shame of this failure beset him from the past, and the failure was caused because he had not been true to the aspirations which took him beyond himself. When he returned to self, the glory departed. And a fine simile of his soul as a young witch whose blue eyes,

>As she stood naked by the river springs,
>Drew down a God,

who, as he sat in the sunshine on her knees singing of heaven, saw the mockery in her eyes and vanished, tells of how the early ravishment departed, slain by self-scorn that followed on self-worship. But one love and reverence remained—that for Shelley, the Sun-treader, and kept him from being "wholly lost." To strengthen this one self-forgetful element, the love of Pauline enters in, and the new impulse brings back something of the ancient joy. "Let me take it," he cries, " and sing on again

>fast as fancies come;
>Rudely, the verse being as the mood it paints,"—

a line which tells us how Browning wished his metrical movement to be judged. This is the exordium, and it is already full of his theory of life—the soul forced from within to aspire to the perfect whole, the necessary failure, the despair, the new impulse to love arising out of the despair; failure making fresh growth, fresh uncontentment. God has sent a new impulse from without; let me begin again.

Then, in the new light, he strips his mind bare. What am I? What have I done? Where am I going?

The first element in his soul, he thinks, is a living personality, linked to a principle of restlessness,

>Which would be all, have, see, know, taste, feel, all.

And this would plunge him into the depths of self were it not for that Imagination in him whose power never fails to bear him beyond himself; and is finally in him a need, a trust, a yearning after God; whom, even when he is most lost, he feels is always acting on him, and at every point of life transcending him.

And Imagination began to create, and made him at one with all men and women of whom he had read (the same motive is repeated in *Sordello*), but especially at one with those out of the Greek world he loved—" a God wandering after Beauty "—a high-crested chief

>Sailing with troops of friends to Tenedos.

Never was anything more clear than these lives he lived beyond himself; and the lines in which he records the vision have all the sharpness and beauty of his after-work—

>I had not seen a work of lofty art,
>Nor woman's beauty nor sweet Nature's face,
>Yet, I say, never morn broke clear as those
>On the dim-clustered isles in the blue sea,
>The deep groves and white temples and wet caves:
>And nothing ever will surprise me now—
>Who stood beside the naked Swift-footed,
>Who bound my forehead with Proserpine's hair.

Yet, having this infinite world of beauty, he aimed low; lost in immediate wants, striving only for the mortal and the possible, while all the time there lived in him, breathing with keen desire, powers which, developed, would make him at one with the infinite Life of God.

But having thus been untrue to his early aspiration, he fell into the sensual life, like Paracelsus, and then, remorseful, sought peace in self-restraint; but no rest, no contentment was gained that way. It is one of Browning's root-ideas that peace is not won by repression of the noble passions, but by letting them loose in full freedom to pursue after their highest aims. Not in restraint, but in the conscious impetuosity of the soul towards the divine realities, is the wisdom of life. Many poems are consecrated to this idea.

So, cleansing his soul by ennobling desire, he sought to realise his dreams in the arts, in the creation and expression of pure Beauty. And he followed Poetry and Music and Painting, and chiefly explored passion and mind in the great poets. Fed at these deep springs, his soul rose into keen life; his powers burst forth, and gazing on all systems and schemes of philosophy and government, he heard ineffable things unguessed by man. All Plato entered into him; he vowed himself to liberty and the new world where "men were to be as gods and earth as heaven." Thus, yet here on earth, not only beyond the earth, he would attain the Perfect. Man also shall attain it; and so thinking, he turned, like Sordello, to look at and learn mankind, pondering "how best life's end might be attained—an end comprising every joy."

And even as he believed, the glory vanished; everything he had hoped for broke to pieces:

> First went my hopes of perfecting mankind,
> Next—faith in them, and then in freedom's self
> And virtue's self, then my own motives, ends
> And aims and loves, and human love went last.

And then, with the loss of all these things of the soul which bear a man's desires into the invisible and unreachable, he gained the world, and success in it. All the powers of the mere Intellect, that grey-haired deceiver whose name is Archimago, were his;—wit, mockery, analytic force, keen reasoning on the visible, the Understanding's absolute belief in itself; its close grasp on what it called facts, and its clear application of knowledge for clear ends. God, too, had vanished in this intellectual satisfaction; and in the temple of his soul, where He had been worshipped, troops of shadows now knelt to the man whose intellect, having grasped all knowledge, was content; and hailed him as king.

The position he describes is like that Wordsworth states in the *Prelude* to have been his, when, after the vanishing of his aspirations for man which followed the imperialistic fiasco of the French Revolution, he found himself without love or hope, but with full power to make an intellectual analysis of nature and of human nature, and was destroyed thereby. It is the same position which Paracelsus attains and which is followed by the same ruin. It is also, so far as its results are concerned, the position of the Soul described by Tennyson in *The Palace of Art*.

Love, emotion, God are shut out. Intellect and knowledge of the world's work take their place. And the result is the slow corrosion of the soul by pride. "I have nursed up energies," says Browning, "they will prey on me." He feels this and breaks away from its death. "My heart must worship," he cries. The "shadows" know this feeling is against them, and they shout in answer:

"Thyself, thou art our king!"

But the end of that is misery. Therefore he begins to aspire again, but still, not for the infinite of perfection beyond, but for a finite perfection on, the earth.

"I will make every joy here my own," he cries, "and then I will die." "I will have one rapture to fill all the soul." "All knowledge shall be mine." It is the aspiration of Paracelsus. "I will live in the whole of Beauty, and here it shall be mine." It is the aspiration of Aprile. "Then, having this perfect human soul, master of all powers, I shall break forth, at some great crisis in history, and lead the world." It is the very aspiration of Sordello.

But when he tries for this, he finds failure at every point. Everywhere he is limited; his soul demands what his body refuses to fulfil; he is always baffled, falling short, chained down and maddened by restrictions; unable to use what he conceives, to grasp as a tool what he can reach in Thought; hating himself; imagining what might be, and driven back from it in despair.

Even in his love for Pauline, in which he has skirted the infinite and known that his soul cannot accept finality—he finds that in him which is still unsatisfied.

What does this puzzle mean? "It means," he answers, "that this earth's life is not my only sphere,

> Can I so narrow sense but that in life
> Soul still exceeds it?"

Yet, he will try again. He has lived in all human life, and his craving is still athirst. He has not yet tried Nature herself. She seems to have undying beauty, and his feeling for her is now, of course, doubled by his love for Pauline. "Come with me," he cries to her, "come out of the world into natural beauty"; and there follows a noble description of a lovely country into which he passes from a mountain glen—morning, noon, afternoon and evening all described—and the emotion of the whole rises till it reaches the topmost height of eagerness and joy, when, suddenly, the whole fire is extinguished—

> I am concentrated—I feel ;
> But my soul saddens when it looks beyond :
> I cannot be immortal, taste all joy.
>
> O God, where do they tend—these struggling aims?
> What would I have? What is this " sleep " which seems
> To bound all? Can there be a " waking " point
> Of crowning life?
>   * * * * *
> And what is that I hunger for but God?

So, having worked towards perfection, having realised that he cannot have it here, he sees at last that the failures of earth are a prophecy of a perfection to come. He claims the infinite beyond. "I believe," he cries, "in God and truth and love. Know my last state is happy, free from doubt or touch of fear."

That is Browning all over. These are the motives of a crowd of poems, varied through a crowd of examples; never better shaped than in the trenchant and magnificent end of *Easter-Day*, where the questions and answers are like the flashing and clashing of sharp scimitars. Out of the same quarry from which *Pauline* was hewn the rest were hewn. They are polished, richly sculptured, hammered into fair form, but the stone is the same. Few have been so consistent as Browning, few so true to their early inspiration. He is among those happy warriors

> Who, when brought
> Among the tasks of real life, have wrought
> Upon the plan that pleased their boyish thought.

This, then, is *Pauline;* I pass on to *Paracelsus*. *Paracelsus*, in order to give the poem a little local colour, opens at Würzburg in a garden, and in the year 1512. But it is not a poem which has to do with any place or any time. It belongs only to the country of the human soul. The young student Paracelsus is sitting with his friends Festus and Michal, on the eve of his departure to conquer the whole world by knowledge. They make a last effort to retain him, but even as he listens to their arguments his eyes are far away—

> As if where'er he gazed there stood a star,

so strong, so deep is desire to attain his aim.

For Paracelsus aims to know the whole of knowledge. Quiet and its charms, this homelike garden of still work, make their appeal in vain. "God has called me," he cries; "these burning desires to know all are his voice in me; and if I stay and plod on here, I reject his call who has marked me from mankind. I must reach pure knowledge. That is my only aim, my only reward."

Then Festus replies: "In this solitariness of aim, all other interests of humanity are left out. Will knowledge, alone, give you enough for life? You, a man!" And again: "You discern your purpose clearly; have you any security of attaining it? Is it not more than mortal power is capable of winning?" Or again: "Have you any knowledge of the path to knowledge?" Or, once more, "Is anything in your mind so clear as this, your own desire to be singly famous?"

"All this is nothing," Paracelsus answers; "the restless force within me will overcome all difficulties. God does not give that fierce energy without giving also that which it desires. And, I am chosen out of all the world to win this glory."

"Why not then," says Festus, "make use of knowledge already gained? Work here; what knowledge will you gain in deserts?"

"I have tried all the knowledge of the past," Paracelsus replies, "and found it a contemptible failure. Others were content with the scraps they won. Not I! I want the whole; the source and sum of divine and human knowledge, and though I craze as even one truth expands its infinitude before me, I go forth alone, rejecting all that others have done, to prove my own soul. I shall arrive at last. And as to mankind, in winning perfect knowledge I shall serve them; but then, all intercourse ends between them and me. I will not be served by those I serve."

"Oh," answers Festus, "is that cause safe which produces carelessness of human love? You have thrown aside all the helps of human knowledge; now you reject all sympathy. No man can thrive who dares to claim to serve the race, while he is bound by no single tie to the race. You would be a being knowing not what Love is—a monstrous spectacle!"

"That may be true," Paracelsus replies, "but for the time I will have nothing to do with feeling. My affections shall remain at rest, and then, *when* I have attained my single aim, when knowledge is all mine, my affections will awaken purified and chastened by my knowledge. Let me, unhampered by sympathy, win my victory. And I go forth certain of victory."

> Are there not, Festus, are there not, dear Michal,
> Two points in the adventure of the diver:
> One—when, a beggar, he prepares to plunge;
> One—when, a prince, he rises with his pearl?
> Festus, I plunge!
> FESTUS.   We wait you when you rise.

So ends the first part, and the second opens ten years afterwards in a Greek Conjurer's house in Constantinople, with Paracelsus writing down the result of his work. And the result is this:

"I have made a few discoveries, but I could not stay to use them. Nought remains but a ceaseless, hungry pressing forward, a vision now and then of truth; and I—I am old before my hour: the adage is true—

> Time fleets, youth fades, life is an empty dream;

and now I would give a world to rest, even in failure!

"This is all my gain. Was it for this," he cries, "I subdued my life, lost my youth, rooted out love; for the sake of this wolfish thirst of knowledge?" No dog, said Faust, in Goethe's poem, driven to the same point by the weariness of knowledge, no dog would longer live this life. My tyrant aim has brought me into a desert; worse still, the purity of my aim is lost. Can I truly say that I have worked for man alone? Sadder still, if I had found that which I sought, should I have had power to use it? O God, Thou who art pure mind, spare my mind. Thus far, I have been a man. Let me conclude, a man! Give me back one hour of my young energy, that I may use and finish what I know.

"And God is good: I started sure of that; and he may still renew my heart.

> True, I am worn;
> But who clothes summer, who is life itself?
> God, that created all things, can renew!"

At this moment the voice of Aprile is heard singing the song of the poets, who, having great gifts, refused to use them, or abused them, or were too weak; and who therefore live apart from God, mourning for ever; who gaze on life, but live no more. He breaks in on Paracelsus, and, in a long passage of overlapping thoughts, Aprile—who would love infinitely and be loved, aspiring to realise every form of love, as Paracelsus has aspired to realise the whole of knowledge—makes Paracelsus feel that love is what he wants. And then, when Paracelsus realises this, Aprile in turn realises that he wants knowledge. Each recognises that he is the complement of the other, that knowledge is worthless without love, and love incapable of realising its aspirations without knowledge—as if love did not contain the sum of knowledge necessary for fine being. Both have failed; and it seems, at first, that they failed because they did not combine their aims. But the chief reason of their failure—and this is, indeed, Browning's main point—is that each of them tried to do more than our limits on earth permit. Paracelsus would have the whole sum of knowledge, Aprile nothing less than the whole of love, and, in this world. It is impossible; yet, were it possible, could they have attained the sum of knowledge and of love on earth and been satisfied therewith, they would have shut out the infinite of knowledge and love beyond them in the divine land, and been, in their satisfaction, more hopelessly lost than they are in their present wretchedness. Failure that leaves an unreached ideal before the soul is in reality a greater boon than success which thinks perfect satisfaction has been reached. Their aim at perfection is right: what is wrong is their view that failure is ruin, and not a prophecy of a greater glory to come. Could they have thought perfection were attained on earth—were they satisfied with anything this world can give, no longer stung with hunger for the infinite—all Paradise, with the illimitable glories, were closed to them!

Few passages are more beautiful in English poetry than that in which Aprile narrates his youthful aspiration: how, loving all things infinitely, he wished to throw them into absolute beauty of form by means of all the arts, for the love of men, and receive from men love for having revealed beauty, and merge at last in God, the Eternal Love. This was his huge aim, his full desire.

Few passages are more pathetic than that in which he tells his failure and its cause. "Time is short; the means of life are limited; we have no means answering to our desires. Now I am wrecked; for the multitudinous images of beauty which filled my mind forbade my seizing upon one which I could have shaped. I often wished to give one to the world, but the others came round and baffled me; and, moreover, I could not leave the multitude of beauty for the sake of one beauty. Unless I could embody all I would embody none.

"And, afterwards, when a cry came from man, 'Give one ray even of your hoarded light to us,' and I tried for man's sake to select one, why, then, mists came—old memories of a thousand sweetnesses, a storm of images—till it was impossible to choose; and so I failed, and life is ended.

"But could I live I would do otherwise. I would give a trifle out of beauty, as an example by which men could guess the rest and love it all; one strain from an angel's song; one flower from the distant land, that men might know that such things were. Then, too, I would put common life into loveliness, so that the lowest hind would find me beside him to put his weakest hope and fear into noble language. And as I thus lived with men, and for them, I should win from them thoughts fitted for their progress, the very commonest of which would come forth in beauty, for they would have been born in a soul filled full of love. This should now be my aim: no longer that desire to embrace the whole of beauty which isolates a man from his fellows; but to realise enough of loveliness to give pleasure to men who desire to love. Therefore, I should live, still aspiring to the whole, still uncontent, but waiting for another life to gain the whole; but at the same time content, for man's sake, to work within the limitations of life; not grieving either for failure, because love given and received makes failure pleasure. In truth, the failure to grasp all on earth makes, if we love, the certainty of a success beyond the earth."

And Paracelsus listening and applying what Aprile says to his old desire to grasp, apart from men, the whole of knowledge as Aprile had desired to grasp the whole of love, learns the truth at last, and confesses it:

> Love me henceforth, Aprile, while I learn
> To love; and, merciful God, forgive us both!
> We wake at length from weary dreams; but both
> Have slept in fairy-land: though dark and drear
> Appears the world before us, we no less
> Wake with our wrists and ankles jewelled still.
> I too have sought to KNOW as thou to LOVE—
> Excluding love as thou refusedst knowledge.

We are halves of a dissevered world, and we must never part till the Knower love, and thou, the Lover, know, and both are saved.

"No, no; that is not all," Aprile answers, and dies. "Our perfection is not in ourselves but in God. Not our strength, but our weakness is our glory. Not in union with me, with earthly love alone, will you find the perfect life. I am not that you seek. It is God the King of Love, his world beyond, and the infinite creations Love makes in it."

But Paracelsus does not grasp that last conclusion. He only understands that he has left out love in his aim, and therefore failed. He does not give up the notion of attainment upon earth. He cannot lose the first imprint of his idea of himself—his lonely grasp of the whole of Knowledge.

The next two parts of the poem do not strengthen

much the main thoughts. Paracelsus tries to work out the lesson learnt from Aprile—to add love to knowledge, to aspire to that fulness in God. But he does not love enough. He despises those who follow him for the sake of his miracles, yet he desires their worship. Moreover, the pride of knowledge still clings to him; he cannot help thinking it higher than love; and the two together drive him into the thought that this world must give him satisfaction. So, he puts aside the ideal aim. But here also he is baffled. Those who follow him as the great teacher ask of him signs. He gives these; and he finds at Basel that he has sunk into the desire of vulgar fame, and prostituted his knowledge; and, sick of this, beaten back from his noble ambitions, he determines to have something at least out of earth, and chooses at Colmar the life of sensual pleasure. "I still aspire," he cries. "I will give the night to study, but I will keep the day for the enjoyment of the senses. Thus, intellect and sense woven together, I shall at least have attained something. If I do not gain knowledge I shall have gained sensual pleasure. Man I despise and hate, and God has deceived me. I take the world." But, even while he says this, his ancient aspiration lives so much in him that he scorns himself for his fall as much as he scorns the crowd.

Then comes the last scene, when, at Salzburg, he returns to find his friend Festus, and to die. In the hour of his death he reviews his whole life, his aims, their failure and the reason of it, and yet dies triumphant for he has found the truth.

I pass over the pathetic delirium in which

Paracelsus thinks that Aprile is present, and cries for his hand and sympathy while Festus is watching by the couch. At last he wakes, and knows his friend, and that he is dying. "I am happy," he cries; "my foot is on the threshold of boundless life; I see the whole whirl and hurricane of life behind me; all my life passes by, and I know its purpose, to what end it has brought me, and whither I am going. I will tell you all the meaning of life. Festus, my friend, tell it to the world.

"There was a time when I was happy; the secret of life was in that happiness." "When, when was that?" answers Festus, "all I hope that answer will decide."

> PAR. When, but the time I vowed myself to man?
> FEST. Great God, thy judgments are inscrutable!

Then he explains. "There are men, so majestical is our nature, who, hungry for joy and truth, win more and more of both, and know that life is infinite progress in God. This they win by long and slow battle. But there are those, of whom I was one"—and here Browning draws the man of genius—"who are born at the very point to which these others, the men of talent, have painfully attained. By intuition genius knows, and I knew at once, what God is, what we are, what life is. Alas! I could not use the knowledge aright. There is an answer to the passionate longings of the heart for fulness, and I knew it. And the answer is this: Live in all things outside of yourself by love and you will have joy. That is the life of God; it ought to be our life. In him it is accomplished and perfect;

but in all created things it is a lesson learned slowly against difficulty.

"Thus I knew the truth, but I was led away from it. I broke down from thinking of myself, my fame, and of this world. I had not love enough, and I lost the truth for a time. But whatever my failures were, I never lost sight of it altogether. I never was content with myself or with the earth. Out of my misery I cried for the joy God has in living outside of himself in love of all things."

Then, thrilled with this thought, he breaks forth into a most noble description—new in English poetry, new in feeling and in thought, enough of itself to lift Browning on to his lofty peak—first of the joy of God in the Universe he makes incessantly by pouring out of himself his life, and, secondly, of the joy of all things in God. "Where dwells enjoyment there is He." But every realised enjoyment looks forward, even in God, to a new and higher sphere of distant glory, and when that is reached, to another sphere beyond—

> thus climbs
> Pleasure its heights for ever and for ever.

Creation is God's joyous self-giving. The building of the frame of earth was God's first joy in Earth. That made him conceive a greater joy—the joy of clothing the earth, of making life therein—of the love which in animals, and last in man, multiplies life for ever.

So there is progress of all things to man, and all created things before his coming have—in beauty, in power, in knowledge, in dim shapes of love and trust in the animals—had prophecies of him which man has realised, hints and previsions, dimly picturing the higher race, till man appeared at last, and one stage of being was complete. But the law of progress does not cease now man has come. None of his faculties are perfect. They also by their imperfection suggest a further life, in which as all that was unfinished in the animals suggested man, so also that which is unfinished in us suggests ourselves in higher place and form. Man's self is not yet Man.

We learn this not only from our own boundless desires for higher life, and from our sense of imperfection. We learn it also when we look back on the whole of nature that was before we were. We illustrate and illuminate all that has been. Nature is humanised, spiritualised by us. We have imprinted ourselves on all things; and this, as we realise it, as we give thought and passion to lifeless nature, makes us understand how great we are, and how much greater we are bound to be. We are the end of nature but not the end of ourselves. We learn the same truth when among us the few men of genius appear; stars in the darkness. We do not say—These stand alone; we never can become as they. On the contrary, we cry: All are to be what these are, and more. They longed for more, and we and they shall have it. All shall be perfected; and then, and not till then, begins the new age and the new life, new progress and new joy. This is the ultimate truth.

"And as in inferior creatures there were prognostics of man—and here Browning repeats himself—so in man there are prognostics of the future and loftier humanity.

> August anticipations, symbols, types
> Of a dim splendour ever on before
> In that eternal cycle life pursues.
> For men begin to pass their nature's bound—

ceaselessly outgrowing themselves in history, and in the individual life—and some, passionately aspiring, run ahead of even the general tendency, and conceive the very highest, and live to reveal it, and in revealing it lift and save those who do not conceive it.

"I, Paracelsus," he cries—and now Browning repeats the whole argument of the poem—"was one of these. To do this I vowed myself, soul and limb.

"But I mistook my means, I took the wrong path, led away by pride. I gazed on power alone, and on power won by knowledge alone. This I thought was the only note and aim of man, and it was to be won, at once and in the present, without any care for all that man had already done. I rejected all the past. I despised it as a record of weakness and disgrace. Man should be all-sufficient now; a single day should bring him to maturity. He has power to reach the whole of knowledge at one leap.

"In that, I mistook the conditions of life. I did not see our barriers; nor that progress is slow; nor that every step of the past is necessary to know and to remember; nor that, in the shade of the past, the present stands forth bright; nor that the future is not to be all at once, but to dawn on us, in zone after zone of quiet progress. I strove to laugh down all the limits of our life, and then the smallest things broke me down—me, who tried to realise the impossible on earth. At last I knew that the power I sought was only God's, and then I prayed to die. All my life was failure.

"At this crisis I met Aprile, and learned my deep mistake. I had left love out; and love and knowledge, and power through knowledge, must go together. And Aprile had also failed, for he had sought love and rejected knowledge. Life can only move when both are hand in hand:

> love preceding
> Power, and with much power, always much more love:
> Love still too straitened in its present means,
> And earnest for new power to set love free.
> I learned this, and supposed the whole was learned.

"But to learn it, and to fulfil it, are two different things. I taught the simple truth, but men would not have it. They sought the complex, the sensational, the knowledge which amazed them. And for this knowledge they praised me. I loathed and despised their praise; and when I would not give them more of the signs and wonders I first gave them, they avenged themselves by casting shame on my real knowledge. Then I was tempted, and became the charlatan; and yet despised myself for seeking man's praise for that which was most contemptible in me. Then I sought for wild pleasure in the senses, and I hated myself still more. And hating myself I came to hate men; and then all that Aprile taught to me was lost.

"But now I know that I did not love enough to trace beneath the hate of men their love. I did not love enough to see in their follies the grain of divine wisdom.

> To see a good in evil, and a hope
> In ill-success; to sympathise, be proud
> Of their half-reasons, faint aspirings, dim
> Struggles for truth, their poorest fallacies,
> Their prejudice and fears and cares and doubts;
> All with a touch of nobleness, despite
> Their error, upward tending all though weak.

"I did not see this, I did not love enough to see this, and I failed.

"Therefore let men regard me, who rashly longed to know all for power's sake; and regard Aprile, the poet, who rashly longed for the whole of love for beauty's sake—and regarding both, shape forth a third and better-tempered spirit, in whom beauty and knowledge, love and power, shall mingle into one, and lead Man up to God, in whom all these four are One. In God alone is the goal.

"Meanwhile I die in peace, secure of attainment. What I have failed in here I shall attain there. I have never, in my basest hours, ceased to aspire; God will fulfil my aspiration:

> If I stoop
> Into a dark tremendous sea of cloud,
> It is but for a time; I press God's lamp
> Close to my breast; its splendour, soon or late,
> Will pierce the gloom: I shall emerge one day.
> You understand me? I have said enough?
>
> Aprile! Hand in hand with you, Aprile!"

And so he dies.

CHAPTER V

THE POET OF ART

THE theory of human life which Browning conceived, and which I attempted in the last chapter to explain out of *Pauline* and *Paracelsus*, underlies the poems which have to do with the arts. Browning as the poet of Art is as fascinating a subject as Browning the poet of Nature; even more so, for he directed of set purpose a great deal of his poetry to the various arts, especially to music and painting. Nor has he neglected to write about his own art. The lover in Pauline is a poet. Paracelsus and Aprile have both touched that art. Sordello is a poet, and so are many others in the poems. Moreover, he treats continually of himself as a poet, and of the many criticisms on his work.

All through this work on the arts, the theory of which we have written appears continuously. It emerges fully in the close of *Easter-Day* It is carefully wrought into poems like *Abt Vogler* and *A Grammarian's Funeral*, in which the pursuit of grammar is conceived of as the pursuit of an art. It is introduced by the way in the midst of subjects belonging to the art of painting, as in *Old Pictures in Florence* and *Andrea del Sarto*. Finally, in those poems which represent in vivid colour and selected personalities special times and forms of art, the theory still appears, but momentarily, as a dryad might show her face in a wood to a poet passing by. I shall be obliged then to touch again and again on this theory of his in discussing Browning as the poet of the arts. This is a repetition which cannot be helped, but for which I request the pardon of my readers.

The subject of the arts, from the time when Caliban "fell to make something" to the re-birth of naturalism in Florence, from the earliest music and poetry to the latest, interested Browning profoundly; and he speaks of them, not as a critic from the outside, but out of the soul of them, as an artist. He is, for example, the only poet of the nineteenth century till we come to Rossetti, who has celebrated painting and sculpture by the art of poetry; and Rossetti did not link these arts to human life and character with as much force and penetration as Browning. Morris, when he wrote poetry, did not care to write about the other arts, their schools or history. He liked to describe in verse the beautiful things of the past, but not to argue on their how and why. Nor did he ever turn in on himself as artist, and ask how he wrote poetry or how he built up a pattern. What he did as artist was to *make*, and when he had made one thing to make another. He ran along like Pheidippides to his goal, without halting for one instant to consider the methods of his running. And all his life long this was his way.

Rossetti described a picture in a sonnet with admirable skill, so admirable that we say to ourselves—" Give me the picture or the sonnet, not both. They blot out one another." But to describe a picture is not to write about art. The one place where he does go down to its means and soul is in his little prose masterpiece, *Hand and Soul*, in which we see the path, the goal, the passion, but not the power of art. But he never, in thought, got, like Browning, to the bottom-joy of it. He does not seem to see, as clearly as Browning saw, that the source of all art was love; and that the expression of love in beautiful form was or ought to be accomplished with that exulting joy which is the natural child of self-forgetfulness. This story of Rossetti's was in prose. In poetry, Rossetti, save in description from the outside, left art alone; and Browning's special work on art, and particularly his poetic studies of it, are isolated in English poetry, and separate him from other poets.

I cannot wish that he had thought less and written less about other arts than poetry. But I do wish he had given more time and trouble to his own art, that we might have had clearer and lovelier poetry. Perhaps, if he had developed himself with more care as an artist in his own art, he would not have troubled himself or his art by so much devotion to abstract thinking and intellectual analysis. A strange preference also for naked facts sometimes beset him, as if men wanted these from a poet. It was as if some scientific demon entered into him for a time and turned poetry out, till Browning got weary of his guest and threw him out of the window. These reversions to some far off Browning in the past, who was deceived into thinking the intellect the king of life, enfeebled and sometimes destroyed the artist in him; and though he escaped for the best part of his poetry from this position, it was not seldom in his later years as a brand plucked from the burning. Moreover, he recognised this tendency in himself; and protested against it, sometimes humorously, sometimes seriously. At least so I read what he means in a number of poems, when he turns, after an overwrought piece of analysis, upon himself, and bursts out of his cobwebs into a solution of the question by passion and imagination. Nevertheless the charm of this merely intellectual play pulled at him continually, and as he could always embroider it with fancy it seemed to him close to imagination; and this belief grew upon him as he got farther away from the warmth and natural truth of youth. It is the melancholy tendency of some artists, as they feel the weakness of decay, to become scientific; and a fatal temptation it is. There is one poem of his in which he puts the whole matter clearly and happily, with a curious and suggestive title, "*Transcendentalism: A Poem in Twelve Books.*"

He speaks to a young poet who will give to men "naked thought, good, true, treasurable stuff, solid matter, without imaginative imagery, without emotion."

> Thought's what they mean by verse, and seek in verse.
> Boys seek for images and melody,
> Men must have reason—so, you aim at men.

It is "quite otherwise," Browning tells him, and he illustrates the matter by a story.

Jacob Böhme did not care for plants. All he cared for was his mysticism. But one day, as if the magic of poetry had slipped into his soul, he heard all the plants talking, and talking to him; and behold, he loved them and knew what they meant. Imagination had done more for him than all his metaphysics. So we give up our days to collating theory with theory, criticising, philosophising, till, one morning, we wake "and find life's summer past."

What remedy? What hope? Why, a brace of rhymes! And then, in life, that miracle takes place which John of Halberstadt did by his magic. We feel like a child; the world is new; every bit of life is run over and enchanted by the wild rose.

> And in there breaks the sudden rose herself,
> Over us, under, round us every side,
> Nay, in and out the tables and the chairs
> And musty volumes, Boehme's book and all—
> Buries us with a glory, young once more,
> Pouring heaven into this shut house of life.
>
> So come, the harp back to your heart again!

I return, after this introduction, to Browning's doctrine of life as it is connected with the arts. It appears with great clearness in *Easter-Day*. He tells of an experience he had when, one night, musing on life, and wondering how it would be with him were he to die and be judged in a moment, he walked on the wild common outside the little Dissenting Chapel he had previously visited on Christmas-Eve and thought of the Judgment. And Common-sense said: "You have done your best; do not be dismayed; you will only be surprised, and when the shock is over you will smile at your fear." And as he thought thus the whole sky became a sea of fire. A fierce and vindictive scribble of red quick flame ran across it, and the universe was burned away. "And I knew," thought Browning, "now that Judgment had come, that I had chosen this world, its beauty, its knowledge, its good—that, though I often looked above, yet to renounce utterly the beauty of this earth and man was too hard for me." And a voice came: "Eternity is here, and thou art judged." And then Christ stood before him and said: "Thou hast preferred the finite when the infinite was in thy power. Earthly joys were palpable and tainted. The heavenly joys flitted before thee, faint, and rare, and taintless. Thou hast chosen those of this world. They are thine."

"O rapture! is this the Judgment? Earth's exquisite treasures of wonder and delight for me!"

"So soon made happy," said the voice. "The loveliness of earth is but like one rose flung from the Eden whence thy choice has excluded thee. The wonders of earth are but the tapestry of the ante-chamber in the royal house thou hast abandoned.

> All partial beauty was a pledge
> Of beauty in its plenitude:
> But since the pledge sufficed thy mood,
> Retain it! plenitude be theirs
> Who looked above!

"O sharp despair! but since the joys of earth fail me, I take art. Art gives worth to nature; it stamps it with man. I'll take the Greek sculpture, the perfect painting of Italy—that world is mine!"

"Then obtain it," said the voice: "the one abstract form, the one face with its one look—all they could manage. Shall I, the illimitable beauty, be judged by these single forms? What of that perfection in their souls these artists were conscious of, inconceivably exceeding all they did? What of their failure which told them an illimitable beauty was before them? What of Michael Angelo now, who did not choose the world's success or earth's perfection, and who now is on the breast of the Divine? All the beauty of art is but furniture for life's first stage. Take it then. But there are those, my saints, who were not content, like thee, with earth's scrap of beauty, but desired the whole. They are now filled with it. Take thy one jewel of beauty on the beach; lose all I had for thee in the boundless ocean."

"Then I take mind; earth's knowledge carries me beyond the finite. Through circling sciences, philosophies and histories I will spin with rapture; and if these fail to inspire, I will fly to verse, and in its dew and fire break the chain which binds me to the earth;—Nay, answer me not, I know what Thou wilt say: What is highest in knowledge, even those fine intuitions which lead the finite into the infinite, and which are best put in noble verse, are but gleams of a light beyond them, sparks from the sum of the whole. I give that world up also, and I take Love. All I ask is leave to love."

"Ah," said the voice, "is this thy final choice? Love is the best; 'tis somewhat late. Yet all the power and beauty, nature and art and knowledge of this earth were only worth because of love. Through them infinite love called to thee; and even now thou clingest to earth's love as all. It is precious, but it exists to bear thee beyond the love of earth into the boundless love of God in me."

At last, beaten to his last fortress, all broken down, he cries :

> Thou Love of God ! Or let me die,
> Or grant what shall seem heaven almost
> Let me not know that all is lost,
> Though lost it be—leave me not tied
> To this despair—this corpse-like bride !
> Let that old life seem mine—no more—
> With limitation as before,
> With darkness, hunger, toil, distress :
> Be all the earth a wilderness !
> Only let me go on, go on,
> Still hoping ever and anon
> To reach one eve the Better Land !

This is put more strongly, as in the line : "Be all the earth a wilderness !" than Browning himself would have put it. But he is in the passion of the man who speaks, and heightens the main truth into an extreme. But the theory is there, and it is especially applied to the love of beauty and therefore to the arts. The illustrations are taken from music and painting, from sculpture and poetry. Only in dwelling too exclusively, as perhaps the situation demands, on the renunciation of this world's successes, he has left out that part of his theory which demands that we should, accepting our limits, work within them for the love of man, but learn from their pressure and pain to transcend them always in the desire of infinite perfection. In *Rabbi Ben Ezra*, a masterpiece of argumentative and imaginative passion—such a poem as only Browning could have written, who, more than other poets, equalised, when most inspired, reasoning, emotions and intuitions into one material for poetry—he applies this view of his to the whole of man's life here and in the world to come, when the

THE POET OF ART

Rabbi in the quiet of old age considers what his life has been, and how God has wrought him through it for eternity. But I leave that poem, which has nothing to do with art, for *Abt Vogler*, which is dedicated to music.

"When Solomon pronounced the Name of God, all the spirits, good and bad, assembled to do his will and build his palace. And when I, Abt Vogler, touched the keys, I called the Spirits of Sound to me, and they have built my palace of music; and to inhabit it all the Great Dead came back, till in the vision I made a perfect music. Nay, for a moment, I touched in it the infinite perfection; but now it is gone; I cannot bring it back. Had I painted it, had I written it, I might have explained it. But in music, out of the sounds something emerges which is above the sounds, and that ineffable thing I touched and lost. I took the well-known sounds of earth, and out of them came a fourth sound, nay, not a sound—but a star. This was a flash of God's will which opened the Eternal to me for a moment; and I shall find it again in the eternal life. Therefore, from the achievement of earth and the failure of it, I turn to God, and in him I see that every image, thought, impulse, and dream of knowledge or of beauty—which, coming whence we know not, flit before us in human life, breathe for a moment, and then depart; which, like my music, build a sudden palace in imagination; which abide for an instant and dissolve, but which memory and hope retain as a ground of aspiration—are not lost to us though they seem to die in their immediate passage. Their music has its home in the Will of God and we shall find them completed there.

All we have willed or hoped or dreamed of good shall exist;
   Not its semblance, but itself; no beauty, nor good, nor power
Whose voice has gone forth, but each survives for the melodist
   When eternity affirms the conception of an hour.
The high that proved too high, the heroic for earth too hard,
   The passion that left the ground to lose itself in the sky,
Are music sent up to God by the lover and the bard;
   Enough that he heard it once: we shall hear it by-and-by.

     *   *   *   *   *

Well, it is earth with me; silence resumes her reign:
   I will be patient and proud, and soberly acquiesce.
Give me the keys. I feel for the common chord again,
   Sliding by semitones, till I sink to the minor,—yes,
And I blunt it into a ninth, and I stand on alien ground,
   Surveying awhile the heights I rolled from into the deep;
Which, hark, I have dared and done, for my resting-place is found,
   The C Major of this life: so, now I will try to sleep.

With that he returns to human life, content to labour in its limits—the common chord is his. But he has been where he shall be, and he is not likely to be satisfied with the C major of life. This, in Browning's thought, is the true comfort and strength of the life of the artist, to whom these fallings from us, vanishings, these transient visits of the infinite Divine, like swallows that pass in full flight, are more common than to other men. They tell him of the unspeakable beauty; they let loose his spirit to fly into the third heaven.

So much for the theory in this poem. As to the artist and his art in it, that is quite a different matter; and as there are few of Browning's poems which reach a higher level than this both in form, thought, and spiritual passion, it may be worth while, for once, to examine a poem of his at large.

Browning's imagination conceived in a moment the musician's experience from end to end; and the form of the experience arose along with the conception. He saw Abt Vogler in the silent church, playing to himself before the golden towers of the organ, and slipping with sudden surprise into a strain which is less his than God's. He saw the vision which accompanied the music, and the man's heart set face to face with the palace of music he had built. He saw him live in it and then pass to heaven with it and lose it. And he saw the close of the experience, with all its scenery in the church and in Abt Vogler's heart, at the same time, in one vision. In this unconscious shaping of his thought into a human incident, with its soul and scenery, is the imagination creating, like a god, a thing unknown, unseen before.

Having thus shaped the form, the imagination passed on to make the ornament. It creates that far-off image of Solomon and his spirits building their palace for the Queen of Sheba which exalts the whole conception and enlarges the reader's imagination through all the legends of the great King—and then it makes, for fresh adornment, the splendid piling up of the sounds into walls of gold, pinnacles, splendours and meteor moons; and lastly, with upward sweeping of its wings, bids the sky to fall in love with the glory of the palace, and the mighty forms of the noble Dead to walk in it. This is the imagination at play with its conception, adorning, glorifying, heightening the full impression, but keeping every imaged ornament misty, impalpable, as in a dream—for so the conception demanded.

And then, to fill the conception with the spirit of humanity, the personal passion of the poet rises and falls through the description, as the music rises and falls. We feel his breast beating against ours; till the time comes when, like a sudden change in a great song, his emotion changes into ecstasy in the outburst of the 9th verse:

Therefore to whom turn I but to thee, the ineffable Name?

It almost brings tears into the eyes. This is art-creation—this is what imagination, intense emotion, and individuality have made of the material of thought—poetry, not prose.

Even at the close, the conception, the imagination, and the personal passion keep their art. The rush upwards of the imaginative feeling dies slowly away; it is as evanescent as the Vision of the Palace, but it dies into another picture of humanity which even more deeply engages the human heart. Browning sees the organ-loft now silent and dark, and the silent figure in it, alone and bowed over the keys. The church is still, but aware of what has been. The golden pipes of the organ are lost in the twilight and the music is over—all the double vision of the third heaven into which he has been caught has vanished away. The form of the thing rightly fits the idea. Then, when the form is shaped, the poet fills it with the deep emotion of the musician's soul, and then with his own emotion; and close as the air to the earth are the sorrow and exultation of Abt Vogler and Browning to the human heart—sorrow for the vanishing and the failure, exultant joy because what has been is but an image of the infinite beauty they will have in God. In the joy they do not sorrow for the failure. It is nothing but an omen of success. Their soul, greater than the vision, takes up common life with patience and silent hope. We hear them sigh and strike the chord of C.

This is lyric imagination at work in lyric poetry. There are two kinds of lyrics among many others. One is where the strong emotion of the poet, fusing all his materials into one creation, comes to a height and then breaks off suddenly. It is like a thunderstorm, which, doubling and redoubling its flash and roar, ends in the zenith with the brightest flash and loudest clang of thunder. There is another kind. It is when the storm of emotion reaches, like the first, its climax, but does not end with it. The lyric passion dies slowly away from the zenith to the horizon, and ends in quietude and beauty, attended by soft colour and gentle sounds; like the thunderstorm which faints with the sunset and gathers its clouds to be adorned with beauty. This lyric of Browning's is a noble example of the second type.

I take another poem, the *Grammarian's Funeral*, to illustrate his art. The main matter of thought in it is the same as that of *Abt Vogler*, with the variation that the central figure is not a musician but a grammarian; that what he pursued was critical knowledge, not beauty, and that he is not a modern, like Abt Vogler, but one of the Renaissance folk, and seized, as men were seized then, with that insatiable curiosity which characterised the outbreak of the New Learning. The matter of thought in it is of less interest to us than the poetic creation wrought out of it, or than the art with which it is done. We see the form into which the imaginative conception is thrown—the group of sorrowing students carrying their master's corpse to the high platform of the mountain, singing what he was, in admiration and honour and delight that he had mastered life and won eternity; a conception full of humanity, as full of the life of the dead master's soul as of the students' enthusiasm. This thrills us into creation, with the poet, as we read. Then the imagination which has made the conception into form adorns it. It creates the plain, the encircling mountains, one cloudy peak higher than the rest; as we mount we look on the plain below; we reach the city on the hill, pass it, and climb the hill-top; there are all the high-flying birds, the meteors, the lightnings, the thickest dew. And we lay our dead on the peak, above the plain. This is the scenery, the imaginative ornament, and all through it we are made to hear the chant of the students; and so lifting is the melody of the verse we seem to taste the air, fresher and fresher as we climb. Then, finally, into the midst of this flows for us the eager intensity of the scholar. Dead as he is, we feel him to be alive; never resting, pushing on incessantly, beating failure beneath his feet, making it the step for further search for the infinite, resolute to live in the dull limits of the present work, but never content save in waiting for that eternity which will fulfil the failure of earth; which, missing earth's success, throws itself on God, dying to gain the highest. This is the passion of the poem, and Browning is in it like a fire. It was his own, his very life. He pours it into the students who rejoice in the death of their master, and he gives it to us as we read the poem. And then, because conception, imagination, and intensity of thought and emotion all here work together, as in *Abt Vogler*, the melody of the poem is lovely, save in one verse which ought to be out of the poem. As to the conclusion, it is priceless. Such a conclusion can only emerge when all that precedes it finely contains it, and I have often thought that it pictures Browning himself. I wish he had been buried on a mountain top, all Italy below him.

> Well, here's the platform, here's the proper place:
> Hail to your purlieus,
> All ye high-flyers of the feathered race,
> Swallows and curlews!
> Here's the top-peak; the multitude below
> Live, for they can, there:
> This man decided not to Live but Know—
> Bury this man there?
>
> Here—here's his place, where meteors shoot, clouds form,
> Lightenings are loosened.
> Stars come and go! Let joy break with the storm,
> Peace let the dew send!
> Lofty designs must close in like effects:
> Loftily lying,
> Leave him—still loftier than the world suspects,
> Living and dying.

This is the artist at work, and I doubt whether all the laborious prose written, in history and criticism, on the revival of learning, will ever express better than this short poem the inexhaustible thirst of the Renaissance in its pursuit of knowledge, or the enthusiasm of the pupils of a New Scholar for his desperate strife to know in a short life the very centre of the Universe.

Another poem on the arts which is mixed up with Browning's theory of life is *Andrea del Sarto*. Into it the theory slips, like an uninvited guest into a dinner-party of whom it is felt that he has some relation to some one of the guests, but for whom no cover is laid. The faulty and broken life of Andrea, in its contrast with his flawless drawing, has been a favourite subject with poets. Alfred de Musset and others have dramatised it, and it seems strange that none of our soul-wrecking and vivisecting novelists have taken it up for their amusement. Browning has not left out a single point of the subject. The only criticism I should make of this admirable poem is that, when we come to the end, we dislike the woman and despise the man more than we pity either of them; and in tragic art-work of a fine quality, pity for human nature with a far-off tenderness in it should remain as the most lasting impression. All the greater artists, even while they went to the bottom of sorrow and wickedness, have done this wise and beautiful thing, and Browning rarely omits it.

The first art-matter in the poem is Browning's sketch of the sudden genesis of a picture. Andrea is sitting with his wife on the window-seat looking out to Fiesole. As he talks she smiles a weary, lovely, autumn smile, and, born in that instant and of her smile, he sees his picture, knows its atmosphere, realises its tone of colour, feels its prevailing sentiment. How he will execute it is another question, and depends on other things; but no better sketch could be given of the sudden spiritual fashion in which great pictures are generated. Here are the lines, and they also strike the keynote of Andrea's soul—that to which his life has brought him.

> You smile? why, there's my picture ready made,
> There's what we painters call our harmony!
> A common greyness silvers everything,—
> All in a twilight, you and I alike—

> You, at the point of your first pride in me
> (That's gone, you know),—but I, at every point;
> My youth, my hope, my art, being all toned down
> To yonder sober pleasant Fiesole.
> There's the bell clinking from the chapel-top;
> That length of convent-wall across the way
> Holds the trees safer, huddled more inside;
> The last monk leaves the garden; days decrease,
> And autumn grows, autumn in everything.
> Eh? the whole seems to fall into a shape
> As if I saw alike my work and self
> And all that I was born to be and do,
> A twilight piece. Love, we are in God's hand.

In God's hand? Yes, but why being free are we so fettered? And here slips in the unbidden guest of the theory. Andrea has chosen earthly love; Lucrezia is all in all; and he has reached absolute perfection in drawing—

> I do what many dream of, all their lives.

He can reach out beyond himself no more. He has got the earth, lost the heaven. He makes no error, and has, therefore, no impassioned desire which, flaming through the faulty picture, makes it greater art than his faultless work. "The soul is gone from me, that vext, suddenly-impassioned, upward-rushing thing, with its play, insight, broken sorrows, sudden joys, pursuing, uncontented life. These men reach a heaven shut out from me, though they cannot draw like me. No praise or blame affects me. I know my handiwork is perfect. But there burns a truer light of God in them. Lucrezia, I am judged."

> Ah, but a man's reach should exceed his grasp,
> Or what's a heaven for? All is silver-grey
> Placid and perfect with my art:—the worse

"Here," he says, "is a piece of Rafael. The arm is out of drawing, and I could make it right. But the passion, the soul of the thing is not in me. Had you, my love, but urged me upward, to glory and God, I might have been uncontent; I might have done it for you. No," and again he sweeps round on himself, out of his excuses, " perhaps not, ' incentives come from the soul's self'; and mine is gone. I've chosen the love of you, Lucrezia, earth's love, and I cannot pass beyond my faultless drawing into the strife to paint those divine imaginations the soul conceives."

That is the meaning of Browning. The faultless, almost mechanical art, the art which might be born of an adulterous connection between science and art, is of little value to men. Not in the flawless painter is true art found, but in those who painted inadequately, yet whose pictures breathe

> Infinite passion and the pain
> Of finite hearts that yearn.

In this incessant strife to create new worlds, and in their creation, which, always ending in partial failure, forces fresh effort, lies, Browning might have said, the excuse for God having deliberately made us defective. Had we been made good, had we no strife with evil ; had we the power to embody at once the beauty we are capable of seeing ; could we have laid our hand on truth, and grasped her without the desperate struggle we have to win one fruit from her tree ; had we had no strong crying and tears, no agony against wrong, against our own passions and their work, against false views of things—we might have been angels ; but we should not have had humanity and all its wild history, and all its work; we should not have had that which, for all I know, may be unique in the universe; no, nor any of the great results of the battle and its misery. Had it not been for the defectiveness, the sin and pain, we should have had nothing of the interest of the long evolution of science, law and government, of the charm of discovery, of pursuit, of the slow upbuilding of moral right, of the vast variety of philosophy. Above all, we should have had none of the great art men love so well, no *Odyssey*, *Divine Comedy*, no *Hamlet*, no *Œdipus*, no Handel, no Beethoven, no painting or sculpture where the love and sorrow of the soul breathe in canvas, fresco, marble and bronze, no, nor any of the great and loving lives who suffered and overcame, from Christ to the poor woman who dies for love in a London lane. All these are made through the struggle and the sorrow. We should not have had, I repeat, humanity; and provided no soul perishes for ever but lives to find union with undying love, the game, with all its terrible sorrow, pays for the candle. We may find out, some day, that the existence and work of humanity, crucified as it has been, are of untold interest and use to the universe —which things the angels desire to look into. If Browning had listened to that view, he would, I think, have accepted it.

Old Pictures in Florence touches another side of his theory. In itself, it is one of Browning's half-humorous poems; a pleasantly-composed piece, glancing here and glancing there, as a man's mind does when leaning over a hill-villa's parapet on a sunny morning in Florence. I have elsewhere quoted its beginning. It is a fine example of his nature-poetry: it creates the scenery and atmosphere of the poem; and the four lines with which the fourth verse closes sketch what Browning thought to be one of his poetic gifts—

> And mark through the winter afternoons,
> By a gift God grants me now and then,
> In the mild decline of those suns like moons,
> Who walked in Florence, besides her men.

This, then, is a poem of many moods, beginning with Giotto's Tower; then wondering why Giotto did not tell the poet who loved him so much that one of his pictures was lying hidden in a shop where some one else picked it up; then, thinking of all Giotto's followers, whose ghosts he imagines are wandering through Florence, sorrowing for the decay of their pictures.

"But at least they have escaped, and have their holiday in heaven, and do not care one straw for our praise or blame. They did their work, they and the great masters. We call them old Masters, but they were new in their time; their old Masters were the Greeks. They broke away from the Greeks and revolutionised art into a new life. In our turn we must break away from them."

And now glides in the theory. "When Greek art reached its perfection, the limbs which infer the soul, and enough of the soul to inform the limbs, were faultlessly represented. Men said the best had been done, and aspiration and growth in art ceased. Content with what had been done, men imitated, but did not create. But man cannot remain without change in a past perfection; for

THE POET OF ART

then he remains in a kind of death. Even with failure, with faulty work, he desires to make new things, and in making, to be alive and feel his life. Therefore Giotto and the rest began to create a fresh aspect of humanity, which, however imperfect in form, would suggest an infinite perfection. The Greek perfection ties us down to earth, to a few forms, and the sooner, if it forbid us to go on, we reject its ideal as the only one, the better for art and for mankind.

> 'Tis a life-long toil till our lump be leaven—
> The better! What's come to perfection perishes.
> Things learned on earth, we shall practise in heaven:
> Works done least rapidly, Art most cherishes.

"The great Campanile is still unfinished;" so he shapes his thoughts into his scenery. Shall man be satisfied in art with the crystallised joy of Apollo, or the petrified grief of Niobe, when there are a million more expressions of joy and grief to render? In that way felt Giotto and his crew. "We will paint the whole of man," they cried, "paint his new hopes and joys and pains, and never pause, because we shall never quite succeed. We will paint the soul in all its infinite variety—bring the invisible full into play. Of course we shall miss perfection—who can get side by side with infinitude?—but we shall grow out of the dead perfection of the past, and live and move, and have our being.

> Let the visible go to the dogs—what matters?"

Thus art began again. Its spring-tide came, dim and dewy; and the world rejoiced.

And that is what has happened again and again in the history of art. Browning has painted a universal truth. It was that which took place when Wordsworth, throwing away the traditions of a century and all the finished perfection, as men thought, of the Augustan age, determined to write of man as man, whatever the issue; to live with the infinite variety of human nature, and in its natural simplicities. What we shall see, he thought, may be faulty, common, unideal, imperfect. What we shall write will not have the conventional perfection of Pope and Gray, which all the cultivated world admires, and in which it rests content—growth and movement dead—but it will be true, natural, alive, running onwards to a far-off goal. And we who write—our loins are accinct, our lights burning, as men waiting for the revelation of the Bridegroom. Wordsworth brought back the soul to Poetry. She made her failures, but she was alive. Spring was blossoming around her with dews and living airs, and the infinite opened before her.

So, too, it was when Turner recreated landscape art. There was the perfect Claudesque landscape, with all its parts arranged, its colours chosen, the composition balanced, the tree here, the river there, the figures in the foreground, the accurate distribution and gradation of the masses of light and shade. "There," the critics said, "we have had perfection. Let us rest in that." And all growth in landscape-art ceased. Then came Turner, who, when he had followed the old for a time and got its good, broke away from it, as if in laughter. "What," he felt, "the infinite of nature is before me; inconceivable change and variety in earth, and sky, and sea—and shall I be tied down to one form of painting landscape, one arrangement of artistic properties? Let the old perfection go." And we had our revolution in landscape art: nothing, perhaps, so faultless as Claude's composition, but life, love of nature, and an illimitable range; incessant change, movement, and aspiration which have never since allowed the landscape artist to think that he has attained.

On another side of the art of painting, Rossetti, Millais, Hunt arose; and they said, "We will paint men as they actually were in the past, in the moments of their passion, and with their emotions on their faces, and with the scenery around them as it was; and whatever background of nature there was behind them, it shall be painted direct from the very work of nature herself, and in her very colours. In doing this our range will become infinite. No doubt we shall fail. We cannot grasp the whole of nature and humanity, but we shall be *in* their life: aspiring, alive, and winning more and more of truth." And the world of art howled at them, as the world of criticism howled at Wordsworth. But a new life and joy began to move in painting. Its winter was over, its spring had begun, its summer was imagined. Their drawing was faulty; their colour was called crude; they seemed to know little or nothing of composition; but the Spirit of Life was in them, and their faults were worth more than the best successes of the school that followed Rafael; for their faults proved that passion, aspiration and originality were again alive:

> Give these, I exhort you, their guerdon and glory
> For daring so much, before they well did it.

If ever the artist should say to himself, "What I

desire has been attained: I can but imitate or follow it"; or if the people who care for any art should think, "The best has been reached; let us be content to rest in that perfection"; the death of art has come.

The next poem belonging to this subject is the second part of *Pippa Passes*. What concerns us here is that Jules, the French artist, loves Phene; and on his return from his marriage pours out his soul to her concerning his art.

In his work, in his pursuit of beauty through his aspiration to the old Greek ideal, he has found his full content—his heaven upon earth. But now, living love of a woman has stolen in. How can he now, he asks, pursue that old ideal when he has the real? how carve Tydeus, with her about the room? He is disturbed, thrilled, uncontent A new ideal rises. How can he now

> Bid each conception stand while, trait by trait,
> My hand transfers its lineaments to stone?
> Will my mere fancies live near you, their truth—
> The live truth, passing and repassing me,
> Sitting beside me?

Before he had seen her, all the varied stuff of Nature, every material in her workshop, tended to one form of beauty, to the human archetype. But now she, Phene, represents the archetype; and though Browning does not express this, we feel that if Jules continue in that opinion, his art will die. Then, carried away by his enthusiasm for his art, he passes, through a statement that nature suggests in all her doings man and his life and his beauty— a statement Browning himself makes in *Paracelsus* —to a description of the capabilities of various stuffs in nature under the sculptor's hand, and especially of marble as having in it the capabilities of all the other stuffs and also something more a living spirit in itself which aids the sculptor and even does some of his work.

This is a subtle thought peculiarly characteristic of Browning's thinking about painting, music, poetry, or sculpture. I believe he felt, and if he did not, it is still true, that the vehicle of any art brought something out of itself into the work of the artist. Abt Vogler feels this as he plays on the instrument he made. Any musician who plays on two instruments knows that the distinct instrument does distinct work, and loves each instrument for its own spirit; because each makes his art, expressed in it, different from his art expressed in another. Even the same art-creation is different in two instruments: the vehicle does its own part of the work. Any painter will say the same, according as he works in fresco or on canvas, in water-colour or in oil. Even a material like charcoal makes him work the same conception in a different way. I will quote the passage; it goes to the root of the matter; and whenever I read it, I seem to hear a well-known sculptor as he talked one night to me of the spiritual way in which marble, so soft and yet so firm, answered like living material to his tool, sending flame into it, and then seemed, as with a voice, to welcome the emotion which, flowing from him through the chisel, passed into the stone.

> But of the stuffs one can be master of,
> How I divined their capabilities!
> From the soft-rinded smoothening facile chalk
> That yields your outline to the air's embrace,

> Half-softened by a halo's pearly gloom :
> Down to the crisp imperious steel, so sure
> To cut its one confided thought clean out
> Of all the world. But marble!—'neath my tools
> More pliable than jelly—as it were
> Some clear primordial creature dug from depths
> In the earth's heart, where itself breeds itself,
> And whence all baser substance may be worked;
> Refine it off to air, you may—condense it
> Down to the diamond ;—is not metal there,
> When o'er the sudden speck my chisel trips?
> —Not flesh, as flake off flake I scale, approach,
> Lay bare those bluish veins of blood asleep?
> Lurks flame in no strange windings where, surprised
> By the swift implement sent home at once,
> Flushes and glowings radiate and hover
> About its track?

But Jules finds that Phene, whom he has been deceived into believing an intelligence equal to his own, does not understand one word he has said, is nothing but an uneducated girl; and his dream of perfection in the marriage of Art and Love vanishes away, and with the deception the aims and hopes of his art as it has been. And Browning makes this happen of set purpose, in order that, having lost satisfaction in his art-ideal, and then his satisfaction in that ideal realised in a woman—having failed in Art and Love—he may pass on into a higher aim, with a higher conception, both of art and love, and make a new world, in the woman and in the art. He is about to accept the failure, to take only to revenge on his deceivers, when Pippa sings as she is passing, and the song touches him into finer issues of thought. He sees that Phene's soul is, like a butterfly, half-loosed from its chrysalis, and ready for flight. The sight and song awake a truer love, for as yet he has loved Phene only through his art. Now he is impassioned with pity for a human soul, and his first new sculpture will be the creation of her soul.

> Shall to produce form out of unshaped stuff
> Be Art—and further, to evoke a soul
> From form be nothing? This new soul is mine!

At last, he is borne into self-forgetfulness by love, and finds a man's salvation. And in that loss of self he drinks of the deep fountain of art. Aprile found that out. Sordello dies as he discovers it, and Jules, the moment he has touched its waters with his lip, sees a new realm of art arise, and loves it with such joy that he knows he will have power to dwell in its heart, and create from its joy.

> One may do whate'er one likes
> In Art; the only thing is, to make sure
> That one does like it—which takes pains to know.

He breaks all his models up. They are paltry, dead things belonging to a dead past. "I begin," he cries, "art afresh, in a fresh world,

> Some unsuspected isle in far-off seas."

The ideal that fails means the birth of a new ideal. The very centre of Browning as an artist is there:

> Held we fall to rise, are baffled to fight better,
> Sleep to wake!

Sordello is another example of his theory, of a different type from Aprile, or that poet in *Pauline* who gave Browning the sketch from which Sordello was conceived. But Browning, who, as I have said, repeated his theory, never repeated his examples: and Sordello is not only clearly varied from Aprile and the person in *Pauline*, but the variations themselves are inventively varied. The complex temperament of Sordello incessantly alters its form, not only as he grows from youth to manhood, but as circumstances meet him. They give him a shock, as a slight blow does to a kaleidoscope, and the whole pattern of his mind changes. But as with the bits of coloured glass in the kaleidoscope, the elements of Sordello's mind remain the same. It is only towards the end of his career, on the forcible introduction into his life of new elements from the outward world, that his character radically changes, and his soul is born. He wins that which he has been without from the beginning. He wins, as we should say, a heart. He not only begins to love Palma otherwise than in his dreams, but with that love the love of man arises—for, in characters like Sordello, personal love, once really stirred, is sure to expand beyond itself—and then, following on the love of man, conscience is quickened into life, and for the first time recognises itself and its duties. In this new light of love and conscience, directed towards humanity, he looks back on his life as an artist, or rather, Browning means us to do so; and we understand that he has done nothing worthy in his art; and that even his gift of imagination has been without the fire of true passion. His aspirations, his phantasies, his songs, done only for his own sake, have been cold, and left the world cold.

He has aspired to a life in the realm of pure imagination, to winning by imagination alone all knowledge and all love, and the power over men which flows from these. He is, in this aspiration, Paracelsus and Aprile in one. But he has neither the sincerity of Paracelsus nor the passion of Aprile. He lives in himself alone, beyond the world of experience, and only not conscious of those barriers which limit our life on which Browning dwells so much, because he does not bring his aspirations or his imaginative work to the test by shaping them outside of himself. He fails, that is, to create anything which will please or endure; fails in the first aim, the first duty of an artist. He comes again and again to the verge of creating something which may give delight to men, but only once succeeds, when by chance, in a moment of excited impulse, caused partly by his own vanity, and partly by the waves of humanity at Palma's *Court of Love* beating on his soul, he breaks for a passing hour into the song which conquers Eglamor. When, at the end, he does try to shape himself without for the sake of men he is too late for this life. He dies of the long struggle, of the revelation of his failure and the reasons of it, of the supreme light which falls on his wasted life; and yet not wasted, since even in death he has found his soul and all it means. His imagination, formerly only intellectual, has become emotional as well; he loves mankind, and sacrifices fame, power, and knowledge to its welfare. He no longer thinks to avoid, by living only in himself, the baffling limitations which inevitably trouble human life; but now desires, working within these limits, to fix his eyes on the ineffable Love; failing but making every failure a ladder on which to climb to higher things. This —the true way of life—he finds out as he dies. To have that spirit, and to work in it, is the very life of art. To pass for ever out of and beyond one's self is to the artist the lesson of Sordello's story.

It is hardly learnt. The self in Sordello, the self of imagination unwarmed by love of men, is driven out of the artist with strange miseries, battles and despairs, and these Browning describes with such inventiveness that at the last one is inclined to say, with all the pitiful irony of Christ, " This kind goeth not forth but with prayer and fasting."

The position in the poem is at root the same as that in Tennyson's *Palace of Art*. These two poets found, about the same time, the same idea, and, independently, shaped it into poems. Tennyson put it into the form of a vision, the defect of which was that it was too far removed from common experience. Browning put it into the story of a man's life. Tennyson expressed it with extraordinary clearness, simplicity, and with a wealth of lovely ornament, so rich that it somewhat overwhelmed the main lines of his conception. Browning expressed it with extraordinary complexity, subtlety, and obscurity of diction. But when we take the trouble of getting to the bottom of *Sordello*, we find ourselves where we do not find ourselves in *The Palace of Art*—we find ourselves in close touch and friendship with a man, living with him, sympathising with him, pitying him, blessing him, angry and delighted with him, amazingly interested in his labyrinthine way of thinking and feeling; we follow with keen interest his education, we see a soul in progress; we wonder what he will do next, what strange turn we shall come to in his mind, what new effort he will make to realise himself; and, loving him right through from his childhood to his death, we are quite satisfied when he dies. At the back of this, and complicating it still more — but, when we arrive at seeing it clearly, increasing the interest of the poem—is a great to-and-fro of humanity at a time when humanity was alive and keen and full of attempting; when men were savagely original, when life was lived to its last drop, and when a new world was dawning. Of all this outside humanity there is not a trace in Tennyson, and Browning could not have got on without it. Of course, it made his poetry difficult. We cannot get excellences without their attendant defects. We have a great deal to forgive in *Sordello*. But for the sake of the vivid humanity we forgive it all.

Sordello begins as a boy, living alone in a castle near Mantua, built in a gorge of the low hills, and the description of the scenery of the castle, without and within, is one example of the fine ornament of which *Sordello* is so full. There, this rich and fertile nature lives, fit to receive delight at every sense, fit to shape what is received into imaginative pictures within, but not without; content with the contemplation of his own imaginings. At first it is Nature from whom Sordello receives impressions, and he amuses himself with the fancies he draws from her. But he never shapes his emotion into actual song. Then tired of Nature, he dreams himself into the skin and soul of all the great men of whom he has read. He becomes them in himself, as Pauline's lover has done before him; but one by one they fade into unreality—for he knows nothing of men—and the last projection of himself into Apollo, the Lord of Poetry, is the most unreal of them all: at which fantasy all the woods and streams and sunshine round Goito are infinitely amused. Thus, when he wants sympathy, he does not go down to Mantua and make song for the crowd of men; he invents in dreams a host of sympathisers, all of whom are but himself in other forms. Even when he aims at perfection, and, making himself Apollo, longs for a Daphne to double his life, his soul is still such stuff as dreams are made of, till he wakes one morning to ask himself: "When will this dream be truth?"

This is the artist's temperament in youth when he is not possessed of the greater qualities of genius—his imaginative visions, his aspirations, his pride in apartness from men, his self-contentment, his sloth, the presence in him of barren imagination, the absence from it of the spiritual, nothing in him which as yet desires, through the sorrow and strife of life, God's infinitude, or man's love; a natural life indeed, forgiveable, gay, sportive, dowered with happy self-love, good to pass through and enjoy, but better to leave behind. But Sordello will not become the actual artist till he lose his self-involvement and find his soul, not only in love of his Daphne but in love of man. And the first thing he will have to do is that which Sordello does not care to do—to embody before men in order to give them pleasure or impulse, to console or exalt them, some of the imaginations he has enjoyed within himself. Nor can Sordello's imagination reach true passion, for it ignores that which chiefly makes the artist; union with the passions of mankind. Only when near to death does he outgrow the boy of Goito, and then we find that he has ceased to be the artist. Thus, the poem is the history of the failure of a man with an artistic temperament to be an artist. Or rather, that is part of the story of the poem, and, as Browning was an artist himself, a part which is of the greatest interest.

Sordello, at the close of the first book, is wearied of dreams. Even in his solitude, the limits of life begin to oppress him. Time fleets, fate is tardy, life will be over before he lives. Then an accident helps him—

> Which breaking on Sordello's mixed content
> Opened, like any flash that cures the blind,
> The veritable business of mankind.

This accident is the theme of the second book. It belongs to the subject of this chapter, for it contrasts two types of the artist, Eglamor and Sordello, and it introduces Naddo, the critic, with a good knowledge of poetry, with a great deal of common sense, with an inevitable sliding into the opinion that what society has stamped must be good—a mixed personage, and a sketch done with Browning's humorous and pitying skill.

The contrast between Eglamor and Sordello runs through the whole poem. Sordello recalls Eglamor at the last, and Naddo appears again and again to give the worldly as well as the common-sense solution of the problems which Sordello makes for himself. Eglamor is the poet who has no genius, whom one touch of genius burns into nothing, but who, having a charming talent, employs it well; and who is so far the artist that what he feels he is able to shape gracefully, and to please mankind therewith; who, moreover loves, enjoys, and is wholly possessed with what he shapes in song. This is good; but then he is quite satisfied with what he does; he has no aspiration, and all the infinitude of beauty is lost to him. And when Sordello takes up his incomplete song, finishes it, inspires, expands what Eglamor thought perfect, he sees at last that he has only a graceful talent, that he has lived in a vain show, like a gnome in a cell of the rock of gold. Genius, momentarily realising itself in Sordello, reveals itself to Eglamor with all its infinities; Heaven and Earth and the universe open on Eglamor, and the revelation of what he is, and of the perfection beyond, kills him. That is a fine, true, and piteous sketch.

But Sordello, who is the man of possible genius, is not much better off. There has been one outbreak into reality at Palma's *Court of Love*. Every one, afterwards, urges him to sing. The critics gather round him. He makes poems, he becomes the accepted poet of Northern Italy. But he cannot give continuous delight to the world. His poems are not like his song before Palma. They have no true passion, being woven like a spider's web out of his own inside. His case then is more pitiable, his failure more complete, than Eglamor's. Eglamor could shape something; he had his own enjoyment, and he gave pleasure to men. Sordello, lured incessantly towards abstract ideals, lost in their contemplation, is smitten, like Aprile, into helplessness by the multitudinousness of the images he sees, refuses to descend into real life and submit to its limitations, is driven into the slothfulness of that dreaming imagination which is powerless to embody its images in the actual song. Sometimes he tries to express himself, longing for reality. When he tries he fails, and instead of making failure a step to higher effort, he falls back impatiently on himself, and is lost in himself. Moreover, he tries always within himself, and with himself for judge. He does not try the only thing which would help him—the submission of his work to the sympathy and judgment of men. Out of touch with any love save love of his own imaginings, he cannot receive those human impressions which kindle the artist into work, nor answer the cry which comes from mankind, with such eagerness, to genius—" Express for us in clear form that which we vaguely feel. Make us see and admire and love." Then he ceases even to love song, because, though he can imagine everything, he can do nothing; and deaf to the voices of men, he despises man. Finally he asks himself, like so many young poets who have followed his way, What is the judgment of the world worth? Nothing at all, he answers. With that ultimate folly, the favourite resort of minor poets, Sordello goes altogether wrong. He pleases nobody, not even himself; spends his time in arguing inside himself why he has not succeeded; and comes to no conclusion, except that total failure is the necessity of the world. At last one day, wandering from Mantua, he finds himself in his old environment, in the mountain cup where Goito and the castle lie. And the old dream, awakened by the old associations, that he was Apollo, Lord of Song, rushed back upon him and enwrapped him wholly. He feels, in the blessed silence, that he is no longer what he has been of late,

> a pettish minstrel meant
> To wear away his soul in discontent,
> Brooding on fortune's malice,

but himself once more, freed from the world of Mantua; alone again, but in his loneliness really more lost than he was at Mantua, as we soon find out in the third book.

I return, in concluding this chapter, to the point which bears most clearly on Browning as the poet of art. The only time when Sordello realises what it is to be an artist is when, swept out of himself by the kindled emotion of the crowd at the *Court of Love* and inspired also by the true emotion of Eglamor's song, which has been made because he loved it—his imagination is impassioned enough to shape for man the thing within him, outside of himself, and to sing for the joy of singing—having forgotten himself in mankind, in their joy and in his own.

But it was little good to him. When he stole home to Goito in a dream, he sat down to think over the transport he had felt, why he felt it, how he was better than Eglamor; and at last, having missed the whole use of the experience (which was to draw him into the service of man within the limits of life but to always transcend the limits in aspiration), he falls away from humanity into his own self again; and perfectly happy for the moment, but lost as an artist and a man, lies lazy, filleted and robed on the turf, with a lute beside him, looking over the landscape below the castle and fancying himself Apollo. This is to have the capacity to be an artist, but it is not to be an artist. And we leave Sordello lying on the grass enjoying himself, but not destined on that account to give any joy to man.

CHAPTER VI

SORDELLO

THE period in which the poem of *Sordello* opens is at the end of the first quarter of the thirteenth century, at the time when the Guelf cities allied themselves against the Ghibellines in Northern Italy. They formed the Lombard League, and took their private quarrels up into one great quarrel—that between the partisans of the Empire and those of the Pope. Sordello is then a young man of thirty years. He was born in 1194, when the fierce fight in the streets of Vicenza took place which Salinguerra describes, as he looks back on his life, in the fourth canto of this poem. The child is saved in that battle, and brought from Vicenza by Adelaide, the second wife of Ezzelino da Romano II.,* to Goito. He is really the son of Salinguerra and Retrude, a connection of Frederick II., but Adelaide conceals this, and brings him up as her page, alleging that he is the son of Elcorte, an archer. Palma (or Cunizza), Ezzelino's daughter by Agnes Este, his first wife, is also at Goito in attendance on Adelaide. Sordello and she meet as girl and boy, and she becomes one of the

* Browning spells this name *Ecelin*, probably for easier use in verse.

dreams with which his lonely youth at Goito is adorned.

At Adelaide's death Palma discovers the real birth of Sordello. She has heard him sing some time before at a Love-court, where he won the prize; where she, admiring, began to love him; and this love of hers has been increased by his poetic fame which has now filled North Italy. She summons him to her side at Verona, makes him understand that she loves him, and urges him, as Salinguerra's son, to take the side of the Ghibellines to whose cause Salinguerra, the strongest military adventurer in North Italy, has now devoted himself. When the poem begins, Salinguerra has received from the Emperor the badge which gives him the leadership of the Ghibelline party in North Italy.

Then Palma, bringing Sordello to see Salinguerra, reveals to the great partisan that Sordello is his son, and that she loves him. Salinguerra, seeing in the union of Palma, daughter of the Lord of Romano, with his son, a vital source of strength to the Emperor's party, throws the Emperor's badge on his son's neck, and offers him the leadership of the Ghibellines. Palma urges him to accept it; but Sordello has been already convinced that the Guelf side is the right one to take for the sake of mankind. Rome, he thinks, is the great uniting power; only by Rome can the cause of peace and the happiness of the people be in the end secured. That cause—the cause of a happy people—is the one thing for which, after many dreams centred in self, Sordello has come to care. He is sorely tempted by the love of Palma and by the power offered him to give up that cause or to palter with it; yet in the end his soul resists the temptation. But the part of his life, in which he has neglected his body, has left him without physical strength; and now the struggle of his soul to do right in this spiritual crisis gives the last blow to his weakened frame. His heart breaks, and he dies at the moment when he dimly sees the true goal of life. This is a masterpiece of the irony of the Fate-Goddess; and a faint suspicion of this irony, underlying life, even though Browning turns it round into final good, runs in and out of the whole poem in a winding thread of thought.

This is the historical background of the poem, and in front of it are represented Sordello, his life, his development as an individual soul, and his death. I have, from one point of view, slightly analysed the first two books of the poem, but to analyse the whole would be apart from the purpose of this book. My object in this and the following chapter is to mark out, with here and there a piece of explanation, certain characteristics of the poem in relation, first, to the time in which it is placed; secondly, to the development of Sordello in contact with that time; and thirdly, to our own time; then to trace the connection of the poem with the poetic evolution of Browning; and finally, to dwell throughout the whole discussion on its poetic qualities.

1. The time in which the poem's thought and action are placed is the beginning of the thirteenth century in North Italy, a period in which the religious basis of life, laid so enthusiastically in the eleventh century, and gradually weakening through the twelfth, had all but faded away for the mediæval

noble and burgher, and even for the clergy. Religion, it is true, was confessed and its dogmas believed in; the Cistercian revival had restored some of its lost influence, but it did not any longer restrain the passions, modify the wickedness, control the ambitions or subdue the world, in the heart of men, as it had done in the eleventh century. There was in Italy, at least, an unbridled licence of life, a fierce individuality, which the existence of a number of small republics encouraged; and, in consequence, a wild confusion of thought and act in every sphere of human life. Moreover, all through the twelfth century there had been a reaction among the artistic and literary men against the theory of life laid down by the monks, and against the merely saintly aims and practice of the religious, of which that famous passage in *Aucassin and Nicolete* is an embodiment. Then, too, the love poetry (a poetry which tended to throw monkish purity aside) started in the midst of the twelfth century; then the troubadours began to sing; and then the love-songs of Germany arose. And Italian poetry, a poetry which tended to repel the religion of the spirit for the religion of enjoyment, had begun in Sicily and Siena in 1172–78, and was nurtured in the Sicilian Court of Frederick II., while Sordello was a youth. All over Europe, poetry drifted into a secular poetry of love and war and romance. The religious basis of life had lost its strength. As to North Italy, where our concern lies, humanity there was weltering like a sea, tossing up and down, with no direction in its waves. It was not till Francis of Assisi came that a new foundation for religious life, a new direction for it, began to be established. As to

Law, Government, Literature, and Art, all their elements were in equal confusion. Every noble, every warrior who reached ascendency, or was born to it, made his own laws and governed as he liked. Every little city had its own fashions and its own aims ; and was continually fighting, driven by jealousy, envy, hatred, or emulation, with its neighbours. War was the incessant business of life, and was carried on not only against neighbouring cities, but by each city in its own streets, from its own towers, where noble fought against noble, citizen with citizen, and servant with servant. Literature was only trying to begin, to find its form, to find its own Italian tongue, to understand what it desired. It took more than a century after Sordello's youth to shape itself into the poetry of Dante and Petrarch, into their prose and the prose of Boccaccio. The *Vita Nuova* was set forth in 1290, 93, the *Decameron* in 1350, 53, and Petrarch was crowned at Rome in 1341. And the arts of sculpture and painting were in the same condition. They were struggling towards a new utterance, but as yet they could not speak.

It is during this period of impassioned confusion and struggle towards form, during this carnival of individuality, that Sordello, as conceived by Browning, a modern in the midst of mediævalism, an exceptional character wholly unfitted for the time, is placed by Browning. And the clash between himself and his age is too much for him. He dies of it ; dies of the striving to find an anchorage for life, and of his inability to find it in this chartless sea. But the world of men, incessantly recruited by new generations, does not die like the individual, and what Sordello could not do, it did. It emerged from this confusion in the thirteenth and fourteenth centuries, with S. Francis, Dante, Petrarch and Boccaccio, the Pisani, Giotto, and the Commonwealth of Florence. Religion, Poetry, Prose, Sculpture, Painting, Government and Law found new foundations. The Renaissance began to dawn, and during its dawn kept, among the elect of mankind, all or nearly all the noble impulses and faith of mediævalism.

This dawn of the Renaissance is nearly a hundred years away at the time of this poem, yet two of its characteristics vitally moved through this transition period; and, indeed, while they continued even to the end of the Renaissance, were powers which brought it about. The first of these was a boundless curiosity about life, and the second was an intense individuality. No one can read the history of the Italian Republics in the thirteenth century without incessantly coming into contact with both these elements working fiercely, confusedly, without apparently either impulse or aim, but producing a wonderful activity of life, out of which, by command as it were of the gods, a new-created world might rise into order. It was as if chaos were stirred, like a cauldron with a stick, that suns and planets, moving by living law, might emerge in beauty. Sordello lived in the first whirling of these undigested elements, and could only dream of what might be; but it was life in which he moved, disorderly life, it is true, but not the dread disorder of decay. Browning paints it with delight.

This unbridled curiosity working in men of unbridled individuality produced a tumbling confusion in life. Men, full of eagerness, each determined to fulfil his own will, tried every kind of life, attempted every kind of pursuit, strove to experience all the passions, indulged their passing impulses to the full, and when they were wearied of any experiment in living passed on to the next, not with weariness but with fresh excitement. Cities, small republics, did the same collectively—Ferrara, Padua, Verona, Mantua, Milan, Parma, Florence, Pisa, Siena, Perugia. Both cities and citizens lived in a nervous storm, and at every impulse passed into furious activity. In five minutes a whole town was up in the market-place, the bells rang, the town banner was displayed, and in an hour the citizens were marching out of the gates to attack the neighbouring city. A single gibe in the streets, or at the church door, interchanged between one noble and another of opposite factions, and the gutters of the streets ran red with the blood of a hundred men. This then was the time of *Sordello*, and splendidly has Browning represented it.

2. Sordello is the image of this curiosity and individuality, but only inwardly. In the midst of this turbulent society Browning creates him with the temperament of a poet, living in a solitary youth, apart from arms and the wild movement of the world. His soul is full of the curiosity of the time. The inquisition of his whole life is, "What is the life most worth living? How shall I attain it, in what way make it mine?" and then, "What sort of lives are lived by other men?" and, finally, "What is the happiest life for the whole?" The curiosity does not drive him, like the rest of the

world, into action in the world. It expands only in thought and dreaming. But however he may dream, however wrapt in self he may be, his curiosity about these matters never lessens for a moment. Even in death it is his ruling passion.

Along with this he shares fully in the impassioned individuality of the time. Browning brings that forward continually. All the dreams of his youth centre in himself; Nature becomes the reflection of himself; all histories of great men he represents as in himself; finally, he becomes to himself Apollo, the incarnation of poetry. But he does not seek to realise his individuality, any more than his curiosity, in action. When he is drawn out of himself at Mantua and sings for a time to please men, he finds that the public do not understand him, and flies back to his solitude, back to his own soul. And Mantua, and love, and adventure all die within him. "I have all humanity," he says, "within myself—why then should I seek humanity?" This is the way the age's passion for individuality shows itself in him. Other men put it into love, war, or adventure. He does not; he puts it into the lonely building-up of his own soul. Even when he is brought into the midst of the action of the time we see that he is apart from it. As he wanders through the turmoil of the streets of Ferrara in Book iv., he is dreaming still of his own life, of his own soul. His curiosity, wars and adventures are within. The various lives he is anxious to live are lived in lonely imaginations. The individuality he realises is in thought. At this point then he is apart from his century—an exceptional temperament set in strong contrast to the world around him—the dreamer face to face with a mass of men all acting with intensity. And the common result takes place; the exceptional breaks down against the steady and terrible pull of the ordinary. It is Hamlet over again, and when Sordello does act it is just as Hamlet does, by a sudden impulse which lifts him from dreaming into momentary action, out of which, almost before he has realised he is acting, he slips back again into dreams. And his action seems to him the dream, and his dream the activity. That saying of Hamlet's would be easy on the lips of Sordello, if we take "bad dreams" to mean for him what they meant for Hamlet the moment he is forced to action in the real world—"I could be bounded in a nut-shell and think myself king of infinite space, had I not bad dreams." When he is surprised into action at the Court of Love at Mantua, and wins the prize of song, he seems to slip back into a sleepy cloud. But Palma, bending her beautiful face over him and giving him her scarf, wins him to stay at Mantua; and for a short time he becomes the famous poet. But he is disappointed. That which he felt himself to be (the supernal greatness of his individuality) is not recognised, and at last he feels that to act and fight his way through a world which appreciates his isolated greatness so little as to dare to criticise him, is impossible. We have seen in the last chapter how he slips back to Goito, to his contemplation of himself in nature, to his self-communion, to the dreams which do not contradict his opinion of himself. The momentary creator perishes in the dreamer. He gives up life, adventure, love, war, and he finally surrenders his art. No more poetry for him.

It is thus that a character feeble for action, but mystic in imagination, acts in the petulance of youth when it is pushed into a clashing, claiming world. In this mood a year passes by in vague content. Yet a little grain of conscience makes him sour. He is vexed that his youth is gone with all its promised glow, pleasure and action; and the vexation is suddenly deepened by seeing a great change in the aspect of nature. "What," he thinks, when he sees the whole valley filled with Mincio in flood, "can Nature in this way renew her youth, and not I? Alas! I cannot so renew myself; youth is over." But if youth be dead, manhood remains; and the curiosity and individuality of the age stir in him again. "I must find," he thinks, "the fitting kind of life. I must make men feel what I am. But how; what do I want for this? I want some outward power to draw me forth and upward, as the moon draws the waters; to lead me to a life in which I may know mankind, in order that I may take out of men all I need to make *myself* into perfect form——a full poet, able to impose my genius on mankind, and to lead them where I will. What force can draw me out of these dreaming solitudes in which I fail to realise my art? Why, there is none so great as love. Palma who smiled on me, she shall be my moon." At that moment, when he is again thrilled with curiosity concerning life, again desirous to realise his individuality in the world of men, a message comes from Palma. "Come, there is much for you to do—come to me at Verona." She lays a political career before him. "Take the Kaiser's cause, you and I together; build a new Italy under the Emperor." And Sordello is fired by the thought, not as yet for the sake of doing good to man, but to satisfy his curiosity in a new life, and to edify his individual soul into a perfection unattained as yet. "I will go," he thinks, "and be the spirit in this body of mankind, wield, animate, and shape the people of Italy, make them the form in which I shall express myself. It is not enough to act, in imagination, all that man is, as I have done. I will now make men act by the force of my spirit: North Italy shall be my body, and thus I shall realise myself"—as if one could, with that self-contemplating motive, ever realise personality.

This, then, is the position of Sordello in the period of history I have pictured, and it carries him to the end of the third book of the poem. It has embodied the history of his youth—of his first contact with the world; of his retreat from it into thought over what he has gone through; and of his reawakening into a fresh questioning—how he shall realise life, how manifest himself in action. "What shall I do as a poet, and a man?"

3. The next thing to be said of *Sordello* is its vivid realisation of certain aspects of mediæval life. Behind this image of the curious dreamer lost in abstractions, and vividly contrasted with it, is the fierce activity of mediæval cities and men in incessant war; each city, each man eager to make his own individuality supreme; and this is painted by Browning at the very moment when the two great parties were formed, and added to personal war the intensifying power of two ideals. This was a field for imagination in which Browning was sure to revel, like a wild creature of the woods on a summer day. He had the genius of places, of portraiture, and of

sudden flashes of action and passion; and the time of which he wrote supplied him with full matter for these several capacities of genius.

When we read in *Sordello* of the fierce outbursts of war in the cities of North Italy, we know that Browning saw them with his eyes and shared their fury and delight. Verona is painted in the first book just as the news arrives that her prince is captive in Ferrara. It is evening, a still and flaming sunset, and soft sky. In dreadful contrast to this burning silence of Nature is the wrath and hate which are seething in the market-place. Group talked with restless group, and not a face

> But wrath made livid, for among them were
> Death's staunch purveyors, such as have in care
> To feast him. Fear had long since taken root
> In every breast, and now these crushed its fruit,
> The ripe hate, like a wine; to note the way
> It worked while each grew drunk! Men grave and grey
> Stood, with shut eyelids, rocking to and fro,
> Letting the silent luxury trickle slow
> About the hollows where a heart should be;
> But the young gulped with a delirious glee
> Some foretaste of their first debauch in blood
> At the fierce news.

Step by step the varying passions, varying with the men of the varied cities of the League assembled at Verona, are smitten out on the anvil of Browning's imagination. Better still is the continuation of the same scene in the third book, when the night has come, and the raging of the people, reaching its height, declares war. Palma and Sordello, who are in the palace looking on the square, lean out to see and hear. On the black balcony beneath them, in the still air, amid a gush of torch-fire, the grey-haired counsellors harangue the people;

> then
> Sea-like that people surging to and fro
> Shouted, "Hale forth the carroch—trumpets, ho,
> A flourish! Run it in the ancient grooves!
> Back from the bell! Hammer—that whom behoves
> May hear the League is up!

Then who will may read the dazzling account of the streets of Ferrara thick with corpses; of Padua, of Bassano streaming blood; of the wells chokeful of carrion, of him who catches in his spur, as he is kicking his feet when he sits on the well and singing, his own mother's face by the grey hair; of the sack of Vicenza in the fourth book; of the procession of the envoys of the League through the streets of Ferrara, with ensigns, war-cars and clanging bells; of the wandering of Sordello at night through the squares blazing with fires, and the soldiers camped around them singing and shouting; of his solitary silent thinking contrasted with their noise and action — and he who reads will know, as if he lived in them, the fierce Italian towns of the thirteenth century.

Nor is his power less when he describes the solitary silent places of mediæval castles, palaces, and their rooms; of the long, statue-haunted, cypress-avenued gardens, a waste of flowers and wild undergrowth. We wander, room by room, through Adelaide's castle at Goito, we see every beam in the ceiling, every figure on the tapestry; we walk with Browning through the dark passages into the dim-lighted chambers of the town palace at Verona, and hang over its balconies; we know the gardens at

Goito, and the lonely woods; and we keep pace with Sordello through those desolate paths and ilex-groves, past the fountains lost in the wilderness of foliage, climbing from terrace to terrace where the broken statues, swarming with wasps, gleam among the leering aloes and the undergrowth, in the garden that Salinguerra made for his Sicilian wife at Ferrara. The words seem as it were to flare the ancient places out before the eyes.

Mixed up with all this painting of towns, castles and gardens there is some natural description. Browning endeavours, it is plain, to keep that within the mediæval sentiment. But that he should succeed in that was impossible. The mediæval folk had little of our specialised sentiment for landscape, and Browning could not get rid of it.

The modern philosophies of Nature do not, however, appear in *Sordello* as they did in *Pauline* or *Paracelsus*. Only once in the whole of *Sordello* is Nature conceived as in analogy with man, and Browning says this in a parenthesis. "Life is in the tempest," he cries, "thought

"Clothes the keen hill-top; mid-day woods are fraught
With fervours":

but, in spite of the mediæval environment, the modern way of seeing Nature enters into all his descriptions. They are none the worse for it, and do not jar too much with the mediæval *mise-en-scène*. We expect our modern sentiment, and Sordello himself, being in many ways a modern, seems to license these descriptions. Most of them also occur when he is on the canvas, and are a background to his thought. Moreover, they are not set descriptions; they are flashed out, as it were, in a few lines, as if they came by chance, and are not pursued into detail. Indeed, they are not done so much for the love of Nature herself, as for passing illustrations of Sordello's ways of thought and feeling upon matters which are not Nature. As such, even in a mediæval poem, they are excusable. And vivid they are in colour, in light, in reality. Some I have already isolated. Here are a few more, just to show his hand. This is the castle and its scenery, described in Book i.:

> In Mantua territory half is slough,
> Half pine-tree forest: maples, scarlet oaks
> Breed o'er the river-beds; even Mincio chokes
> With sand the summer through: but 'tis morass
> In winter up to Mantua's walls. There was,
> Some thirty years before this evening's coil,
> One spot reclaimed from the surrounding spoil,
> Goito; just a castle built amid
> A few low mountains; firs and larches hid
> Their main defiles, and rings of vineyard bound
> The rest. Some captured creature in a pound,
> Whose artless wonder quite precludes distress,
> Secure beside in its own loveliness,
> So peered, with airy head, below, above
> The castle at its toils, the lapwings love
> To glean among at grape time.

And this is the same place from the second book:

> And thus he wandered, dumb
> Till evening, when he paused, thoroughly spent
> On a blind hill-top: down the gorge he went,
> Yielding himself up as to an embrace.
> The moon came out; like features of a face,
> A querulous fraternity of pines,
> Sad blackthorn clumps, leafless and grovelling vines
> Also came out, made gradually up
> The picture; 'twas Goito's mountain-cup
> And castle.

And here, from Book iii., is Spring when Palma, dreaming of the man she can love, cries that the waking earth is in a thrill to welcome him—

> " Waits he not the waking year?
> His almond-blossoms must be honey-ripe
> By this; to welcome him fresh runnels stripe
> The thawed ravines; because of him the wind
> Walks like a herald."

This is May from Book ii.; and afterwards, in the third book, the months from Spring to Summer—

> My own month came;
> 'Twas a sunrise of blossoming and May.
> Beneath a flowering laurel thicket lay
> Sordello; each new sprinkle of white stars
> That smell fainter of wine than Massic jars
> Dug up at Baiæ, when the south wind shed
> The ripest, made him happier.
>
> Not any strollings now at even-close
> Down the field path, Sordello! by thorn-rows
> Alive with lamp-flies, swimming spots of fire
> And dew, outlining the black cypress-spire
> She waits you at, Elys, who heard you first
> Woo her, the snow month through, but, ere she durst
> Answer 'twas April. Linden-flower-time long
> Her eyes were on the ground; 'tis July, strong
> Now; and, because white dust-clouds overwhelm
> The woodside, here, or by the village elm
> That holds the moon, she meets you, somewhat pale.

And here are two pieces of the morning, one of the wide valley of Naples; another with which the poem ends, pure modern, for it does not belong to Sordello's time, but to our own century. This is from the fourth book.

> Broke
> Morning o'er earth; he yearned for all it woke—
> From the volcano's vapour-flag, winds hoist
> Black o'er the spread of sea,—down to the moist
> Dale's silken barley-spikes sullied with rain,
> Swayed earthwards, heavily to rise again.

And this from the last book—

> Lo, on a heathy brown and nameless hill
> By sparkling Asolo, in mist and chill,
> Morning just up, higher and higher runs
> A child barefoot and rosy. See! the sun's
> On the square castle's inner-court's low wall
> Like the chine of some extinct animal
> Half-turned to earth and flowers; and through the haze,
> (Save where some slender patches of grey maize
> Are to be over-leaped) that boy has crossed
> The whole hill-side of dew and powder-frost
> Matting the balm and mountain camomile.
> Up and up goes he, singing all the while
> Some unintelligible words to beat
> The lark, God's poet, swooning at his feet.

As alive, and even clearer in outline than these natural descriptions, are the portraits in *Sordello* of the people of the time. No one can mistake them for modern folk. I do not speak of the portrait of Sordello—that is chiefly of the soul, not of the body—but of the personages who fill the background, the heads of noble houses, the warriors, priests, soldiers, singers, the women, and chiefly Adelaide and Palma. These stand before us as Tintoret or Veronese might have painted them had they lived on into the great portrait-century. Their dress, their attitudes, their sudden gestures, their eyes, hair, the trick of their mouths, their armour, how they walked and talked and read and wrote, are all done in quick touches and jets of colour. Each is distinct from the others, each a type. A multitude of cabinet sketches of men are made in the market-places, in castle rooms, on the roads, in the gardens, on the bastions of the towns. Take as one example the Pope's Legate:

> With eyes, like fresh-blown thrush-eggs on a thread,
> Faint-blue and loosely floating in his head,
> Large tongue, moist open mouth; and this long while
> That owner of the idiotic smile
> Serves them!

Nor does Browning confine himself to personages of Sordello's time. There are admirable portraits, but somewhat troubled by unnecessary matter, of Dante, of Charlemagne, of Hildebrand. One elaborate portrait is continued throughout the poem. It is that of Salinguerra, the man of action as contrasted with Sordello the dreamer. Much pains are spent on this by Browning. We see him first in the streets of Ferrara.

>   Men understood
> Living was pleasant to him as he wore
> His careless surcoat, glanced some missive o'er,
> Propped on his truncheon in the public way.

Then at the games at Mantua, when he is told Sordello will not come to sing a welcome to him. What cares he for poet's whims?

> The easy-natured soldier smiled assent,
> Settled his portly person, smoothed his chin,
> And nodded that the bull-bait might begin.

Then mad with fighting frenzy in the sacking of Vicenza, then in his palace nursing his scheme to make the Emperor predominant, then pacing like a lion, hot with hope of mastering all Italy, when he finds out that Sordello is his son: "hands clenched, head erect, pursuing his discourse—crimson ear, eyeballs suffused, temples full fraught."

Then in the fourth book there is a long portrait of him which I quote as a full specimen of the power with which Browning could paint a partisan of the thirteenth century. Though sixty years old, Salinguerra looked like a youth—

> So agile, quick
> And graceful turned the head on the broad chest
> Encased in pliant steel, his constant vest,
> Whence split the sun off in a spray of fire
> Across the room; and, loosened of its tire
> Of steel, that head let breathe the comely brown
> Large massive locks discoloured as if a crown
> Encircled them, so frayed the basnet where
> A sharp white line divided clean the hair;
> Glossy above, glossy below, it swept
> Curling and fine about a brow thus kept
> Calm, laid coat upon coat, marble and sound:
> This was the mystic mark the Tuscan found,
> Mused of, turned over books about. Square-faced,
> No lion more; two vivid eyes, enchased
> In hollows filled with many a shade and streak
> Settling from the bold nose and bearded cheek.
> Nor might the half-smile reach them that deformed
> A lip supremely perfect else—unwarmed,
> Unwidened, less or more; indifferent
> Whether on trees or men his thoughts were bent,
> Thoughts rarely, after all, in trim and train
> As now a period was fulfilled again:
> Of such, a series made his life, compressed
> In each, one story serving for the rest.

This is one example of a gallery of vivid portraiture in all Browning's work, such as Carlyle only in the nineteenth century has approached in England. It is not a national, but an international gallery of portraits. The greater number of the portraits are Italian, and they range over all classes of society from the Pope to the peasant. Even Bishop Blougram has the Italian subtlety, and, like the Monsignore in *Pippa Passes*, something of the politic morality of Machiavelli. But Israel, Greece, France, Spain, Germany, and the days before the world was brought together, furnish him with men drawn as alive. He has painted their souls, but others have done this kind of painting as well, if not so minutely. But no others have painted so livingly the outside of men—their features one by one, their carriage, their gestures, their clothing, their walk, their body. All the colours of their dress and eyes and lips are given. We see them live and move and have their being. It is the same with his women, but I keep these for further treatment.

4. The next thing I have to say about *Sordello* concerns what I call its illustrative episodes. Browning, wishing to illuminate his subject, sometimes darts off from it into an elaborate simile as Homer does. But in Homer the simile is carefully set, and explained to be a comparison. It is not mixed up with the text. It is short, rarely reaching more than ten lines. In Browning, it is glided into without any preparation, and at first seems part of the story. Nor are we always given any intimation of its end. And Browning is led away by his imaginative pleasure in its invention to work it up with adventitious ornament of colour and scenery; having, in his excitement of invention, lost all power of rejecting any additional touch which occurs to him, so that the illustration, swelling out into a preposterous length, might well be severed from the book and made into a separate poem. Moreover, these long illustrations are often but faintly connected with the subject they are used to illumine; and they delay the movement of the poem while they confuse the reader. The

worst of these, worst as an illustration, but in itself an excellent fragment to isolate as a picture-poem, is the illustration of the flying slave who seeks his tribe beyond the Mountains of the Moon. It is only to throw light on a moment of Salinguerra's discursive thought, and is far too big for that. It is more like an episode than an illustration. I quote it not only to show what I mean, but also for its power. It is in Bk. iv.

> As, shall I say, some Ethiop, past pursuit
> Of all enslavers, dips a shackled foot
> Burnt to the blood, into the drowsy black
> Enormous watercourse which guides him back
> To his own tribe again, where he is king ;
> And laughs because he guesses, numbering
> The yellower poison-wattles on the pouch
> Of the first lizard wrested from its couch
> Under the slime (whose skin, the while, he strips
> To cure his nostril with, and festered lips,
> And eyeballs bloodshot through the desert-blast)
> That he has reached its boundary, at last
> May breathe ;—thinks o'er enchantments of the South
> Sovereign to plague his enemies, their mouth,
> Eyes, nails, and hair ; but, these enchantments tried
> In fancy, puts them soberly aside
> For truth, projects a cool return with friends,
> The likelihood of winning mere amends
> Ere long ; thinks that, takes comfort silently,
> Then, from the river's brink, his wrongs and he,
> Hugging revenge close to their hearts, are soon
> Off-striding for the Mountains of the Moon."

The best of these is where he illustrates the restless desire of a poet for the renewal of energy, for finding new worlds to sing. The poet often seems to stop his work, to be satisfied. "Here I will rest," he says, "and do no more." But he only waits for a fresh impulse.

> 'Tis but a sailor's promise, weather-bound :
> " Strike sail, slip cable, here the bark be moored
> For once, the awning stretched, the poles assured !
> Noontide above ; except the wave's crisp dash,
> Or buzz of colibri, or tortoise' splash,
> The margin's silent : out with every spoil
> Made in our tracking, coil by mighty coil,
> This serpent of a river to his head
> I' the midst ! Admire each treasure, as we spread
> The bank, to help us tell our history
> Aright ; give ear, endeavour to descry
> The groves of giant rushes, how they grew
> Like demons' endlong tresses we sailed through,
> What mountains yawned, forests to give us vent
> Opened, each doleful side, yet on we went
> Till . . . may that beetle (shake your cap) attest
> The springing of a land-wind from the West ! "
> —Wherefore ? Ah yes, you frolic it to-day !
> To-morrow, and the pageant moved away
> Down to the poorest tent-pole, we and you
> Part company : no other may pursue
> Eastward your voyage, be informed what fate
> Intends, if triumph or decline await
> The tempter of the everlasting steppe !

This, from Book iii., is the best because it is closer than the rest to the matter in hand ; but how much better it might have been ! How curiously overloaded it is, how difficult what is easy has been made !

The fault of these illustrations is the fault of the whole poem. *Sordello* is obscure, Browning's idolaters say, by concentration of thought. It is rather obscure by want of that wise rejection of unnecessary thoughts which is the true concentration. It is obscure by a reckless misuse of the ordinary rules of language. It is obscure by a host of parentheses introduced to express thoughts which are only suggested, half-shaped, and which are frequently interwoven with parentheses introduced into the original parentheses. It is obscure by the worst punctuation I ever came across, but this was improved in the later editions. It is obscure by multitudinous fancies put in whether they have to do with the subject or not, and by multitudinous deviations within those fancies. It is obscure by Browning's effort to make words express more than they are capable of expressing.

It is no carping criticism to say this of Browning's work in *Sordello*, because it is the very criticism his after-practice as an artist makes. He gave up these efforts to force, like Procrustes, language to stretch itself or to cut itself down into forms it could not naturally take; and there is no more difficulty in most of his earlier poems than there is in *Paracelsus*. Only a little of the Sordellian agonies remains in them, only that which was natural to Browning's genius. The interwoven parentheses remain, the rushes of invention into double and triple illustrations, the multiplication of thought on thought; but for these we may even be grateful. Opulence and plenitude of this kind are not common; we are not often granted a man who flings imaginations, fancies and thoughts from him as thick and bright as sparks from a grinder's wheel. It is not every poet who is unwilling to leave off, who finds himself too full to stop. "These bountiful wits," as Lamb said, "always give full measure, pressed down, and running over."

CHAPTER VII

BROWNING AND SORDELLO

THERE are certain analogies between Browning as a poet and the Sordello of the poem; between his relation to the world of his time and that of Sordello to his time; and finally, between Browning's language in this poem and the change in the Italian language which he imputes to the work of Sordello. This chapter will discuss these analogies, and close with an appreciation of Browning's position between the classic and romantic schools of poetry.

The analogies of which I write may be denied, but I do not think they can be disproved. Browning is, no doubt, separate from Sordello in his own mind, but underneath the young poet he is creating, he is continually asking himself the same question which Sordello asks—What shall I do as an artist? To what conclusion shall I come with regard to my life as a poet? It is no small proof of this underlying personal element in the first three books of the poem that at the end of the third book Browning flings himself suddenly out of the mediæval world and the men he has created, and waking into 1835–40 at Venice, asks himself—What am I writing, and why? What is my aim in being a poet? Is it worth my while to go on with Sordello's story, and why is it worth the telling? In fact, he allows us to think that he has been describing in Sordello's story a transitory phase of his own career. And then, having done this, he tells how he got out of confusion into clearer light.

The analogy between Browning's and Sordello's time is not a weak one. The spirit of the world, between 1830 and 1840 in England, resembled in many ways the spirit abroad at the beginning of the thirteenth century. The country had awakened out of a long sleep, and was extraordinarily curious not only with regard to life and the best way to live it, but also with regard to government, law, the condition of the people, the best kind of religion and how best to live it, the true aims of poetry and how it was to be written, what subjects it should work on, what was to be the mother-motive of it, that is, what was the mother-motive of all the arts. And this curiosity deepened from year to year for fifty years. But even stronger than the curiosity was the eager individualism of this time, which extended into every sphere of human thought and action, and only began about 1866 to be balanced by an equally strong tendency towards collectivism.

These two elements in the time-spirit did not produce, in a settled state like England, the outward war and confusion they produced in the thirteenth century, though they developed after 1840, in '48, into a European storm—but they did produce a confused welter of mingled thoughts concerning the sources and ends of human life, the action it should take, and why it should take it. The poetry of Arnold and Clough represents with great clearness the further development in the soul of man of this confusion. I think that Browning has represented in the first three books of *Sordello* his passage through this tossing sea of thought.

He had put into *Paracelsus* all that he had worked out with clearness during his youth; his theory of life is stated with lucidity in that poem. But when it was finished, and he had entered, like Sordello from Goito into Mantua, into the crowd and clash of the world; when, having published *Pauline* and *Paracelsus*, he had, like Sordello, met criticism and misunderstanding, his Paracelsian theory did not seem to explain humanity as clearly as he imagined. It was only a theory; Would it stand the test of life among mankind, be a saving and healing prophecy? Life lay before him, now that the silent philosophising of poetic youth was over, in all its inexplicable, hurried, tormented, involved, and multitudinously varied movement. He had built up a transcendental building* in *Paracelsus*. Was it all to fall in ruin? No answer came when he looked forth on humanity over whose landscape the irony of the gods, a bitter mist, seemed to brood. At what then shall he aim as a poet? What shall be his subject-matter? How is life to be lived?

Then he thought that he would, as a poet, describe his own time and his own soul under the character of Sordello, and place Sordello in a time more stormy than his own. And he would make Sordello of an exceptional temper like himself, and

---

* He makes a simile of this in *Sordello*. See Book iii. before his waking up in Venice, the lines beginning
"Rather say
My transcendental platan!"

to clash with *his* time as he was then clashing with his own. With these thoughts he wrote the first books of *Sordello*, and Naddo, the critic of Sordello's verses, represents the critics of Paracelsus and the early poems. I have experienced, he says of himself in *Sordello*, something of the spite of fate.

Then, having done this, he leaves Sordello at the end of the third book, and turns, beset with a thousand questions, to himself and his art in a personal digression. Reclining on a ruined palace-step at Venice, he thinks of Eglamor who made a flawless song, the type of those who reach their own perfection here; and then of Sordello who made a song which stirred the world far more than Eglamor's, which yet was not flawless, not perfect; but because of its imperfection looked forward uncontented to a higher song. Shall he, Browning the poet, choose Eglamor or Sordello; even though Sordello perish without any achievement? And he chooses to sail for ever towards the infinite, chooses the imperfection which looks forward. A sailor who loves voyaging may say, when weather-bound, " Here rest, unlade the ship, sleep on this grassy bank." 'Tis but a moment on his path; let the wind change, and he is away again, whether triumph or shipwreck await him, for ever

> The tempter of the everlasting steppe.

That much is then settled for life and for poetry. And in that choice of endless aspiration Browning confirms all that he thought, with regard to half of his theory of life, in *Paracelsus*. This is his first thought for life, and it is embodied in the whole of Sordello's career. Sordello is never content with earth, either when he is young, or when he passes into the world, or when he dies not having attained or been already perfect—a thought which is as much at the root of romanticism as of Christianity. Then comes the further question: To whom shall I dedicate the service of my art? Who shall be my motive, the Queen whom I shall love and write of; and he thinks of Sordello who asks that question and who, for the time, answers "Palma," that is, the passion of love.

"But now, shall I, Browning, take as my Queen"—and he symbolises his thought in the girls he sees in the boats from his palace steps—"that girl from Bassano, or from Asolo, or her from Padua; that is, shall I write of youth's love, of its tragic or its comedy, of its darkness, joy and beauty only? No, he answers, not of that stuff shall I make my work, but of that sad dishevelled ghost of a girl, half in rags, with eyes inveterately full of tears; of wild, worn, care-bitten, ravishing, piteous, and pitiful Humanity, who begs of me and offers me her faded love in the street corners. She shall be my Queen, the subject of my song, the motive of my poetry. She may be guilty, warped awry from her birth, and now a tired harlotry; but she shall rest on my shoulder and I shall comfort her. She is false, mistaken, degraded, ignorant, but she moves blindly from evil to good, and from lies to truth, and from ignorance to knowledge, and from all to love; and all her errors prove that she has another world in which, the errors being worked through, she will develop into perfectness. Slowly she moves, step by step; but not a millionth part is here done of what she will do at last. That is the matter of my poetry, which, in its infinite change and hopes, I shall express in my work. I shall see it, say what I have seen, and it may be

> Impart the gift of seeing to the rest.

Therefore I have made Sordello, thus far, with all his weakness and wrong—

> moulded, made anew
> A Man, and give him to be turned and tried,
> Be angry with or pleased at."

And then Browning severs himself from Sordello. After this retirement of thought into himself, described as taking place in Venice during an hour, but I dare say ranging over half a year in reality, he tells the rest of Sordello's story from the outside, as a spectator and describer.

Browning has now resolved to dedicate his art, which is his life, to love of Humanity, of that pale dishevelled girl, unlovely and lovely, evil and good; and to tell the story of individual men and women, and of as many as possible; to paint the good which is always mixed with their evil; to show that their failures and sins point to a success and goodness beyond, because they emerged from aspiration and aspiration from the divinity at the root of human nature. But to do this, a poet must not live like Sordello, in abstractions, nor shrink from the shock of men and circumstance, nor refuse to take men and life as they are—but throw himself into the vital present, with its difficulties, baffling elements and limitations; take its failures for his own; go through them while he looks beyond them, and, because he looks beyond them, never lose hope, or retreat from life, or cease to fight his way onward. And, to support him in this, there is but one thing—infinite love, pity, and sympathy for mankind, increased, not lessened by knowledge of the sins and weakness, the failure and despairs of men. This is Browning's second thought for life. But this is the very thing Sordello, as conceived by Browning, did not and could not do. He lived in abstractions and in himself; he tried to discard his human nature, or to make it bear more than it could bear. He threw overboard the natural physical life of the body because it limited, he thought, the outgoings of the imaginative soul, and only found that in weakening the body he enfeebled the soul. At every point he resented the limits of human life and fought against them. Neither would he live in the world allotted to him, nor among the men of his time, nor in its turmoil; but only in imagination of his own inner world, among men whom he created for himself, of which world he was to be sole king. He had no love for men; they wearied, jarred, and disturbed his ideal world. All he wanted was their applause or their silence, not their criticism, not their affection. And of course human love and sympathy for men and insight into them, departed from him, and with them his art departed. He never became a true poet.

It is this failure, passing through several phases of life in which action is demanded of Sordello, that Browning desired to record in the last three books of the poem. And he thinks it worth doing because it is human, and the record of what is human is always of worth to man. He paints Sordello's passage through phase after phase of thought and act in the outside world, in all of which he seems for the moment to succeed or to touch the verge of success, but in which his neglect of the needs of the body and the uncontentment of his soul produce failure. At last, at the very moment of death he knows why he failed, and sees, as through a glass darkly, the failure making the success of the world to come. The revelation bursts his heart.

And now what is the end, what is the result for man of this long striving of Sordello? Nothing! Nothing has been done. Yet no, there is one result. The imperfect song he made when he was young at Goito, in the flush of happiness, when he forgot himself in love of nature and of the young folk who wandered rejoicing through the loveliness of nature —that song is still alive, not in the great world among the noble women and warriors of the time, but on the lips of the peasant girls of Asolo who sing it on dewy mornings when they climb the castle hill. This is the outcome of Sordello's life, and it sounds like irony on Browning's lips. It is not so; the irony is elsewhere in the poem, and is of another kind. Here, the conclusion is,—that the poem, or any work of art, made in joy, in sympathy with human life, moved by the love of loveliness in man or in nature, lives and lasts in beauty, heals and makes happy the world. And it has its divine origin in the artist's loss of himself in humanity, and his finding of himself, through union with humanity, in union with God the eternal poet. In this is hidden the life of an artist's greatness. And here the little song, which gives joy to a child, and fits in with and enhances its joy, is greater in the eyes of the immortal judges than all the glory of the world which Sordello sought so long for himself alone. It is a truth Browning never failed to record, the greatness and power of the things of love; for, indeed, love being infinite and omnipotent, gives to its smallest expression the glory of all its qualities.

The second of these analogies between Browning and Sordello relates to Browning's treatment of the English language in the poem of *Sordello* and what he pictures Sordello as doing for the Italian language in the poem. The passage to which I refer is about half-way in the second book. As there is no real ground for representing Sordello as working any serious change in the Italian tongue of literature except a slight phrase in a treatise of Dante's, the representation is manifestly an invention of Browning's added to the character of Sordello as conceived by himself. As such it probably comes out of, and belongs to, his own experience. The Sordello who acts thus with language represents the action of Browning himself at the time he was writing the poem. If so, the passage is full of interest.

All we know about Sordello as a poet is that he wrote some Italian poems. Those by which he was famous were in Provençal. In Dante's treatise on the use of his native tongue, he suggests that Sordello was one of the pioneers of literary Italian. So, at least, Browning seems to infer from the passage, for he makes it the motive of his little "excursus" on Sordello's presumed effort to strike out a new form and method in poetic language.

Nothing was more needed than such an effort if any fine literature were to arise in Italy. In this unformed but slowly forming thirteenth century the language was in as great a confusion—and, I may say, as individual (for each poet wrote in his own dialect) as the life of the century.

What does Browning make Sordello do? He has brought him to Mantua as the accepted master of song; and Sordello burns to be fully recognised as the absolute poet. He has felt for some time that while he cannot act well he can imagine action well. And he sings his imaginations. But there is at the root of his singing a love of the applause of the people more than a love of song for itself. And he fails to please. So Sordello changes his subject and sings no longer of himself in the action of the heroes he imagines, but of abstract ideas, philosophic dreams and problems. The very critics cried that he had left human nature behind him. Vexed at his failure, and still longing to catch the praise of men, that he may confirm his belief that he is the loftiest of poets, he makes another effort to amaze the world. "I'll write no more of imaginary things," he cries; "I will catch the crowd by reorganising the language of poetry, by new arrangements of metre and words, by elaborate phraseology, especially by careful concentration of thought into the briefest possible frame of words. I will take the stuff of thought—that is, the common language—beat it on the anvil into new shapes, break down the easy flow of the popular poetry, and scarcely allow a tithe of the original words I have written to see the light,

> welding words into the crude
> Mass from the new speech round him, till a rude
> Armour was hammered out, in time to be
> Approved beyond the Roman panoply
> Melted to make it.

That is, he dissolved the Roman dialect to beat out of it an Italian tongue. And in this new armour of language he clothed his thoughts. But the language broke away from his thoughts: neither expressed them nor made them clear. The people failed to understand his thought, and at the new ways of using language the critics sneered. "Do get back," they said, "to the simple human heart, and tell its tales in the simple language of the people."

I do not think that the analogy can be missed. Browning is really describing—with, perhaps, a half-scornful reference to his own desire for public appreciation—what he tried to do in *Sordello* for the language in which his poetry was to be written. I have said that when he came to write *Sordello* his mind had fallen back from the clear theory of life laid down in *Paracelsus* into a tumbled sea of troubled thoughts; and *Sordello* is a welter of thoughts tossing up and down, now appearing, then disappearing, and then appearing again in conjunction with new matter, like objects in a sea above which a cyclone is blowing. Or we may say that his mind, before and during the writing of *Sordello*, was like the thirteenth century, pressing blindly in vital disturbance towards an unknown goal. That partly accounts for the confused recklessness of the language of the poem. But a great many of the tricks Browning now played with his poetic language were deliberately done. He had tried—like Sordello at the Court of Love—a love-poem in *Pauline*. It had not succeeded. He had tried in *Paracelsus* to expose an abstract theory of life, as Sordello had tried writing on abstract imaginings. That also had failed. Now he determined—as he represents Sordello doing—to alter his whole way of writing. "I will concentrate now," he thought, "since they say I am too loose and too diffuse; cut away nine-tenths of all I write, and leave out every word I can possibly omit. I will not express completely what I think; I shall only suggest it by an illustration. And if anything occur to me likely to illuminate it, I shall not add it afterwards but insert it in a parenthesis. I will make a new tongue for my poetry." And the result was the style and the strange manner in which *Sordello* was written. This partly excuses its obscurity, if deliberation can be an excuse for a bad manner in literature. Malice prepense does not excuse a murder, though it makes it more interesting. Finally, the manner in which *Sordello* was written did not please him. He left it behind him, and *Pippa Passes*, which followed *Sordello*, is as clear and simple as its predecessor is obscure in style.

Thirdly, the language of *Sordello*, and, in a lesser degree, that of all Browning's poetry, proves—if his whole way of thought and passion did not also prove it—that Browning was not a classic, that he deliberately put aside the classic traditions in poetry. In this he presents a strong contrast to Tennyson. Tennyson was possessed by those traditions. His masters were Homer, Vergil, Milton and the rest of those who wrote with measure, purity, and temperance; and from whose poetry proceeded a spirit of order, of tranquillity, of clearness, of simplicity; who were reticent in ornament, in illustration, and stern in rejection of unnecessary material. None of these classic excellences belong to Browning, nor did he ever try to gain them, and that was, perhaps, a pity. But, after all, it would have been of no use had he tried for them. We cannot impose from without on ourselves that which we have not within; and Browning was, in spirit, a pure romantic, not a classic. Tennyson never allowed what romanticism he possessed to have its full swing. It always wore the classic dress, submitted itself to the classic traditions, used the classic forms. In the *Idylls of the King* he took a romantic story; but nothing could be more unromantic than many of the inventions and the characters; than the temper, the morality, and the conduct of the poem. The Arthurian poets, Malory himself, would have jumped out their skin with amazement, even with indignation, had they read it. And a great deal of this oddity, this unfitness of the matter to the manner, arose from the romantic story being expressed in poetry written in accordance with classic traditions. Of course, there were other sources for these inharmonies in the poem, but that was one, and not the least of them.

Browning had none of these classic traditions. He had his own matter, quite new stuff it was; and he made his own manner. He did not go back to the old stories, but, being filled with the romantic spirit, embodied it in new forms, and drenched with it his subjects, whether he took them from ancient, mediæval, Renaissance, or modern life. He felt, and truly, that it is of the essence of romanticism to be always arising into new shapes, assimilating itself, century by century, to the needs, the thought and the passions of growing mankind; progressive, a lover of change; in steady opposition to that dull conservatism the tendency to which besets the classic literature.

Browning had the natural faults of the romantic poet; and these are most remarkable when such a poet is young. The faults are the opposites of the classic poet's excellences: want of measure, want of proportion, want of clearness and simplicity, want of temperance, want of that selective power which knows what to leave out or when to stop. And these frequently become positive and end in actual disorder of composition, huddling of the matters treated of into ill-digested masses, violence in effects and phrase, bewildering obscurity, sought-out even desperate strangeness of subject and expression, uncompromising individuality, crude ornament, and fierce colour. Many examples of these faults are to be found in *Sordello* and throughout the work of Browning. They are the extremes into which the Romantic is frequently hurried.

But, then, Browning has the natural gifts and excellences of the romantic poet, and these elements make him dearer than the mere Classic to a multitude of imaginative persons. One of them is endless and impassioned curiosity, for ever unsatisfied, always finding new worlds of thought and feeling into which to make dangerous and thrilling voyages of discovery—voyages that are filled from end to end with incessantly changing adventure, or delight in that adventure. This enchants the world. And it is not only in his subjects that the romantic poet shows his curiosity. He is just as curious of new methods of tragedy, of lyric work, of every mode of poetry; of new ways of expressing old thoughts; new ways of treating old metres; of the invention of new metres and new ways of phrasing; of strange and startling word-combinations, to clothe fittingly the strange and startling things discovered in human nature, in one's own soul, or in the souls of others. In ancient days such a temper produced the many tales of invention which filled the romantic cycles.

Again and again, from century to century, this romantic spirit has done its re-creating work in the development of poetry in France, Germany, Italy, Spain, and England. And in 1840, and for many years afterwards, it produced in Browning, and for our pleasure, his dramatic lyrics as he called them; his psychological studies, which I may well call excursions, adventures, battles, pursuits, retreats, discoveries of the soul; for in the soul of man lay, for Browning, the forest of Broceliande, the wild country of Morgan le Fay, the cliffs and moors of Lyonnesse. It was there, over that unfooted country, that Childe Roland rode to the Dark Tower. Nor can anything be more in the temper of old spiritual romance—though with a strangely modern *mise-en-scène*—than the great adventure on the dark common with Christ in *Christmas-Eve and Easter-Day*.

Another root of the romantic spirit was the sense of, and naturally the belief in, a world not to be felt of the senses or analysed by the understanding; which was within the apparent world as its substance or soul, or beyond it as the power by which it existed; and this mystic belief took, among poets, philosophers, theologians, warriors and the common people, a thousand forms, ranging from full-schemed philosophies to the wildest superstitions. It tended, in its extremes, to make this world a shadow, a dream; and our life only a real life when it habitually dwelt in the mystic region mortal eye could not see, whose voices mortal ear could not receive. Out of this root, which shot its first fibres into the soul of humanity in the days of the earliest savage and separated him by an unfathomable gulf from the brute, arose all the myths and legends and mystic stories which fill romance. Out of it developed the unquenchable thirst of those of the romantic temper for communion with the spiritual beings of this mystic world; a thirst which, however repressed for a time, always arises again; and is even now arising among the poets of to-day.

In Browning's view of the natural world some traces of this element of the romantic spirit may be distinguished, but in his poetry of Man it scarcely appears. Nor, indeed, is he ever the true mystic. He had too much of the sense which handles daily life; he saw the facts of life too clearly, to fall into the vaguer regions of mysticism. But one part of its region, and of the romantic spirit, so incessantly recurs in Browning that it may be said to underlie the whole of his work. It is that into which the thoughts and passions of the romantic poets in all ages ran up, as into a goal—the conception of a perfect world, beyond this visible, in which the noble hopes, loves and work of humanity—baffled, limited, and ruined here—should be fulfilled and satisfied. The Greeks did not frame this conception as a people, though Plato outreached towards it; the Romans had it not, though Vergil seems to have touched it in hours of inspiration. The Teutonic folk did not possess it till Christianity invaded them. Of course, it was alive like a beating heart in Christianity, that most romantic of all religions. But the Celtic peoples did conceive it before Christianity and with a surprising fulness, and wherever they went through Europe they pushed it into the thought, passions and action of human life. And out of this conception, which among the Irish took form as the Land of Eternal Youth, love and joy, where human trouble ceased, grew that element in romance which is perhaps the strongest in it—the hunger for eternity, for infinite perfection of being, and, naturally, for unremitting pursuit of it; and among Christian folk for a life here which should fit them for perfect life to come. Christian romance threw itself with fervour into that ideal, and the pursuit, for example, of the Holy Grail is only one of the forms of this hunger for eternity and perfection.

Browning possessed this element of romance with remarkable fulness, and expressed it with undiminished ardour for sixty years of poetic work. From *Pauline* to *Asolando* it reigns supreme. It is the fountain-source of *Sordello*—by the pervasiveness of which the poem consists. Immortal life in God's perfection! Into that cry the Romantic's hunger for eternity had developed in the soul of Browning. His heroes, in drama and lyric, in

Paracelsus and *Sordello*, pass into the infinite, there to be completed.

And if I may here introduce a kind of note, it is at this moment that we ought to take up the *Purgatorio*, and see Sordello as Dante saw him in that flowery valley of the Ante-Purgatory when he talked with Dante and Vergil. He is there a very different person from the wavering creature Browning drew. He is on the way to that perfect fulfilment in God which Browning desired for him and all mankind.

Nevertheless, in order to complete this statement, Browning, in his full idea of life, was not altogether a romantic. He saw there was a great danger that the romantic mysticism might lead its pursuers to neglect the duties of life, or lessen their interest in the drama of mankind. Therefore he added to his cry for eternity and perfection, his other cry: "Recognise your limitations, and work within them, while you must never be content with them. Give yourself in love and patience to the present labour of mankind; but never imagine for a moment that it ends on earth." He thus combined with the thirst of the romantic for eternity the full ethical theory of life, as well as the classic poet's determination to represent the complete aspect of human life on earth. At this point, but with many fantastic deviations due to his prevailing romanticism, he was partly of the classic temper. The poem of *Sordello* is not without an image of this temper, set vigorously in contrast with Sordello himself. This is Salinguerra, who takes the world as it is, and is only anxious to do what lies before him day by day. His long soliloquy, in which for the moment he indulges in dreams, ends in the simple resolution to fight on, hour by hour, as circumstances call on him.

Browning's position, then, is a combination of the romantic and classical, of the Christian and ethical, of the imaginative and scientific views of human life; of the temper which says, "Here only is our life, here only our concern," and that which says, "Not here, but hereafter is our life." "Here, and hereafter," answered Browning. "Live within earth's limits with all your force; never give in, fight on; but always transcend your fullest action in aspiration, faith and love."

It amuses me sometimes the way he is taken by his readers. The romantic and the Christian folk often claim him as the despiser of this world, as one who bids us live wholly for the future, or in the mystic ranges of thought and passion. The scientific, humanitarian, and ethical folk accept that side of him which agrees with their views of human life—views which exclude God, immortality, and a world beyond—that is, they take as the whole of Browning the lesser part of his theory of life. This is not creditable to their understanding, though it is natural enough. We may accept it as an innocent example of the power of a strong bias in human nature. But it is well to remember that the romantic, Christian, mystic elements of human life are more important in Browning's eyes than the ethical or scientific; that the latter are nothing to him without the former; that the best efforts of the latter for humanity are in his belief not only hopeless, but the stuff that dreams are made of, without the former. In the combination of both is Browning's message to mankind.

CHAPTER VIII

THE DRAMAS

OF the great poets who, not being born dramatists, have attempted to write dramas in poetry, Browning was the most persevering. I suppose that, being conscious of his remarkable power in the representation of momentary action and of states of the soul, he thought that he could harmonise into a whole the continuous action of a number of persons, and of their passions in sword-play with one another; and then conduct to a catastrophe their interaction. But a man may be capable of writing dramatic lyrics and dramatic romances without being capable of writing a drama. Indeed, so different are the two capabilities that I think the true dramatist could not write such a lyric or romance as Browning calls dramatic; his genius would carry one or the other beyond the just limits of this kind of poetry into his own kind. And the writer of excellent lyrics and romances of this kind will be almost sure to fail in real drama. I wish, in order to avoid confusion of thought, that the term "dramatic" were only used of poetry which belongs to drama itself. I have heard Chaucer called dramatic. It is a complete misnomer. His genius would have for ever been unable to produce a good drama. Had he lived in Elizabeth's time, he would, no doubt, have tried to write one, but he must have failed. The genius for story-telling is just the genius which is incapable of being a fine dramatist. And the opposite is also true. Shakespeare, great as his genius was, would not have been able to write a single one of the Canterbury Tales. He would have been driven into dramatising them.

Neither Tennyson nor Browning had dramatic genius—that is, the power to conceive, build, co-ordinate and finish a drama. But they thought they had, and we may pardon them for trying their hand. I can understand the hunger and thirst which beset great poets, who had, like these two men, succeeded in so many different kinds of poetry, to succeed also in the serious drama, written in poetry. It is a legitimate ambition; but poets should be acquainted with their limitations, and not waste their energies or our patience on work which they cannot do well. That men like Tennyson and Browning, who were profoundly capable of understanding what a great drama means, and is; who had read what the master-tragedians of Greece have done; who knew their Shakespeare, to say nothing of the other Elizabethan dramatists; who had seen Molière on the stage; who must have felt how the thing ought to be done, composed, and versed; that they, having written a play like *Harold* or *Strafford*, should really wish to stage it, or having heard and seen it on the stage should go on writing more dramas, would seem incomprehensible, were it not that power to do one thing very well is so curiously liable to self-deceit.

The writing of the first drama is not to be blamed. It would be unnatural not to try one's hand. It is the writing of the others which is amazing in men like Tennyson and Browning. They ought to have felt, being wiser than other men in poetry, that they had no true dramatic capacity. Other poets who also tried the drama did know themselves better. Byron wrote several dramas, but he made little effort to have them represented on the stage. He felt they were not fit for that; and, moreover, such scenic poems as *Manfred* and *Cain* were not intended for the stage, and do not claim to be dramas in that sense. To write things of this kind, making no claim to public representation, with the purpose of painting a situation of the soul, is a legitimate part of a poet's work, and among them, in Browning's work, might be classed *In a Balcony*, which I suppose his most devoted worshipper would scarcely call a drama.

Walter Scott, than whom none could conduct a conversation better in a novel, or make more living the clash of various minds in a critical event, whether in a cottage or a palace; whom one would select as most likely to write a drama well—had self-knowledge enough to understand, after his early attempts, that true dramatic work was beyond his power. Wordsworth also made one effort, and then said good-bye to drama. Coleridge tried, and staged *Remorse*. It failed and deserved to fail. To read it is to know that the writer had no sense of an audience in his mind as he wrote it—a fatal want in a dramatist. Even its purple patches of fine poetry and its noble melody of verse did not redeem it. Shelley did better than these brethren of his, and that is curious. One would say, after reading his previous poems, that he was the least likely of men to write a true drama. Yet the *Cenci* approaches that goal, and the fragment of *Charles the First* makes so great a grip on the noble passions and on the intellectual eye, and its few scenes are so well woven, that it is one of the unfulfilled longings of literature that it should have been finished. Yet Shelley himself gave it up. He knew, like the others, that the drama was beyond his power.

Tennyson and Browning did not so easily recognise their limits. They went on writing dramas, not for the study, which would have been natural and legitimate, but for the stage. This is a curious psychological problem, and there is only one man who could have given us, if he had chosen, a poetic study of it, and that is Browning himself. I wish, having in his mature age read *Strafford* over, and then read his other dramas—all of them full of the same dramatic weaknesses as *Strafford*—he had analysed himself as "the poet who would be a dramatist and could not." Indeed, it is a pity he did not do this. He was capable of smiling benignly at himself, and sketching himself as if he were another man; a thing of which Tennyson, who took himself with awful seriousness, and walked with himself as a Druid might have walked in the sacred grove of Mona, was quite incapable.

However, the three important dramas of Tennyson are better, as dramas, than Browning's. That is natural enough. For Browning's dramas were written when he was young, when his knowledge of the dramatic art was small, and when his intellectual powers were not fully developed. Tennyson wrote his when his knowledge of the Drama was great, and when his intellect had undergone years of careful training. He studied the composition and architecture of the best plays; he worked at the stage situations; he created a blank verse for his plays quite different from that he used in his poems, and a disagreeable thing it is; he introduced songs, like Shakespeare, at happy moments; he imitated the old work, and at the same time strove hard to make his own original. He laboured at the history, and *Becket* and *Harold* are painfully historical. History should not master a play, but the play the history. The poet who is betrayed into historical accuracy so as to injure the development of his conception in accordance with imaginative truth, is lost; and *Harold* and *Becket* both suffer from Tennyson falling into the hands of those critical historians whom Tennyson consulted.

Nevertheless, by dint of laborious intellectual work, but not by the imagination, not by dramatic genius, Tennyson arrived at a relative success. He did better in these long dramas than Coleridge, Wordsworth, Scott or Byron. *Queen Mary*, *Harold*, and *Becket* get along in one's mind with some swiftness when one reads them in an armchair by the fire. Some of the characters are interesting and wrought with painful skill. We cannot forget the pathetic image of Queen Mary, which dwells in the mind when the play has disappeared; nor the stately representation in *Becket* of the mighty and overshadowing power of Rome, claiming as its own possession the soul of the world. But the minor characters; the action; the play of the characters, great and small, and of the action and circumstance together towards the catastrophe—these things were out of Tennyson's reach, and still more out of Browning's. They could both build up characters, and Browning better than Tennyson; they could both set two people to talk together, and by their talk to reveal their character to us; but to paint action, and the action of many men and women moving to a plotted end; to paint human life within the limits of a chosen subject, changing and tossing and unconscious of its fate, in a town, on a battlefield, in the forum, in a wild wood, in the king's palace or a shepherd farm; and to image this upon the stage, so that nothing done or said should be unmotived, unrelated to the end, or unnatural; of that they were quite incapable, and Browning more incapable than Tennyson.

There is another thing to say. The three long dramas of Tennyson are better as dramas than the long ones of Browning. But the smaller dramatic pieces of Browning are much better than the smaller ones of Tennyson. *The Promise of May* is bad in dialogue, bad in composition, bad in delineation of character, worst of all in its subject, in its plot, and in its motives. *The Cup,* and *The Falcon,* a beautiful story beautifully written by Boccaccio, is strangely dulled, even vulgarised, by Tennyson. The *Robin Hood* play has gracious things in it, but as a drama it is worthless, and it is impossible to forgive Tennyson for his fairies. All these small plays are dreadful examples of what a great poet may do when he works in a vehicle —if I may borrow a term from painting—for which he has no natural capacity, but for which he thinks he has. He is then like those sailors, and meets justly the same fate, who think that because they can steer a boat admirably, they can also drive a coach and four. The love scene in *Becket* between Rosamund and Henry illustrates my meaning. It was a subject in itself that Tennyson ought to have done well, and would probably have done well in another form of poetry; but, done in a form for which he had no genius, he did it badly. It is the worst thing in the play. Once, however, he did a short drama fairly well. *The Cup* has some dramatic movement, its construction is clear, its verse imaginative, its scenery well conceived; and its motives are simple and easily understood. But then, as in *Becket*, Irving stood at his right hand, and advised him concerning dramatic changes and situations. Its passion is, however, cold; it leaves us unimpressed.

On the contrary, Browning's smaller dramatic pieces — I cannot call them dramas — are much better than those of Tennyson. *Pippa Passes, A Soul's Tragedy, In a Balcony*, stand on a much higher level, aim higher, and reach their aim more fully than Tennyson's shorter efforts. They have not the qualities which fit them for representation, but they have those which fit them for thoughtful and quiet reading. No one thinks much of the separate personalities; our chief interest is in following Browning's imagination as it invents new phases of his subject, and plays like a sword in sunlight, in and out of these phases. As poems of the soul in severe straits, made under a quasi-dramatic form, they reach a high excellence, but all that we like best in them, when we follow them as situations of the soul, we should most dislike when represented on the stage.

Strafford is, naturally, the most immature of the dramas, written while he was still writing *Paracelsus*, and when he was very young. It is strange to compare the greater part of its prosaic verse with the rich poetic verse of *Paracelsus*; and this further illustrates how much a poet suffers when he writes in a form which is not in his genius. There are only a very few passages in *Strafford* which resemble poetry until we come to the fifth Act, where Browning passes from the jerky, allusive but rhythmical prose of the previous acts into that talk between Strafford and his children which has poetic charm, clearness and grace. The change does not last long, and when Hollis, Charles and Lady Carlisle, followed by Pym, come in, the whole Act is in confusion. Nothing is clear, except absence of the clearness required for a drama. But the previous Acts are even more obscure; not indeed for their readers, but for hearers in a theatre who—since they are hurried on at once to new matter—are forced to take in on the instant what the dramatist means. It would be impossible to tell at first hearing what the chopped-up sentences, the interrupted phrases, the interjected "nots" and "buts" and "yets" are intended to convey. The conversation is mangled. This vice does not prevail in the other dramas to the same extent as in *Strafford*. Browning had learnt his lesson, I suppose, when he saw *Strafford* represented. But it sorely prevails in *Colombe's Birthday*.

Strafford is brought before us as a politician, as the leader of the king's side in an austere crisis of England's history. The first scene puts the great quarrel forward as the ground on which the drama is to be wrought. An attempt is made to represent the various elements of the popular storm in the characters of Pym, Hampden, the younger Vane and others, and especially in the relations between Pym and Strafford, who are set over, one against the other, with some literary power. But the lines on which the action is wrought are not simple. No audience could follow the elaborate network of intrigue which, in Browning's effort to represent too much of the history, he has made so confused. Strong characterisation perishes in this effort to write a history rather than a drama. What we chiefly see of the crisis is a series of political intrigues at the Court carried out by base persons, of whom the queen is the basest, to ruin Strafford; the futility of Strafford's sentimental love of the king, whom he despises while he loves him; Strafford's blustering weakness and blindness when he forces his way into the Parliament House, and the contemptible meanness of Charles. The low intrigues of the Court leave the strongest impression on the mind, not the mighty struggle, not the fate of the Monarchy and its dark supporter.

Browning tries—as if he had forgotten that which should have been first in his mind—to lift the main struggle into importance in the last Act. but he fails. That which ought to be tragic is merely sentimental. Indeed, sentimentality is the curse of the play. Strafford's love of the king is almost maudlin. The scenes between Strafford and

Pym in which their ancient friendship is introduced are over-sentimentalised, not only for their characters, but for the great destinies at stake. Even at the last, when Pym and Strafford forgive each other and speak of meeting hereafter, good sense is violated, and the natural dignity of the scene, and the characters of the men. Strafford is weaker here, if that were possible, than he is in the rest of the drama. Nothing can be more unlike the man.

Pym is intended to be especially strong. He is made a blusterer. He was a gentleman, but in this last scene he is hateful. As to Charles, he was always a selfish liar, but he was not a coward, and a coward he becomes in this play. He, too, is sentimentalised by his uxoriousness. Lady Carlisle is invented. I wish she had not been. Strafford's misfortunes were deep enough without having her in love with him. I do not believe, moreover, that any woman in the whole world from the very beginning was ever so obscure in her speech to the man she loves as Lady Carlisle was to Strafford. And the motive of her obscurity—that if she discloses the King's perfidy she robs Strafford of that which is dearest to him—his belief in the King's affection for him—is no doubt very fine, but the woman was either not in love who argued in that way, or a fool; for Strafford knew, and lets her understand that he knew, the treachery of the King. But Browning meant her to be in love, and to be clever.

The next play Browning wrote, undeterred by the fate of *Strafford*, was *King Victor and King Charles*. The subject is historical, but it is modified by Browning, quite legitimately, to suit his own purposes. In itself the plot is uninteresting. King Victor, having brought the kingdom to the verge of ruin, abdicates and hands the crown to his son, believing him to be a weak-minded person whose mistakes will bring him—Victor—back to the throne, when he can throw upon the young king the responsibility of the mess he has himself made of the kingdom. Charles turns out to be a strong character, sets right the foreign affairs of the kingdom, and repairs his father's misgovernment. Then Victor, envious and longing for power, conspires to resume the throne, and taken prisoner, begs back the crown. Charles, touched as a son, and against his better judgment, restores his father, who immediately and conveniently dies. It is a play of court intrigue and of politics, and these are not made interesting by any action, such as we call dramatic, in the play. From end to end there is no inter-movement of public passion. There are only four characters. D'Ormea, the minister, is a mere stick in a prime-minister's robes and serves Victor and Charles with equal ease, in order to keep his place. He is not even subtle in his *rôle*. When we think what Browning would have made of him in a single poem, and contrast it with what he has made of him here, we are again impressed with Browning's strange loss of power when he is writing drama. Victor and Charles are better drawn than any characters in *Strafford;* and Polyxena is a great advance on Lady Carlisle. But this piece is not a drama; it is a study of soul-situations, and none of them are of any vital importance. There is far too great an improbability in the conception of Charles. A weak man in private becomes a strong man in public life. To represent him, having known and felt his strength, as relapsing into his previous weakness when it endangers all his work, is quite too foolish. He did not do it in history. Browning, with astonishing want of insight, makes him do it here, and adds to it a foolish anger with his wife because she advises him against it. And the reason he does it and is angry with his wife, is a merely sentimental one—a private, unreasoning, childish love of his father, such a love as Strafford is supposed to have for Charles I.—the kind of love which intruded into public affairs ruins them, and which, being feeble and for an unworthy object, injures him who gives it and him who receives it. Even as a study of characters, much more as a drama, this piece is a failure, and the absence of poetry in it is amazing.

The Return of the Druses approaches more nearly to a true drama than its predecessors; it is far better written; it has several fine motives which are intelligently, but not dramatically, worked out; and it is with great joy that one emerges at last into a little poetry. Browning, having more or less invented his subject, is not seduced, by the desire to be historical, to follow apparent instead of imaginative truth; nor are we wearied by his unhappy efforts to analyse, in disconnected conversations, political intrigue. Things are in this play as the logic of imaginative passion wills, as Browning's conception drove him. But, unfortunately for its success as a true drama, Browning doubles and redoubles the motives which impel his characters. Djabal, Anael, Loys, have, all of them, two different and sometimes opposite aims working in them. They are driven now by one, now by the other, and the changes of speech and action made by the different motives surging up, alternately or together, within their will, are so swift and baffling that an audience would be utterly bewildered. It is amusing to follow the prestidigitation of Browning's intellect creating this confused battle in souls as long as one reads the play at home, though even then we wonder why he cannot, at least in a drama, make a simple situation. If he loved difficult work, this would be much more difficult to do well than the confused situation he has not done well. Moreover, the simplified situation would be effective on the stage ; and it would give a great opportunity for fine poetry. As it is, imaginative work is replaced by intellectual exercises, poetry is lost in his analysis of complex states of feeling. However, this involved in-and-out of thought is entertaining to follow in one's study if not on the stage. It is done with a loose power no one else in England possessed, and our only regret is that he did not bridle and master his power. Finally, with regard to this play, I should like to isolate from it certain imaginative representations of characters which embody types of the men of the time, such as the Prefect and the Nuncio. The last interview between Loys and the Prefect, taken out of the drama, would be a little masterpiece of characterisation.

The Blot in the Scutcheon is the finest of all these

dramas. It might well be represented on the stage as a literary drama before those who had already read it, and who would listen to it for its passion and poetry; but its ill-construction and the unnaturalness of its situations will always prevent, and justly, its public success as a drama. It is full of pathetic and noble poetry; its main characters are clearly outlined and of a refreshing simplicity. It has few obtrusive metaphysical or intellectual subtleties—things which Browning could not keep out of his dramas, but which only a genius like Shakespeare can handle on the stage. It has real intensity of feeling, and the various passions interlock and clash together with some true dramatic interaction. Their presentation awakens our pity, and wonder for the blind fates of men. The close leaves us in sorrow, yet in love with human nature. The pathos of the catastrophe is the most pathetic thing in Browning. I do not even except the lovely record of Pompilia. The torture of the human heart, different but equal, of Tresham and Mildred in the last scene, is exceedingly bitter in its cry—too cruel almost to hear and know, were it not relieved by the beauty of their tenderness and forgiveness in the hour of death. They die of their pain, but die loving, and are glad to die. They have all of them—Mildred, Tresham, and Mertoun—sinned as it were by error. Death unites them in righteousness, loveliness and love. A fierce, swift storm sweeps out of a clear heaven upon them, destroys them, and saves them. It is all over in three days. They are fortunate; their love deserved that the ruin should be brief, and the reparation be transferred, in a moment, to the grave justice of eternity.

The first two acts bear no comparison with the third. The first scene, with all the servants, only shows how Browning failed in bringing a number of characters together, and in making them talk with ease and connectedly. Then, in two acts, the plot unfolds itself. It is a marvel of bad construction, grossly improbable, and offends that popular common sense of what is justly due to the characters concerned and to human nature itself, to which a dramatist is bound to appeal.

Mildred and Mertoun have loved and sinned. Mertoun visits her every night. Gerard, an old gamekeeper, has watched him climbing to her window, and he resolves to tell this fatal tale to Tresham, Mildred's brother, whose strongest feeling is pride in the unblemished honour of his house. Meantime Mertoun has asked Tresham for Mildred's hand in marriage, and these lovers, receiving his consent, hope that their sin will be purged. Then Gerard tells his story. Tresham summons Mildred. She confesses the lover, and Tresham demands his name. To reveal the name would have saved the situation, as we guess from Tresham's character. His love would have had time to conquer his pride. But Mildred will not tell the name, and when Tresham says: "Then what am I to say to Mertoun?" she answers, "I will marry him." This, and no wonder, seems the last and crowning dishonour to Tresham, and he curses, as if she were a harlot, the sister whom he passionately loves.

This is a horrible situation which Browning had no right to make. The natural thing would be for Mildred to disclose that her lover and Lord Mertoun, whom she was to marry, were one and the same.

There is no adequate reason, considering the desperate gravity of the situation, for her silence; it ought to be accounted for and it is not, nor could it be. Her refusal to tell her lover's name, her confession of her dishonour and at the same time her acceptance of Mertoun as a husband at her brother's hands, are circumstances which shock probability and common human nature.

Then it is not only this which irritates a reader; it is also the stupidity of Tresham. That also is most unnatural. He believes that the girl whom he has loved and honoured all his life, whose purity was as a star to him, will accept Mertoun while she was sinning with another! He should have felt that this was incredible, and immediately understood, as Guendolen does, that her lover and Mertoun were the same. Dulness and blindness so improbable are unfitting in a drama, nor does the passion of his overwhelming pride excuse him. The central situation is a protracted irritation. Browning was never a good hand at construction, even in his poems. His construction is at its very worst in this drama.

But now, when we have, with wrath, accepted this revolting situation—which, of course, Browning made in order to have his tragic close, but which a good dramatist would have arranged so differently—we pass into the third act, the tragic close; and that is simple enough in its lines, quite naturally wrought out, beautifully felt, and of exquisite tenderness. Rashness of wrath and pride begin it; Mertoun is slain by Tresham as he climbs to Mildred's window, though why he should risk her honour any more when she is affianced to him is another of Browning's maddening improbabilities. And then wrath and pride pass away, and sorrow and love and the joy of death are woven together in beauty. If we must go through the previous acts to get to this, we forgive, for its sake, their wrongness. It has turns of love made exquisitely fair by inevitable death, unfathomable depths of feeling. We touch in these last scenes the sacred love beyond the world in which forgiveness is forgotten.

Colombe's Birthday is of all these plays the nearest to a true drama. It has been represented in America as well as in England, and its skilful characterisation of Valence, Colombe, and Berthold has won deserved praise; but it could not hold the stage. The subject is too thin. Colombe finds out on her birthday that she is not the rightful heir to the Duchy; but as there is some doubt, she resolves to fight the question. In her perplexities she is helped and supported by Valence, an advocate from one of the cities of the Duchy, who loves her, but whom she believes to serve her from loyalty alone. Berthold, the true heir, to avoid a quarrel, offers to marry Colombe, not because he loves her, but as a good piece of policy. She then finds out that she loves Valence, and refusing the splendid alliance, leaves the court a private person, with love and her lover. This slight thing is spun out into five acts by Browning's metaphysics of love and friendship. There is but little action, or pressure of the characters into one another. The intriguing courtiers are dull, and their talk is not knit together. The only thing alive in them is their universal meanness. That meanness, it is true, enhances the magnanimity of Valence and Berthold, but its dead level in so many commonplace persons lowers the dramatic interest of the piece. The play is rather an interesting conversational poem about the up-growing of love between two persons of different but equally noble character; who think love is of more worth than power or wealth, and who are finally brought together by a bold, rough warrior who despises love in comparison with policy. Its real action takes place in the hearts of Valence and Colombe, not in the world of human life; and what takes place in their hearts is at times so quaintly metaphysical, so curiously apart from the simplicities of human love, so complicated, even beyond the complexity of the situation—for Browning loved to pile complexity on complexity—that it makes the play unfit for public representation but all the more interesting for private reading. But, even in the quiet of our room, we ask why Browning put his subject into a form which did not fit it; why he overloaded the story of two souls with a host of characters who have no vital relation to it, and, having none, are extremely wearisome? It might have been far more successfully done in the form of *In a Balcony*, which Browning himself does not class as a drama.

Luria, the last of the dramas in date of composition, may be said to have no outward action, except in one scene where Tiburzio breaks in suddenly to defend Luria, who, like a wounded stag, stands at bay among the dogs and hunters who suspect his fidelity to Florence. It is a drama of inward action, of changes in the souls of men. The full purification of Luria is its one aim, and the motive of Luria himself is a single motive. The play occupies one day only, and passes in one place.

Luria is a noble Moor who commands the armies of Florence against Pisa, and conquers Pisa. He is in love with the city of Florence as a man is with a woman. Its beauty, history, great men, and noble buildings attract his Eastern nature, by their Northern qualities, as much as they repel his friend and countryman Husain. He lives for her with unbroken faithfulness, and he dies for her with piteous tenderness when he finds out that Florence distrusts him. When he is suspected of treachery, his heart breaks, and to explain his broken heart, he dies. There is no other way left to show to Florence that he has always been true to her. And at the moment of his death, all who spied on him, distrusted and condemned him, are convinced of his fidelity. Even before he dies, his devotion to his ideal aim, his absolute unselfishness, have won over and ennobled all the self-interested characters which surround him—Puccio, the general who is jealous of him; Domizia, the woman who desires to use him as an instrument of her hate to Florence; even Braccio, the Macchiavellian Florentine who thinks his success must be dangerous to the state. Luria conquers them all. It is the triumph of self-forgetfulness. And the real aim of the play is not dramatic. It is too isolated an aim to be dramatic. It is to build up and image the noble character of Luria, and it reaches that end with dignity.

The other characters are but foils to enhance the

solitary greatness of Luria. Braccio is a mere voice, a theory who talks, and, at the end, when he becomes more human, he seems to lose his intelligence. The Secretaries have no individuality. Domizia causes nothing, and might with advantage be out of the play. However, when, moved by the nobleness of Luria, she gives up her revenge on Florence, she speaks well, and her outburst is poetical. Puccio is a real personage, but a poor fellow. Tiburzio is a pale reflection of Luria. Husain alone has some personality, but even his Easternness, which isolates him, is merged in his love of Luria. All of them only exist to be the scaffolding by means of which Luria's character is built into magnificence, and they disappear from our sight, like scaffolding, when the building is finished.

There are fine things in the poem: the image of Florence; its men, its streets, its life as seen by the stranger-eyes of Luria; the contrast between the Eastern and the Latin nature; the picture of hot war; the sudden friendship of Luria and Tiburzio, the recognition in a moment of two high hearts by one another; the picture of Tiburzio fighting at the ford, of Luria tearing the letter among the shamed conspirators; the drawing of the rough honest soldier-nature in Puccio, and, chief of all, the vivid historic painting of the time and the type of Italian character at the time of the republics.

The first part of *A Soul's Tragedy* is written in poetry and the second in prose. The first part is dull but the second is very lively and amusing; so gay and clever that we begin to wish that a good deal of Browning's dramas had been written in prose. And the prose itself, unlike his more serious prose in his letters and essays, is good, clear, and of an excellent style. The time of the play is in the sixteenth century; but there is nothing in it which is special to that time: no scenery, no vivid pictures of street life, no distinct atmosphere of the period. It might just as well be of the eighteenth or nineteenth century. The character of Chiappino may be found in any provincial town. This compound of envy, self-conceit, superficial cleverness and real silliness is one of our universal plagues, and not uncommon among the demagogues of any country. And he contrasts him with Ogniben, the Pope's legate, another type, well known in governments, skilled in affairs, half mocking, half tolerant of the "foolish people," the alluring destroyer of all self-seeking leaders of the people. He also is as common as Chiappino, as modern as he is ancient. Both are representative types, and admirably drawn. They are done at too great length, but Browning could not manage them as well in Drama as he would have done in a short piece such as he placed in *Men and Women*. Why this little thing is called *A Soul's Tragedy* I cannot quite understand. That title supposes that Chiappino loses his soul at the end of the play. But it is plain from his mean and envious talk at the beginning with Eulalia that his soul is already lost. He is not worse at the end, but perhaps on the way to betterment. The tragedy is then in the discovery by the people that he who was thought to be a great soul is a fraud. But that conclusion was not Browning's intention. Finally, if this be a tragedy it is clothed with comedy. Browning's humour was never more wise, kindly, worldly and biting than in the second act, and Ogniben may well be set beside Bishop Blougram. It would be a privilege to dine with either of them.

Every one is in love with *Pippa Passes*, which appeared immediately after *Sordello*. It may have been a refreshment to Browning after the complexities and metaphysics of *Sordello*, to live for a time with the soft simplicity of Pippa, with the clear motives of the separate occurrences at Asolo, with the outside picturesque world, and in a lyric atmosphere. It certainly is a refreshment to us. It is a pity so little was done by Browning in this pleasant, graceful, happy way. The substance of thought in it and its intellectual force are just as strong as in *Sordello* or *Paracelsus*, and are concerned, especially in the first two pieces, with serious and weighty matters of human life. Beyond the pleasure the poem gives, its indirect teaching is full of truth and beauty; and the things treated of belong to many phases of human life, and touch their problems with poetic light and love. Pippa herself, in her affectionate, natural goodness, illuminates the greater difficulties of life in a single day more than Sordello or Paracelsus could in the whole course of their lives.

It may be that there are persons who think lightly of *Pippa Passes* in comparison with *Fifine at the Fair*, persons who judge poetry by the difficulties they find in its perusal. But *Pippa Passes* fulfils the demands of the art of poetry, and produces in the world the high results of lovely and noble poetry. The other only does these things in part;

and when *Fifine at the Fair* and even *Sordello* are in the future only the study of pedants, *Pippa Passes* will be an enduring strength and pleasure to all who love tenderly and think widely. And those portions of it which belong to Pippa herself, the most natural, easy and simplest portions, will be the sources of the greatest pleasure and the deepest thought. Like Sordello's song, they will endure for the healing, comforting, exalting and impelling of the world.

I have written of her and of other parts of the poem elsewhere. It only remains to say that nowhere is the lyric element in Browning's genius more delightfully represented than in this little piece of mingled song and action. There is no better love-lyric in his work than

> You'll love me yet!—and I can tarry
> Your love's protracted growing;

and the two snatches of song which Pippa sings when she is passing under Ottima's window and the Monsignore's—"The year's at the spring" and "Overhead the tree-tops meet"—possess, independent of the meaning of the words and their poetic charm, a freshness, dewiness, morning ravishment to which it is difficult to find an equal. They are filled with youth and its delight, alike of the body and the soul. What Browning's spirit felt and lived when he was young and his heart beating with the life of the universe, is in them, and it is their greatest charm.

CHAPTER IX

POEMS OF THE PASSION OF LOVE

WHEN we leave *Paracelsus, Sordello* and the *Dramas* behind, and find ourselves among the host of occasional poems contained in the *Dramatic Lyrics* and *Romances*, in *Men and Women*, in *Dramatis Personæ*, and in the later volumes, it is like leaving an unencumbered sea for one studded with a thousand islands. Every island is worth a visit and different from the rest. Their variety, their distinct scenery, their diverse inhabitants, the strange surprises in them, are as continual an enchantment for the poetic voyager as the summer isles of the Pacific. But while each of them is different from the rest, yet, like the islands in the Pacific, they fall into groups; and to isolate these groups is perhaps the best way to treat so varied a collection of poems. To treat them chronologically would be a task too long and wearisome for a book. To treat them zoologically, if I may borrow that term, is possible, and may be profitable. This chapter is dedicated to the poems which relate to Love.

Commonly speaking, the term *Love Poems* does not mean poems concerning the absolute Love, or the love of Ideas, such as Truth or Beauty, or Love of mankind or one's own country, or the loves that belong to home, or the love of friends, or even married love unless it be specially bound up, as it is in Browning's poem of *By the Fireside*, with antenuptial love—but poems expressing the isolating passion of one sex for the other; chiefly in youth, or in conditions which resemble those of youth, whether moral or immoral. These celebrate the joys and sorrows, rapture and despair, changes and chances, moods, fancies, and imaginations, quips and cranks and wanton wiles, all the tragedy and comedy, of that passion, which is half of the sense and half of the spirit, sometimes wholly of the senses and sometimes wholly of the spirit. It began, in one form of it, among the lower animals and still rules their lives; it has developed through many thousand years of humanity into myriads of shapes in and outside of the soul; into stories whose varieties and multitudes are more numerous than the stars of heaven or the sand of the seashore; and yet whose multitudinous changes and histories have their source in two things only—in the desire to generate, which is physical; in the desire to forget self in another, which is spiritual. The union of both these desires into one passion of thought, act and feeling is the fine quintessence of this kind of love; but the latter desire alone is the primal motive of all the other forms of love, from friendship and maternal love to love of country, of mankind, of ideas, and of God.

With regard to love-poems of the sort we now discuss, the times in history when they are most written are those in which a nation or mankind renews its youth. Their production in the days of

Elizabeth was enormous, their passion various and profound, their fancy elaborate, their ornament extravagant with the extravagance of youth; and, in the hands of the greater men, their imagination was as fine as their melody. As that age grew older they were not replaced but were dominated by more serious subjects; and though love in its fantasies was happily recorded in song during the Caroline period, passion in English love-poetry slowly decayed till the ideas of the Revolution, before the French outbreak, began to renew the youth of the world. The same career is run by the individual poet. The subject of his youth is the passion of love, as it was in Browning's *Pauline*. The subjects of his manhood are serious with other thought and feeling, sad with another sadness, happy with another happiness. They traverse a wider range of human feeling and thought, and when they speak of love, it is of love in its wiser, steadier, graver and less selfish forms. It was so with Browning, who far sooner than his comrades, escaped from the tangled wilderness of youthful passion. It is curious to think that so young a creature as he was in 1833 should have left the celebration of the love of woman behind him, and only written of the love which his *Paracelsus* images in Aprile. It seems a little insensitive in so young a man. But I do not think Browning was ever quite young save at happy intervals; and this falls in with the fact that his imagination was more intellectual than passionate; that while he felt love, he also analysed, even dissected it, as he wrote about it; that it scarcely ever carried him away so far as to make him forget everything but itself. Perhaps once or twice, as in *The Last Ride Together*, he may have drawn near to this absorption, but even then the man is thinking more of his own thoughts than of the woman by his side, who must have been somewhat wearied by so silent a companion. Even in *By the Fireside*, when he is praising the wife whom he loved with all his soul, and recalling the moment of early passion while yet they looked on one another and felt their souls embrace before they spoke—it is curious to find him deviating from the intensity of the recollection into a discussion of what might have been if she had not been what she was—a sort of *excursus* on the chances of life which lasts for eight verses—before he returns to that immortal moment. Even after years of married life, a poet, to whom passion has been in youth supreme, would scarcely have done that. On the whole, his poetry, like that of Wordsworth, but not so completely, is destitute of the love-poem in the ordinary sense of the word; and the few exceptions to which we might point want so much that exclusiveness of a lover which shuts out all other thought but that of the woman, that it is difficult to class them in that species of literature. However, this is not altogether true, and the main exception to it is a curious piece of literary and personal history. Those who read *Asolando*, the last book of poems he published, were surprised to find with what intensity some of the first poems in it described the passion of sexual love. They are fully charged with isolated emotion; other thoughts than those of love do not intrude upon them. Moreover, they have a sincere lyric note. It is impossible, unless by a miracle of imagination, that these could have been written when he was about eighty years of age. I believe, though I do not know, that he wrote them when he was quite a young man; that he found them on looking over his portfolios, and had a dim and scented pleasure in reading and publishing them in his old age. He mentions in the preface that the book contains both old and new poems. The new are easily isolated, and the first poem, the introduction to the collection, is of the date of the book. The rest belong to different periods of his life. The four poems to which I refer are *Now*, *Summum Bonum*, *A Pearl—A Girl*, and *Speculative*. They are beautiful with a beauty of their own; full of that natural abandonment of the whole world for one moment with the woman loved, which youth and the hours of youth in manhood feel. I should have been sorry if Browning had not shaped into song this abandonment. He loved the natural, and was convinced of its rightness; and he had, as I might prove, a tenderness for it even when it passed into wrong. He was the last man in the world to think that the passion of noble sexual love was to be despised. And it is pleasant to find, at the end of his long poetic career, that, in a serious and wise old age, he selected, to form part of his last book, poems of youthful and impassioned love, in which the senses and the spirit met, each in their pre-eminence.

The two first of these, *Now* and *Summum Bonum*, must belong to his youth, though from certain turns of expression and thought in them, it seems that Browning worked on them at the time he published them. I quote the second for its lyric charm, even though the melody is ruthlessly broken.

> All the breath and the bloom of the year in the bag of one bee:
> All the wonder and wealth of the mine in the heart of one gem:
> In the core of one pearl all the shade and the shine of the sea:
> Breath and bloom, shade and shine,—wonder, wealth, and —how far above them—
> Truth, that's brighter than gem,
> Trust, that's purer than pearl,—
> Brightest truth, purest trust in the universe—all were for me
> In the kiss of one girl.

The next two poems are knit to this and to *Now* by the strong emotion of earthly love, of the senses as well as of the spirit, for one woman; but they differ in the period at which they were written. The first, *A Pearl—A Girl*, recalls that part of the poem *By the Fireside*, when one look, one word, opened the infinite world of love to Browning. If written when he was young, it has been revised in after life.

> A simple ring with a single stone
> To the vulgar eye no stone of price:
> Whisper the right word, that alone—
> Forth starts a sprite, like fire from ice,
> And lo, you are lord (says an Eastern scroll)
> Of heaven and earth, lord whole and sole
> Through the power in a pearl.
>
> A woman ('tis I this time that say)
> With little the world counts worthy praise
> Utter the true word—out and away
> Escapes her soul: I am wrapt in blaze,
> Creation's lord, of heaven and earth
> Lord whole and sole—by a minute's birth—
> Through the love in a girl!

The second — *Speculative* — also describes a moment of love-longing, but has the characteristics of his later poetry. It may be of the same date as the book, or not much earlier. It may be of his later manhood, of the time when he lost his wife. At any rate, it is intense enough. It looks back on the love he has lost, on passion with the woman he loved. And he would surrender all—Heaven, Nature, Man, Art—in this momentary fire of desire; for indeed such passion is momentary. Momentariness is the essence of the poem. "Even in heaven I will cry for the wild hours now gone by—Give me back the Earth and Thyself." *Speculative*, he calls it, in an after irony.

> Others may need new life in Heaven—
>   Man, Nature, Art—made new, assume!
> Man with new mind old sense to leaven,
>   Nature—new light to clear old gloom,
> Art that breaks bounds, gets soaring-room.
>
> I shall pray: "Fugitive as precious—
>   Minutes which passed,—return, remain!
> Let earth's old life once more enmesh us,
>   You with old pleasure, me—old pain,
> So we but meet nor part again!"

Nor was this reversion to the passion of youthful love altogether a new departure. The lyrics in *Ferishtah's Fancies* are written to represent, from the side of emotion, the intellectual and ethical ideas worked out in the poems. The greater number of them are beautiful, and they would gain rather than lose if they were published separately from the poems. Some are plainly of the same date as the poems. Others, I think, were written in Browning's early time, and the preceding poems are made to fit them. But whatever be their origin, they nearly all treat of love, and one of them with a crude claim on the love of the senses alone, as if that—as if the love of the body, even alone—were not apart from the consideration of a poet who wished to treat of the whole of human nature. Browning, when he wished to make a thought or a fact quite plain, frequently stated it without any of its modifications, trusting to his readers not to mistake him; knowing indeed, that if they cared to find the other side—in this case the love which issues from the senses and the spirit together, or from the spirit alone—they would find it stated just as soundly and clearly. He meant us to combine both statements, and he has done so himself with regard to love.

When, however, we have considered these exceptions, it still remains curious how little the passionate Love-poem, with its strong personal touch, exists in Browning's poetry. One reason may be that Love-poems of this kind are naturally lyrical, and demand a sweet melody in the verse, and Browning's genius was not especially lyrical, nor could he inevitably command a melodious movement in his verse. But the main reason is that he was taken up with other and graver matters, and chiefly with the right theory of life; with the true relation of God and man; and with the picturing—for absolute Love's sake, and in order to win men to love one another by the awakening of pity—of as much of humanity as he could grasp in thought and feeling. Isolated and personal love was only a small part of this large design.

One personal love, however, he possessed fully and intensely. It was his love for his wife, and three poems embody it. The first is *By the Fireside*. It does not take rank as a true love lyric; it is too long, too many-motived for a lyric. It is a meditative poem of recollective tenderness wandering through the past; and no poem written on married love in England is more beautiful. The poet, sitting silent in the room where his wife sits with him, sees all his life with her unrolled, muses on what has been, and is, since she came to bless his life, or what will be, since she continues to bless it; and all the fancies and musings which, in a usual love lyric, would not harmonise with the intensity of love-passion in youth, exactly fit in with the peace and satisfied joy of a married life at home with God and nature and itself. The poem is full of personal charm. Quiet thought, profound feeling and sweet memory like a sunlit mist, soften the aspect of the room, the image of his wife, and all the thoughts, emotions and scenery described. It is a finished piece of art.

The second of these poems is the Epilogue to the volumes of *Men and Women*, entitled *One Word More*. It also is a finished piece of art, carefully conceived, upbuilded stone by stone, touch by touch, each separate thought with its own emotion, each adding something to the whole, each pushing Browning's emotion and picture into our souls, till the whole impression is received. It is full, and full to the brim, with the long experience of peaceful joy in married love. And the subtlety of the close of it, and of Browning's play with his own fancy about the moon, do not detract from the tenderness of it; for it speaks not of transient passion but of the love of a whole life lived from end to end in music.

The last of these is entitled *Prospice*. When he wrote it he had lost his wife. It tells what she had made of him; it reveals alike his steadfast sadness that she had gone from him and the steadfast resolution, due to her sweet and enduring power, with which, after her death, he promised, bearing with him his sorrow and his memory of joy, to stand and withstand in the battle of life, ever a fighter to the close—and well he kept his word. It ends with the expression of his triumphant certainty of meeting her, and breaks forth at last into so great a cry of pure passion that ear and heart alike rejoice. Browning at his best, Browning in the central fire of his character, is in it.

> Fear death?—to feel the fog in my throat,
>   The mist in my face,
> When the snows begin, and the blasts denote
>   I am nearing the place,
> The power of the night, the press of the storm,
>   The post of the foe;
> Where he stands, the Arch Fear in a visible form,
>   Yet the strong man must go:
> For the journey is done and the summit attained
>   And the barriers fall,
> Though a battle's to fight ere the guerdon be gained,
>   The reward of it all.
> I was ever a fighter, so—one fight more,
>   The best and the last!
> I would hate that Death bandaged my eyes, and forbore,
>   And bade me creep past.
> No! let me taste the whole of it, fare like my peers
>   The heroes of old,
> Bear the brunt, in a minute pay glad life's arrears
>   Of pain, darkness and cold.
> For sudden the worst turns the best to the brave,
>   The black minute's at end,
> And the elements' rage, the fiend-voices that rave,
>   Shall dwindle, shall blend,
> Shall change, shall become first a peace out of pain,
>   Then a light, then thy breast,
> O thou soul of my soul! I shall clasp thee again,
>   And with God be the rest!

Leaving now these personal poems on Love, we come to those we may call impersonal. They are poems about love, not in its simplicities, but in its subtle moments—moments that Browning loved to analyse, and which he informed not so much with the passion of love, as with his profound love of human nature. He describes in them, with the seriousness of one who has left youth behind, the moods of love, its changes, vagaries, certainties, failures and conquests. It is a man writing, not of the love of happy youth, but of love tossed on the stormy seas of manhood and womanhood, and modified from its singular personal intensity by the deeper thought, feeling and surprising chances of our mortal life. Love does not stand alone, as in the true love lyric, but with many other grave matters. As such it is a more interesting subject for Browning. For Love then becomes full of strange turns, unexpected thoughts, impulses unknown before creating varied circumstances, and created by them; and these his intellectual spirituality delighted to cope with, and to follow, labyrinth after labyrinth. I shall give examples of these separate studies, which have always an idea beyond the love out of which the poem arises. In some of them the love is finally absorbed in the idea. In all of them their aim is beyond the love of which they speak.

Love among the Ruins tells of a lover going to meet his sweetheart. There are many poems with this expectant motive in the world of song, and no motive has been written of with greater emotion. If we are to believe these poems, or have ever waited ourselves, the hour contains nothing but her presence, what she is doing, how she is coming, why she delays, what it will be when she comes— a thousand things, each like white fire round her image. But Browning's lover, through nine verses, cares only for the wide meadows over which he makes his way and the sheep wandering over them, and their flowers and the ruins in the midst of them; musing on the changes and contrasts of the world—the lonely land and the populous glory which was of old in the vast city. It is only then, and only in two lines, that he thinks of the girl who is waiting for him in the ruined tower. Even then his imagination cannot stay with her, but glances from her instantly—thinking that the ancient king stood where she is waiting, and looked, full of pride, from the high tower on his splendid city. When he has elaborated this second excursion of thought he comes at last to the girl. Then is the hour of passion, but even in its fervour he draws a conclusion, belonging to a higher world than youthful love, as remote from it as his description of the scenery and the ruins. "Splendour of arms, triumph of wealth, centuries of glory and pride, they are nothing to love. Love is best." It is a general, not a particular conclusion. In a true Love-poem it would be particular.

Another poem of waiting love is *In Three Days*. And this has the spirit of a true love lyric in it. It reads like a personal thing; it breathes exaltation; it is quick, hurried, and thrilled. The delicate fears of chance and change in the three days, or in the years to come, belong of right and nature to the waiting, and are subtly varied and condensed. It is, however, the thoughtful love of a man who can be metaphysical in love, not the excluding mastery of passion.

Two in the Campagna is another poem in which love passes away into a deeper thought than love—a strange and fascinating poem of twofold desire. The man loves a woman and desires to be at peace with her in love, but there is a more imperative passion in his soul—to rest in the infinite, in accomplished perfection. And his livelong and vain pursuit of this has wearied him so much that he has no strength left to realise earthly love. Is it possible that she who now walks with him in the Campagna can give him in her love the peace of the infinite which he desires, and if not, why—where is the fault? For a moment he seems to catch the reason, and asks his love to see it with him and to grasp it. In a moment, like the gossamer thread he traces only to see it vanish, it is gone—and nothing is left, save

> Infinite passion, and the pain
> Of finite hearts that yearn.

Least of all is the woman left. She has quite disappeared. This is not a Love-poem at all, it is the cry of Browning's hunger for eternity in the midst of mortality, in which all the hunger for earthly love is burnt to dust.

The rest are chiefly studies of different kinds of love, or of crises in love; moments in its course, in its origin or its failure. There are many examples in the shorter dramatic pieces, as *In a Balcony*; and even in the longer dramas certain sharp climaxes of love are recorded, not as if they belonged to the drama, but as if they were distinct studies introduced by chance or caprice. In the short poems called "dramatic" these studies are numerous, and I group a few of them together according to their motives, leaving out some which I shall hereafter treat of when I come to discuss the women in Browning. *Evelyn Hope* has nothing to do with the passion of love. The physical element of love is entirely excluded by the subject. It is a beautiful expression of a love purely spiritual, to be realised in its fulness only after death, spirit with spirit, but yet to be kept as the master of daily life, to whose law all thought and action are referred. The thought is noble, the expression of it simple, fine, and clear. It is, moreover, close to truth— there are hundreds of men who live quietly in love of that kind, and die in its embrace.

In *Cristina* the love is just as spiritual, but the motive of the poem is not one, as in *Evelyn Hope*, but two. The woman is not dead, and she has missed her chance. But the lover has not. He has seen her and in a moment loved her. She also looked on him and felt her soul matched by his as they "rushed together." But the world carried her away and she lost the fulness of life. He, on the contrary, kept the moment for ever, and with it, her and all she might have been with him.

> Her soul's mine: and thus grown perfect,
> I shall pass my life's remainder.

This is not the usual Love-poem. It is a love as spiritual, as mystic, even more mystic, since the woman lives, than the lover felt for Evelyn Hope.

The second motive in *Cristina* of the lover who meets the true partner of his soul or hers, and either seizes the happy hour and possesses joy for ever, or misses it and loses all, is a favourite with

Browning. He repeats it frequently under diverse circumstances, for it opened out so many various endings, and afforded so much opportunity for his beloved analysis. Moreover, optimist as he was in his final thought of man, he was deeply conscious of the ironies of life, of the ease with which things go wrong, of the impossibility of setting them right from without. And in the matter of love he marks in at least four poems how the moment was held and life was therefore conquest. Then in *Youth and Art*, in *Dis Aliter Visum*, in *Bifurcation*, in *The Lost Mistress*, and in *Too Late*, he records the opposite fate, and in characters so distinct that the repetition of the motive is not monotonous. These are studies of the Might-have-beens of love.

Another motive, used with varied circumstance in three or four poems, but fully expanded in *James Lee's Wife*, is the discovery, after years of love, that love on one side is lost irretrievably. Another motive is, that rather than lose love men or women will often sacrifice their conscience, their reason, or their liberty. This sacrifice, of all that makes our nobler being for the sake of personal love alone, brings with it, because the whole being is degraded, the degradation, decay, and death of personal love itself.

Another set of poems describes with fanciful charm, sometimes with happy gaiety, love at play with itself. True love makes in the soul an unfathomable ocean in whose depths are the imaginations of love, serious, infinite, and divine. But on its surface the light of jewelled fancies plays—a thousand thousand sunny memories and hopes, flying thoughts and dancing feelings. A poet would be certain to have often seen this happy crowd, and to desire to trick them out in song. So Browning does in his poem, *In a Gondola.* The two lovers, with the dark shadow of fate brooding over them, sing and muse and speak alternately, imaging in swift and rival pictures made by fancy their deep-set love; playing with its changes, creating new worlds in which to place it, but always returning to its isolated individuality; recalling how it began, the room where it reached its aim, the pictures, the furniture, the balcony, her dress, all the scenery, in a hundred happy and glancing pictures; while interlaced through their gaiety—and the gaiety made keener by the nearness of dark fate—is coming death, death well purchased by an hour of love. Finally, the lover is stabbed and slain, and the pity of it throws back over the sunshine of love's fancies a cloud of tears. This is the stuff of life that Browning loved to paint—interwoven darkness and brightness, sorrow and joy trembling each on the edge of the other, life playing at ball, as joyous as Nausicaa and her maids, on a thin crust over a gulf of death.

Just such another poem—of the sportiveness of love, only this time in memory, not in present pleasure, is to be found in *A Lovers' Quarrel,* and the quarrel is the dark element in it. Browning always feels that mighty passion has its root in tragedy, and that it seeks relief in comedy. The lover sits by the fireside alone, and recalls, forgetting pain for a moment, the joyful play they two had together, when love expressed its depth of pleasure in dramatic fancies. Every separate picture is done in Browning's impressionist way. And when the glad memories are over, and the sorrow returns, passion leaps out—

>   It is twelve o'clock:
>   I shall hear her knock
> In the worst of a storm's uproar,
>   I shall pull her through the door,
> I shall have her for evermore!

This is partly a study of the memory of love; and Browning has represented, without any sorrow linked to it, memorial love in a variety of characters under different circumstances, so that, though the subject is the same, the treatment varies. A charming instance of this is *The Flower's Name;* easy to read, happy in its fancy, in its scenery, in the subtle play of deep affection, in the character of its lover, in the character of the girl who is remembered—a good example of Browning's power to image in a few verses two human souls so clearly that they live in our world for ever. *Meeting at Night—Parting at Morning* is another reminiscence, mixed up with the natural scenery of the meeting and parting, a vivid recollection of a fleeting night of passion, and then the abandonment of its isolation for a wider, fuller life with humanity. I quote it for the fine impassioned way in which human feeling and natural scenery are fused together.

MEETING AT NIGHT.

> The grey sea and the long black land;
>   And the yellow half-moon large and low;
> And the startled little waves that leap
> In fiery ringlets from their sleep,
>   As I gain the cove with pushing prow,
> And quench its speed i' the slushy sand.

Then a mile of warm sea-scented beach;
   Three fields to cross till a farm appears;
A tap at the pane, the quick sharp scratch
And blue spurt of a lighted match,
   And a voice less loud, through its joys and fears,
Than the two hearts beating each to each!

Parting at Morning.

Round the cape of a sudden came the sea,
   And the sun looked over the mountain's rim:
   And straight was a path of gold for him,
And the need of a world of men for me.

The poem entitled *Confessions* is another of these memories, in which a dying man, careless of death, careless of the dull conventions of the clergyman, cares for nothing but the memory of his early passion for a girl one happy June, and dies in comfort of the sweetness of the memory, though he thinks—

How sad and bad and mad it was.

Few but Browning would have seen, and fewer still have recorded, this vital piece of truth. It represents a whole type of character—those who in a life of weary work keep their day of love, even when it has been wrong, as their one poetic, ideal possession, and cherish it for ever. The wrong of it disappears in the ideal beauty which now has gathered round it, and as it was faithful, unmixed with other love, it escapes degradation. We see, when the man images the past and its scenery out of the bottles of physic on the table, how the material world had been idealised to him all his life long by this passionate memory—

Do I view the world as a vale of tears?
Ah, reverend sir, not I.

It might be well to compare with this another treatment of the memory of love in *St. Martin's Summer*. A much less interesting and natural motive rules it than *Confessions;* and the characters, though more " in society " than the dying man, are grosser in nature; gross by their inability to love, or by loving freshly to make a new world in which the old sorrow dies or is transformed. There is no humour in the thing, though there is bitter irony. But there is humour in an earlier poem—*A Serenade at the Villa*, where, in the last verse, the bitterness of wrath and love together (a very different bitterness from that of *St. Martin's Summer*), breaks out, and is attributed to the garden gate. The night-watch and the singing is over; she must have heard him, but she gave no sign. He wonders what she thought, and then, because he was only half in love, flings away—

> Oh how dark your villa was,
> Windows fast and obdurate!
> How the garden grudged me grass
> Where I stood—the iron gate
> Ground its teeth to let me pass!

It is impossible to notice all these studies of love, but they form, together, a book of transient phases of the passion in almost every class of society. And they show how Browning, passing through the world, from the Quartier Latin to London drawing-rooms, was continually on the watch to catch, store up, and reproduce a crowd of motives for poetry which his memory held and his imagination shaped.

There is only one more poem, which I cannot pass by in this group of studies. It is one of sacred and personal memory, so much so that it is probable the loss of his life lies beneath it. It rises into that highest poetry which fuses together into one form a hundred thoughts and a hundred emotions, and which is only obscure from the mingling of their multitude. I quote it, I cannot comment on it.

> Never the time and the place
>   And the loved one all together!
> This path—how soft to pace!
>   This May—what magic weather!
> Where is the loved one's face?
> In a dream that loved one's face meets mine
>   But the house is narrow, the place is bleak
> Where, outside, rain and wind combine
>   With a furtive ear, if I strive to speak,
>   With a hostile eye at my flushing cheek,
> With a malice that marks each word, each sign!
>   O enemy sly and serpentine,
>   Uncoil thee from the waking man!
>   Do I hold the Past
>   Thus firm and fast
>   Yet doubt if the Future hold I can?
> This path so soft to pace shall lead
> Through the magic of May to herself indeed!
> Or narrow if needs the house must be,
> Outside are the storms and strangers: we—
>   Oh, close, safe, warm sleep I and she,
>   —I and she!

That, indeed, is passionate enough.

Then there is another group — tales which embody phases of love. *Count Gismond* is one of these. It is too long, and wants Browning's usual force. The outline of the story was, perhaps, too simple to interest his intellect, and he needed in writing poetry not only the emotional subject, but that there should be something in or behind the emotion through the mazes of which his intelligence might glide like a serpent.*

The Glove is another of these tales—a good example of the brilliant fashion in which Browning could, by a strange kaleidoscopic turn of his subject, give it a new aspect and a new ending. The world has had the tale before it for a very long time. Every one had said the woman was wrong and the man right; but here, poetic juggler as he is, Browning makes the woman right and the man wrong, reversing the judgment of centuries. The best of it is, that he seems to hold the truth of the thing. It is amusing to think that only now, in the other world, if she and Browning meet, will she find herself comprehended.

Finally, as to the mightier kinds of love, those supreme forms of the passion, which have neither beginning nor end; to which time and space are but names; which make and fill the universe; the least grain of which predicates the whole; the spirit of which is God Himself; the breath of whose life is immortal joy, or sorrow which means joy; whose vision is Beauty, and whose activity is Creation—these, united in God, or divided among men into their three great entities—love of ideas for their truth and beauty; love of the natural universe, which is God's garment; love of humanity, which is God's child—these pervade the whole of Browning's poetry as the heat of the sun pervades the earth and every little grain upon it. They make its warmth

* There is one simple story at least which he tells quite admirably, *The Pied Piper of Hamelin*. But then, that story, if it is not troubled by intellectual matter, is also not troubled by any deep emotion. It is told by a poet who becomes a child for children.

and life, strength and beauty. They are too vast to be circumscribed in a lyric, represented in a drama, bound up even in a long story of spiritual endeavour like *Paracelsus*. But they move, in dignity, splendour and passion, through all that he deeply conceived and nobly wrought; and their triumph and immortality in his poetry are never for one moment clouded with doubt or subject to death. This is the supreme thing in his work. To him Love is the Conqueror, and Love is God.

CHAPTER X

THE PASSIONS OTHER THAN LOVE

THE poems on which I have dwelt in the last chapter, though they are mainly concerned with love between the sexes, illustrate the other noble passions, all of which, such as joy, are forms of, or rather children of, self-forgetful love. They do not illustrate the evil or ignoble passions—envy, jealousy, hatred, base fear, despair, revenge, avarice and remorse—which, driven by the emotion that so fiercely and swiftly accumulates around them, master the body and soul, the intellect and the will, like some furious tyrant, and in their extremes hurry their victim into madness. Browning took some of these terrible powers and made them subjects in his poetry. Short, sharp-outlined sketches of them occur in his dramas and longer poems. There is no closer image in literature of long-suppressed fear breaking out into its agony of despair than in the lines which seal Guido's pleading in the *The Ring and the Book*.

> Life is all!
> I was just stark mad,—let the madman live
> Pressed by as many chains as you please pile!
> Don't open! Hold me from them! I am yours,
> I am the Grand Duke's—no, I am the Pope's!
> Abate,—Cardinal,—Christ,—Maria,—God, . . .
> Pompilia, will you let them murder me?

But there is no elaborate, long-continued study of these sordid and evil things in Browning. He was not one of our modern realists who love to paddle and splash in the sewers of humanity. Not only was he too healthy in mind to dwell on them, but he justly held them as not fit subjects for art unless they were bound up with some form of pity, as jealousy and envy are in Shakespeare's treatment of the story of Othello; or imaged along with so much of historic scenery that we lose in our interest in the decoration some of the hatefulness of the passion. The combination, for example, of envy and hatred resolved on vengeance in *The Laboratory* is too intense for any pity to intrude, but Browning realises not only the evil passions in the woman but the historical period also and its temper; and he fills the poem with scenery which, though it leaves the woman first in our eyes, yet lessens the malignant element. The same, but of course with the difference Browning's variety creates, may be said of the story of the envious king, where envy crawls into hatred, hatred almost motiveless—the *Instans Tyrannus*. A faint vein of humour runs through it. The king describes what has been; his hatred has passed. He sees how small and fanciful it was, and the illustrations he uses to express it tell us that; though they carry with them also the contemptuous intensity of his past hatred. The swell of the hatred remains, though the hatred is past. So we are not left face to face with absolute evil, with the corruption hate engenders in the soul. God has intervened, and the worst of it has passed away.

Then there is the study of hatred in the *Soliloquy*

of the Spanish Cloister. The hatred is black and deadly, the instinctive hatred of a brutal nature for a delicate one, which, were it unrelieved, would be too vile for the art of poetry. But it is relieved, not only by the scenery, the sketch of the monks in the refectory, the garden of flowers, the naughty girls seated on the convent bank washing their black hair, but also by the admirable humour which ripples like laughter through the hopes of his hatred, and by the brilliant sketching of the two men. We see them, know them, down to their little tricks at dinner, and we end by realising hatred, it is true, but in too agreeable a fashion for just distress.

In other poems of the evil passions the relieving element is pity. There are the two poems entitled *Before* and *After*, that is, before and after the duel. *Before* is the statement of one of the seconds, with curious side-thoughts introduced by Browning's mental play with the subject, that the duel is absolutely necessary. The challenger has been deeply wronged; and he cannot and will not let forgiveness intermit his vengeance. The man in us agrees with that; the Christian in us says, "Forgive, let God do the judgment." But the passion for revenge has here its way and the guilty falls. And now let Browning speak—Forgiveness is right and the vengeance-fury wrong. The dead man has escaped, the living has not escaped the wrath of conscience; pity is all.

> Take the cloak from his face, and at first
>   Let the corpse do its worst!
>
> How he lies in his rights of a man!
>   Death has done all death can.
> And, absorbed in the new life he leads,
>   He recks not, he heeds

> Nor his wrong nor my vengeance; both strike
>   On his senses alike,
> And are lost in the solemn and strange
>   Surprise of the change.
>
> Ha, what avails death to erase
>   His offence, my disgrace?
> I would we were boys as of old
>   In the field, by the fold:
> His outrage, God's patience, man's scorn
>   Were so easily borne!
>
> I stand here now, he lies in his place;
>   Cover the face.

Again, there are few studies in literature of contempt, hatred and revenge more sustained and subtle than Browning's poem entitled *A Forgiveness;* and the title marks how, though the justice of revenge was accomplished on the woman, yet that pity, even love for her, accompanied and followed the revenge. Our natural revolt against the cold-blooded work of hatred is modified, when we see the man's heart and the woman's soul, into pity for their fate. The man tells his story to a monk in the confessional, who has been the lover of his wife. He is a statesman absorbed in his work, yet he feels that his wife makes his home a heaven, and he carries her presence with him all the day. His wife takes the first lover she meets, and, discovered, tells her husband that she hates him. "Kill me now," she cries. But he despises her too much to hate her; she is not worth killing. Three years they live together in that fashion, till one evening she tells him the truth. "I was jealous of your work. I took my revenge by taking a lover, but I loved you, you only, all the time, and lost you—

>   I thought you gave
> Your heart and soul away from me to slave
> At statecraft. Since my right in you seemed lost,
> I stung myself to teach you, to your cost,
> What you rejected could be prized beyond
> Life, heaven, by the first fool I threw a fond
> Look on, a fatal word to.

"Ah, is that true, you loved and still love? Then contempt perishes, and hate takes its place. Write your confession, and die by my hand. Vengeance is foreign to contempt, you have risen to the level at which hate can act. I pardon you, for as I slay hate departs—and now, sir," and he turns to the monk—

>   She sleeps, as erst
> Beloved, in this your church: ay, yours!

and drives the poisoned dagger through the grate of the confessional into the heart of her lover.

This is Browning's closest study of hate, contempt, and revenge. But bitter and close as it is, what is left with us is pity for humanity, pity for the woman, pity for the lover, pity for the husband.

Again, in the case of Sebald and Ottima in *Pippa Passes*, pity also rules. Love passing into lust has led to hate, and these two have slaked their hate and murdered Luca, Ottima's husband, They lean out of the window of the shrub-house as the morning breaks. For the moment their false love is supreme. Their crime only creeps like a snake, half asleep, about the bottom of their hearts; they recall their early passion and try to brazen it forth in the face of their murder, which now rises, dreadful and more dreadful, into threatening life in their soul. They reanimate their hate of Luca to lower their remorse, but at every instant his blood stains their speech. At last, while Ottima loves on, Sebald's dark horror turns to hatred of her he loved, till she lures him back into desire of her again. The momentary lust cannot last, but Browning shoots it into prominence that the outburst of horror and repentance may be the greater.

> I kiss you now, dear Ottima, now and now!
> This way? Will you forgive me—be once more
> My great queen?

At that moment Pippa passes by, singing:

> The year's at the spring
> And day's at the morn;
> Morning's at seven;
> The hill-side's dew-pearled;
> The lark's on the wing;
> The snail's on the thorn;
> God's in his heaven—
> All's right with the world!

Something in it smites Sebald's heart like a hammer of God. He repents, but in the cowardice of repentance curses her. That baseness I do not think Browning should have introduced, no, nor certain carnal phrases which, previously right, now jar with the spiritual passion of repentance. But his fury with her passes away into the passion of despair—

> My brain is drowned now—quite drowned: all I feel
> Is . . . is, at swift recurring intervals,
> A hurry-down within me, as of waters
> Loosened to smother up some ghastly pit:
> There they go—whirls from a black fiery sea!

lines which must have been suggested to Browning by verses, briefer and more intense, in Webster's

Duchess of Malfi. Even Ottima, lifted by her love, which purifies itself in wishing to die for her lover, repents.

> Not me,—to him, O God, be merciful!

Thus into this cauldron of sin Browning steals the pity of God. We know they will be saved, so as by fire.

Then there is the poem on the story of *Cristina and Monaldeschi;* a subject too odious, I think, to be treated lyrically. It is a tale of love turned to hatred, and for good cause, and of the pitiless vengeance which followed. Browning has not succceded in it; and it may be so because he could get no pity into it. The Queen had none. Monaldeschi deserved none—a coward, a fool, and a traitor! Nevertheless, more might have been made of it by Browning. The poem is obscure and wandering, and the effort he makes to grip the subject reveals nothing but the weakness of the grip. It ought not to have been published.

And now I turn to passions more delightful, that this chapter may close in light and not in darkness—passions of the imagination, of the romantic regions of the soul. There is, first, the longing for the mystic world, the world beneath appearance, with or without reference to eternity. Secondly, bound up with that, there is the longing for the unknown, for following the gleam which seems to lead us onward, but we know not where. Then, there is the desire, the deeper for its constant suppression, for escape from the prison of a worldly society, from its conventions and maxims of morality, its barriers of custom and rule, into liberty and unchartered life. Lastly, there is that longing to discover and enjoy the lands of adventure and romance which underlies and wells upwards through so much of modern life, and which has never ceased to send its waters up to refresh the world. These are romantic passions. On the whole, Browning does not often touch them in their earthly activities. His highest romance was beyond this world. It claimed eternity, and death was the entrance into its enchanted realm. When he did bring romantic feeling into human life, it was for the most part in the hunger and thirst, which, as in *Abt Vogler*, urged men beyond the visible into the invisible. But now and again he touched the Romantic of Earth. *Childe Roland*, *The Flight of the Duchess*, and some others, are alive with the romantic spirit.

But before I write of these, there are a few lyrical poems, written in the freshness of his youth, which are steeped in the light of the story-telling world; and might be made by one who, in the morning of imagination, sat on the dewy hills of the childish world. They are full of unusual melody, and are simple and wise enough to be sung by girls knitting in the sunshine while their lovers bend above them. One of these, a beautiful thing, with that touch of dark fate at its close which is so common in folk-stories, is hidden away in *Paracelsus*. "Over the sea," it begins:

> Over the sea our galleys went,
> With cleaving prows in order brave
> To a speeding wind and a bounding wave,
> A gallant armament:

> Each bark built out of a forest-tree
>   Left leafy and rough as first it grew,
> And nailed all over the gaping sides,
> Within and without, with black bull-hides,
> Seethed in fat, and suppled with flame,
> To bear the playful billows' game.

It is made in a happy melody, and the curious mingling in the tale, as it continues, of the rudest ships, as described above, with purple hangings, cedar tents, and noble statues,

> A hundred shapes of lucid stone,

and with gentle islanders from Græcian seas, is characteristic of certain folk-tales, especially those of Gascony. That it is spoken by Paracelsus as a parable of the state of mind he has reached, in which he clings to his first fault with haughty and foolish resolution, scarcely lessens the romantic element in it. That is so strong that we forget that it is meant as a parable.

There is another song which touches the edge of romance, in which Paracelsus describes how he will bury in sweetness the ideal aims he had in youth, building a pyre for them of all perfumed things; and the last lines of the verse I quote leave us in a castle of old romance—

> And strew faint sweetness from some old
>   Egyptian's fine worm-eaten shroud
> Which breaks to dust when once unrolled;
>   Or shredded perfume, like a cloud
> From closet long to quiet vowed,
> With mothed and dropping arras hung,
> Mouldering her lute and books among,
> As when a queen, long dead, was young.

The other is a song, more than a song, in *Pippa Passes*, a true piece of early folk-romance, with a faint touch of Greek story, wedded to Eastern and mediæval elements, in its roving imaginations. It is admirably pictorial, and the air which broods over it is the sunny and still air which, in men's fancy, was breathed by the happy children of the Golden Age. I quote a great part of it:

> A King lived long ago,
> In the morning of the world,
> When earth was nigher heaven than now:
> And the King's locks curled,
> Disparting o'er a forehead full
> As the milk-white space 'twixt horn and horn
> Of some sacrificial bull—
> Only calm as a babe new-born:
> For he was got to a sleepy mood,
> So safe from all decrepitude,
> Age with its bane, so sure gone by,
> (The gods so loved him while he dreamed)
> That, having lived thus long, there seemed
> No need the King should ever die.

LUIGI. No need that sort of King should ever die!

> Among the rocks his city was:
> Before his palace, in the sun,
> He sat to see his people pass,
> And judge them every one
> From its threshold of smooth stone.
> They haled him many a valley-thief
> Caught in the sheep-pens, robber chief
> Swarthy and shameless, beggar, cheat,
> Spy-prowler, or rough pirate found
> On the sea-sand left aground;
> * * * * *
> These, all and every one,
> The King judged, sitting in the sun.

LUIGI. That King should still judge sitting in the sun!

> His councillors, on left and right,
> Looked anxious up,—but no surprise
> Disturbed the King's old smiling eyes
> Where the very blue had turned to white.

> 'Tis said, a Python scared one day
> The breathless city, till he came,
> With forky tongue and eyes on flame,
> Where the old King sat to judge alway;
> But when he saw the sweepy hair
> Girt with a crown of berries rare
> Which the god will hardly give to wear
> To the maiden who singeth, dancing bare
> In the altar-smoke by the pine-torch lights,
> At his wondrous forest rites,—
> Seeing this, he did not dare
> Approach the threshold in the sun,
> Assault the old king smiling there.
> Such grace had kings when the world begun!

Then there are two other romantic pieces, not ringing with this early note, but having in them a wafting scent of the Provençal spirit. One is the song sung by Pippa when she passes the room where Jules and Phene are talking—the song of Kate, the Queen. The other is the cry Rudel, the great troubadour, sent out of his heart to the Lady of Tripoli whom he never saw, but loved. The subject is romantic, but that, I think, is all the romance in it. It is not Rudel who speaks but Browning. It is not the twelfth but the nineteenth century which has made all that analysis and overworked illustration.

There remain, on this matter, *Childe Roland* and the *Flight of the Duchess*. I believe that *Childe Roland* emerged, all of a sudden and to Browning's surprise, out of the pure imagination, like the Sea-born Queen; that Browning did not conceive it beforehand; that he had no intention in it, no reason for writing it, and no didactic or moral aim in it. It was not even born of his will. Nor does he seem to be acquainted with the old story on the subject which took a ballad form in Northern England. The impulse to write it was suddenly awakened in him by that line out of an old song the Fool quotes in *King Lear*. There is another tag of a song in *Lear* which stirs a host of images in the imagination; and out of which some poet might create a romantic lyric:

Still through the hawthorn blows the cold wind.

But it does not produce so concrete a set of images as *Childe Roland to the Dark Tower came*. Browning has made that his own, and what he has done is almost romantic. Almost romantic, I say, because the peculiarities of Browning's personal genius appear too strongly in *Childe Roland* for pure romantic story, in which the idiosyncrasy of the poet, the personal element of his fancy, are never dominant. The scenery, the images, the conduct of the tales of romance, are, on account of their long passage through the popular mind, impersonal.

Moreover, Browning's poem is too much in the vague. The romantic tales are clear in outline; this is not. But the elements in the original story entered, as it were of their own accord, into Browning. There are several curious, unconscious reversions to folk-lore which have crept into his work like living things which, seeing Browning engaged on a story of theirs, entered into it as into a house of their own, and without his knowledge. The wretched cripple who points the way; the blind and wicked horse; the accursed stream; the giant mountain range, all the peaks alive, as if in a nature myth; the crowd of Roland's predecessors turned to stone by their failure; the sudden revealing of the tower where no tower had been, might all be matched out of folk-stories. I think I have heard that Browning wrote the poem at a breath one morning; and it reads as if, from verse to verse, he did not know what was coming to his pen. This is very unlike his usual way; but it is very much the way in which tales of this kind are unconsciously up-built.

Men have tried to find in the poem an allegory of human life; but Browning had no allegorising intention. However, as every story which was ever written has at its root the main elements of human nature, it is always possible to make an allegory out of any one of them. If we like to amuse ourselves in that fashion, we may do so; but we are too bold and bad if we impute allegory to Browning. *Childe Roland* is nothing more than a gallop over the moorlands of imagination; and the skies of the soul, when it was made, were dark and threatening storm. But one thing is plain in it: it is an outcome of that passion for the mystical world, for adventure, for the unknown, which lies at the root of the romantic tree.

The *Flight of the Duchess* is full of the passion of escape from the conventional; and no where is Browning more original or more the poet. Its manner is exactly right, exactly fitted to the character and condition of the narrator, who is the Duke's huntsman. Its metrical movement is excellent, and the changes of that movement are in harmony with the things and feelings described. It is astonishingly swift, alive, and leaping; and it delays, as a stream, with great charm, when the emotion of the subject is quiet, recollective, or deep. The descriptions of Nature in the poem are some of the most vivid and true in Browning's work. The sketches of animal life—so natural on the lips of the teller of the story—are done from the keen observation of a huntsman, and with his love for the animals he has fed, followed and slain. And, through it all, there breathes the romantic passion—to be out of the world of custom and commonplace, set free to wander for ever to an unknown goal; to drink the air of adventure and change; not to know to-day what will take place to-morrow, only to know that it will be different; to ride on the top of the wave of life as it runs before the wind; to live with those who live, and are of the same mind; to be loved and to find love the best good in the world; to be the centre of hopes and joys among those who may blame and give pain, but who are never indifferent; to have many troubles, but always to pursue their far-off good; to wring the life out of them, and, at the last, to have a new life, joy and freedom in another and a fairer world. But let Browning tell the end:

> So, at the last shall come old age,
> Decrepit as befits that stage;
> How else would'st thou retire apart
> With the hoarded memories of thy heart,
> And gather all to the very least
> Of the fragments of life's earlier feast,
> Let fall through eagerness to find
> The crowning dainties yet behind?
> Ponder on the entire past
> Laid together thus at last,
> When the twilight helps to fuse
> The first fresh with the faded hues,
> And the outline of the whole
> Grandly fronts for once thy soul.

> And then as, 'mid the dark, a gleam
> Of yet another morning breaks,
> And, like the hand which ends a dream,
> Death, with the might of his sunbeam,
> Touches the flesh, and the soul awakes,
> Then——

Then the romance of life sweeps into the world beyond. But even in that world the duchess will never settle down to a fixed life. She will be, like some of us, a child of the wandering tribes of eternity.

This romantic passion which never dies even in our modern society, is embodied in the gipsy crone who, in rags and scarcely clinging to life, suddenly lifts into youth and queenliness, just as in a society, where romance seems old or dead, it springs into fresh and lovely life. This is the heart of the poem, and it is made to beat the more quickly by the wretched attempt of the duke and his mother to bring back the observances of the Middle Ages without their soul. Nor even then does Browning leave his motive. The huntsman has heard the gipsy's song; he has seen the light on his mistress' face as she rode away—the light which is not from sun or star—and the love of the romantic world is born in him. He will not leave his master; there his duty lies. "I must see this fellow his sad life through." But then he will go over the mountains, after his lady, leaving the graves of his wife and children, into the unknown, to find her, or news of her, in the land of the wanderers. And if he never find her, if, after pleasant journeying, earth cannot give her to his eyes, he will still pursue his quest in a world where romance and formality are not married together.

So I shall find out some snug corner,
Under a hedge, like Orson the wood-knight,
Turn myself round and bid the world Good Night;
And sleep a sound sleep till the trumpet's blowing
Wakes me (unless priests cheat us laymen)
To a world where will be no further throwing
Pearls before swine that can't value them.   Amen.

CHAPTER XI

IMAGINATIVE REPRESENTATIONS

ALL poems might be called "imaginative representations." But the class of poems in Browning's work to which I give that name stands apart. It includes such poems as *Cleon, Caliban on Setebos, Fra Lippo Lippi*, the *Epistle of Karshish*, and they isolate themselves, not only in Browning's poetry, but in English poetry. They have some resemblance in aim and method to the monologues of Tennyson, such as the *Northern Farmer* or *Rizpah*, but their aim is much wider than Tennyson's, and their method far more elaborate and complex.

What do they represent? To answer this is to define within what limits I give them the name of "imaginative representations." They are not only separate studies of individual men as they breathed and spoke; face, form, tricks of body recorded; intelligence, character, temper of mind, spiritual aspiration made clear—Tennyson did that; they are also studies of these individual men—Cleon, Karshish and the rest—as general types, representative images, of the age in which they lived; or of the school of art to which they belonged; or of the crisis in theology, religion, art, or the social movement which took place while the men they paint were alive, and which these men led, or formed, or followed. That is their main element, and it defines them.

They are not dramatic. Their action and ideas are confined to one person, and their circumstance and scenery to one time and place. But Browning, unlike Tennyson, filled the background of the stage on which he placed his single figure with a multitude of objects, or animals, or natural scenery, or figures standing round or in motion; and these give additional vitality and interest to the representation. Again, they are short, as short as a soliloquy or a letter or a conversation in a street. Shortness belongs to this form of poetic work—a form to which Browning gave a singular intensity. It follows that they must not be argumentative beyond what is fitting. Nor ought they to glide into the support of a thesis, or into didactic addresses, as *Bishop Blougram* and *Mr. Sludge* do. These might be called treatises, and are apart from the kind of poem of which I speak. They begin, indeed, within its limits, but they soon transgress those limits; and are more properly classed with poems which, also representative, have not the brevity, the scenery, the lucidity, the objective representation, the concentration of the age into one man's mind, which mark out these poems from the rest, and isolate them into a class of their own.

The voice we hear in them is rarely the voice of Browning; nor is the mind of their personages his mind, save so far as he is their creator. There are a few exceptions to this, but, on the whole, Browning has, in writing these poems, stripped himself of his own personality. He had, by creative power, made these men; cast them off from himself, and put them into their own age. They talk their minds out in character with their age. Browning seems to watch them, and to wonder how they got out of his hands and became men. That is the impression they make, and it predicates a singular power of imagination. Like the Prometheus of Goethe, the poet sits apart, moulding men and then endowing them with life. But he cannot tell, any more than Prometheus, what they will say and do after he has made them. He does tell, of course, but that is not our impression. Our impression is that they live and talk of their own accord, so vitally at home they are in the country, the scenery, and the thinking of the place and time in which he has imagined them.

Great knowledge seems required for this, and Browning had indeed an extensive knowledge not so much of the historical facts, as of the tendencies of thought which worked in the times wherein he placed his men. But the chief knowledge he had, through his curious reading, was of a multitude of small intimate details of the customs, clothing, architecture, dress, popular talk and scenery of the towns and country of Italy from the thirteenth century up to modern times. To every one of these details—such as are found in *Sordello*, in *Fra Lippo Lippi*, in the *Bishop orders his Tomb at St. Praxed's Church*—his vivid and grasping imagination gave an uncommon reality.

But even without great knowledge such poems may be written, if the poet have imagination, and the power to execute in metrical words what has been imagined. *Theology in the Island* and the prologue to a *Death in the Desert* are examples of this. Browning knew nothing of that island in the undiscovered seas where Prosper dwelt, but he made all the scenery of it and all its animal life, and he re-created Caliban. He had never seen the cave in the desert where he placed John to die, nor the sweep of rocky hills and sand around it, nor the Bactrian waiting with the camels. Other poets, of course, have seen unknown lands and alien folks, but he has seen them more vividly, more briefly, more forcibly. His imagination was objective enough.

But it was as subjective as it was objective. He saw the soul of Fra Lippo Lippi and the soul of his time as vividly as he saw the streets of Florence at night, the watch, the laughing girls, and the palace of the Medici round the corner. It was a remarkable combination, and it is by this combination of the subjective and objective imagination that he draws into some dim approach to Shakespeare; and nowhere closer than in these poems.

Again, not only the main character of each of these poems, but all the figures introduced (sometimes only in a single line) to fill up the background, are sketched with as true and vigorous a pencil as the main figure; are never out of place or harmony with the whole, and are justly subordinated. The young men who stand round the Bishop's bed when he orders his tomb, the watchmen in *Fra Lippo Lippi*, the group of St. John's disciples, are as alive, and as much in tune with the whole, as the servants and tenants of Justice

Shallow. Again, it is not only the lesser figures, but the scenery of these poems which is worth our study. That also is closely fitted to the main subject. The imagination paints it for that, and nothing else. It would not fit any other subject. For imagination, working at white heat, cannot do what is out of harmony; no more than a great musician can introduce a false chord. All goes together in these poems—scenery, characters, time, place and action.

Then, also, the extent of their range is remarkable. Their subjects begin with savage man making his god out of himself. They pass through Greek mythology to early Christian times; from Artemis and Pan to St. John dying in the desert. Then, still in the same period, while Paul was yet alive, he paints another aspect of the time in Cleon the rich artist, the friend of kings, who had reached the top of life, included all the arts in himself, yet dimly craved for more than earth could give. From these times the poems pass on to the early and late Renaissance, and from that to the struggle for freedom in Italy, and from that to modern life in Europe. This great range illustrates the penetration and the versatility of his genius. He could place us with ease and truth at Corinth, Athens or Rome, in Paris, Vienna or London; and wherever we go with him we are at home.

One word more must be said about the way a great number of these poems arose. They leaped up in his imagination full-clad and finished at a single touch from the outside. *Caliban upon Setebos* took its rise from a text in the Bible which darted into his mind as he read the *Tempest*. *Cleon* arose as he read that verse in St. Paul's speech at Athens, "As certain also of your own poets have said." I fancy that *An Epistle of Karshish* was born one day when he read those two stanzas in *In Memoriam* about Lazarus, and imagined how the subject would come to him. *Fra Lippo Lippi* slipped into his mind one day at the Belle Arti at Florence as he stood before the picture described in the poem, and walked afterwards at night through the streets of Florence. These fine things are born in a moment, and come into our world from poet, painter, and musician, full-grown; built, like Aladdin's palace, with all their jewels, in a single night. They are inexplicable by any scientfiic explanation, as inexplicable as genius itself. When have the hereditarians explained Shakespeare, Mozart, Turner? When has the science of the world explained the birth of a lyric of Burns, a song of Beethoven's, or a drawing of Raffaelle? Let these gentlemen veil their eyes, and confess their inability to explain the facts. For it is fact they touch. "Full fathom five thy father lies"—that song of Shakespeare exists. The overture to Don Giovanni is a reality. We can see the Bacchus and Ariadne at the National Gallery and the Theseus at the Museum. These are facts; but they are a million million miles beyond the grasp of any science. Nay, the very smallest things of their kind, the slightest water-colour sketch of Turner, a half-finished clay sketch of Donatello, the little song done in the corner of a provincial paper by a working clerk in a true poetic hour, are not to be fathomed by the most far-descending plummet of the scientific understanding. These things are in that superphysical world into which, however closely he saw and dealt with his characters in the world of the senses, the conscience, or the understanding, Browning led them all at last.

The first of these poems is *Natural Theology on the Island; or, Caliban upon Setebos*. Caliban, with the instincts and intelligence of an early savage, has, in an hour of holiday, set himself to conceive what Setebos, his mother's god, is like in character. He talks out the question with himself, and because he is in a vague fear lest Setebos, hearing him soliloquise about him, should feel insulted and swing a thunder-bolt at him, he not only hides himself in the earth, but speaks in the third person, as if it was not he that spoke; hoping in that fashion to trick his God.

Browning, conceiving in himself the mind and temper of an honest, earthly, imaginative savage—who is developed far enough to build nature-myths in their coarse early forms—architectures the character of Setebos out of the habits, caprices, fancies, likes and dislikes, and thoughts of Caliban; and an excellent piece of penetrative imagination it is. Browning has done nothing better, though he has done as well.

But Browning's Caliban is not a single personage. No one savage, at no one time, would have all these thoughts of his God. He is the representative of what has been thought, during centuries, by many thousands of men; the concentration into one mind of the ground-thoughts of early theology. At one point, as if Browning wished to sketch the beginning of a new theological period, Caliban represents a more advanced thought than savage man conceives.

This is Caliban's imagination of a higher being than Setebos who is the capricious creator and power of the earth—of the "Quiet," who is master of Setebos and whose temper is quite different; who also made the stars, things which Caliban, with a touch of Browning's subtle thought, separates from the sun and moon and earth. It is plain from this, and from the whole argument which is admirably conducted, that Caliban is an intellectual personage, too long neglected; and Prospero, could he have understood his nature, would have enjoyed his conversation. Renan agreed with Browning in this estimate of his intelligence, and made him the foundation of a philosophical play.

There is some slight reason for this in Shakespeare's invention. He lifts Caliban in intellect, even in feeling, far above Trinculo, Stephano, the Boatswain and the rest of the common men. The objection, however, has been made that Browning makes him too intelligent. The answer is that Browning is not drawing Caliban only, but embodying in an imagined personage the thoughts about God likely to be invented by early man during thousands of years—and this accounts for the insequences in Caliban's thinking. They are not the thoughts of one but of several men. Yet a certain poetic unity is given to them by the unity of place. The continual introduction of the landscape to be seen from his refuge knits the discursive thinking of the savage into a kind of unity. We watch him lying in the thick water-slime of the hollow, his head on the rim of it propped by his hands, under the cave's mouth, hidden by the gadding gourds and vines; looking out to sea and watching the wild animals that pass him by—and out of this place he does not stir.

In Shakespeare's *Tempest* Caliban is the gross, brutal element of the earth and is opposed to Ariel, the light, swift, fine element of the air. Caliban curses Prospero with the evils of the earth, with the wicked dew of the fen and the red plague of the sea-marsh. Browning's Caliban does not curse at all. When he is not angered, or in a caprice, he is a good-natured creature, full of animal enjoyment. He loves to lie in the cool slush, like a lias-lizard, shivering with earthy pleasure when his spine is tickled by the small eft-things that course along it,

> Run in and out each arm, and make him laugh.

The poem is full of these good, close, vivid realisations of the brown prolific earth.

Browning had his own sympathy with Caliban Nor does Shakespeare make him altogether brutish. He has been so educated by his close contact with nature that his imagination has been kindled. His very cursing is imaginative:

> As wicked dew as e'er my mother brushed
> With raven's feather from unwholesome fen
> Drop on you both; a south-west blow on you
> And blister you all o'er.

Stephano and Trinculo, vulgar products of civilisation, could never have said that. Moreover, Shakespeare's Caliban, like Browning's, has the poetry of the earth-man in him. When Ariel plays, Trinculo and Stephano think it must be the devil, and Trinculo is afraid: but Caliban loves and enjoys the music for itself:

> Be not afear'd; the isle is full of noises,
> Sounds and sweet airs, that give delight and hurt not.
> Sometimes a thousand twangling instruments
> Will hum about mine ears, and sometimes voices
> That, if I then had waked after long sleep,
> Will make me sleep again.

Stephano answers, like a modern millionaire:

> This will prove a brave kingdom for me, where I shall have my music for nothing.

Browning's Caliban is also something of a poet, and loves the Nature of whom he is a child. We are not surprised when he

> looks out o'er yon sea which sunbeams cross
> And recross till they weave a spider web
> (Meshes of fire some great fish breaks at times)

though the phrase is full of a poet's imagination, for so the living earth would see and feel the sea. It belongs also to Caliban's nearness to the earth that he should have the keenest of eyes for animals, and that poetic pleasure in watching their life which, having seen them vividly, could describe them vividly. I quote one example from the poem; there are many others:

> 'Thinketh, He made thereat the sun, this isle,
> Trees and the fowls here, beast and creeping thing.
> Yon otter, sleek-wet, black, lithe as a leech;
> Yon auk, one fire-eye in a ball of foam,
> That floats and feeds; a certain badger brown
> He hath watched hunt with that slant white-wedge eye
> By moonlight; and the pie with the long tongue
> That pricks deep into oakwarts for a worm,
> And says a plain word when she finds her prize,
> But will not eat the ants; the ants themselves
> That build a wall of seeds and settled stalks
> About their hole—

There are two more remarks to make about this

poem. First, that Browning makes Caliban create a dramatic world in which Miranda, Ariel, and he himself play their parts, and in which he assumes the part of Prosper. That is, Caliban invents a new world out of the persons he knows, but different from them, and a second self outside himself. No lower animal has ever conceived of such a creation. Secondly, Browning makes Caliban, in order to exercise his wit and his sense of what is beautiful, fall to making something—a bird, an insect, or a building which he ornaments, which satisfies him for a time, and which he then destroys to make a better. This is art in its beginning; and the highest animal we know of is incapable of it. We know that the men of the caves were capable of it. When they made a drawing, a piece of carving, they were unsatisfied until they had made a better. When they made a story out of what they knew and saw, they went on to make more. Creation, invention, art—this, independent entirely of the religious desire, makes the infinite gulf which divides man from the highest animals.

I do not mean, in this book, to speak of the theology of Caliban, though the part of the poem which concerns the origin of sacrifice is well worth our attention. But the poem may be recommended to those theological persons who say there is no God; and to that large class of professional theologians, whose idea of a capricious, jealous, suddenly-angered God, without any conscience except his sense of power to do as he pleases, is quite in harmony with Caliban's idea of Setebos.

The next of these " imaginative representations " is the poem called *Cleon*. Cleon is a rich and famous artist of the Grecian isles, alive while St. Paul was still making his missionary journeys, just at the time when the Græco-Roman culture had attained a height of refinement, but had lost originating power; when it thought it had mastered all the means for a perfect life, but was, in reality, trembling in a deep dissatisfaction on the edge of its first descent into exhaustion. Then, as everything good had been done in the art of the past, cultivated men began to ask "Was there anything worth doing?" "Was life itself worth living?"; questions never asked by those who are living. Or "What is life in its perfection, and when shall we have it?"; a question also not asked by those who live in the morning of a new æra, when the world—as in Elizabeth's days, as in 1789, as perhaps it may be in a few years—is born afresh; but which is asked continually in the years when a great movement of life has passed its culminating point and has begun to decline. Again and again the world has heard these questions; in Cleon's time, and when the Renaissance had spent its force, and at the end of the reign of Louis XIV., and before Elizabeth's reign had closed, and about 1820 in England, and of late years also in our society. This is the temper and the time that Browning embodies in Cleon, who is the incarnation of a culture which is already feeling that life is going out of it.

Protus, the king, has written to him, and the poem is Cleon's answer to the king. Browning takes care, as usual, to have his background of scenery quite clear and fair. It is a courtyard to Cleon's house in one of the sprinkled isles—

Lily on lily, that o'erlace the sea,
And laugh their pride when the light wave lisps " Greece."

I quote it; it marks the man and the age of luxurious culture.

> They give thy letter to me, even now;
> I read and seem as if I heard thee speak.
> The master of thy galley still unlades
> Gift after gift; they block my court at last
> And pile themselves along its portico
> Royal with sunset, like a thought of thee;
> And one white she-slave from the group dispersed
> Of black and white slaves (like the chequer work
> Pavement, at once my nation's work and gift,
> Now covered with this settle-down of doves),
> One lyric woman, in her crocus vest
> Woven of sea-wools, with her two white hands
> Commends to me the strainer and the cup
> Thy lip hath bettered ere it blesses mine.

But he is more than luxurious. He desires the highest life, and he praises the king because he has acknowledged by his gifts the joy that Art gives to life; and most of all he praises him, because he too aspires, building a mighty tower, not that men may look at it, but that he may gaze from its height on the sun, and think what higher he may attain. The tower is the symbol of the cry of the king's soul.

Then he answers the king's letter. "It is true, O king, I am poet, sculptor, painter, architect, philosopher, musician; all arts are mine. Have I done as well as the great men of old? No, but I have combined their excellences into one man, into myself.

> " I have not chanted verse like Homer, no—
> Nor swept string like Terpander—no—nor carved
> And painted men like Phidias and his friend:
> I am not great as they are, point by point.

> But I have entered into sympathy
> With these four, running these into one soul,
> Who, separate, ignored each other's art.
> Say, is it nothing that I know them all?

"This, since the best in each art has already been done, was the only progress possible, and I have made it. It is not unworthy, king!

"Well, now thou askest, if having done this, 'I have not attained the very crown of life; if I cannot now comfortably and fearlessly meet death? 'I, Cleon, leave,' thou sayest, 'my life behind me in my poems, my pictures; I am immortal in my work. What more can life desire?'"

It is the question so many are asking now, and it is the answer now given. <u>What better immortality than in one's work left behind to move in men?</u> What more than this can life desire? But Cleon does not agree with that. "If thou, O king, with the light now in thee, hadst looked at creation before man appeared, thou wouldst have said, 'All is perfect so far.' But questioned if anything more perfect in joy might be, thou wouldst have said, 'Yes; a being may be made, unlike these who do not know the joy they have, who shall be conscious of himself, and know that he is happy. Then his life will be satisfied with daily joy.'" O king, thou wouldst have answered foolishly. The higher the soul climbs in joy the more it sees of joy, and when it sees the most, it perishes. Vast capabilities of joy open round it; it craves for all it presages; desire for more deepening with every attainment. And then the body intervenes. Age, sickness, decay, forbid attainment. Life is inadequate to joy. What have the gods done? It cannot be their malice, no, nor carelessness; but—to let us see oceans of joy, and only give us power to hold a cupful—is that to live? It is misery, and the more of joy my artist nature makes me capable of feeling, the deeper my misery.

"But then, O king, thou sayest 'that I leave behind me works that will live; works, too, which paint the joy of life.' Yes, but to show what the joy of life is, is not to have it. If I carve the young Phœbus, am I therefore young? I can write odes of the delight of love, but grown too grey to be beloved, can I have its delight? That fair slave of yours, and the rower with the muscles all a ripple on his back who lowers the sail in the bay, can write no love odes nor can they paint the joy of love; but they can have it—not I."

The knowledge, he thinks, of what joy is, of all that life can give, which increases in the artist as his feebleness increases, makes his fate the deadlier. What is it to him that his works live? He does not live. The hand of death grapples the throat of life at the moment when he sees most clearly its infinite possibilities. Decay paralyses his hand when he knows best how to use his tools. It is accomplished wretchedness.

I quote his outburst. It is in the soul of thousands who have no hope of a life to come.

> "But," sayest thou—(and I marvel, I repeat,
> To find thee trip on such a mere word) "what
> Thou writest, paintest, stays; that does not die:
> Sappho survives, because we sing her songs,
> And Æschylus, because we read his plays!"
> Why, if they live still, let them come and take
> Thy slave in my despite, drink from thy cup,
> Speak in my place! "Thou diest while I survive?"—

> Say rather that my fate is deadlier still,
> In this, that every day my sense of joy
> Grows more acute, my soul (intensified
> By power and insight) more enlarged, more keen;
> While every day my hairs fall more and more,
> My hand shakes, and the heavy years increase—
> The horror quickening still from year to year,
> The consummation coming past escape
> When I shall know most, and yet least enjoy—
> When all my works wherein I prove my worth,
> Being present still to mock me in men's mouths,
> Alive still, in the praise of such as thou,
> I, I the feeling, thinking, acting man,
> The man who loved his life so overmuch,
> Sleep in my urn. It is so horrible
> I dare at times imagine to my need
> Some future state revealed to us by Zeus,
> Unlimited in capability
> For joy, as this is in desire of joy,
> —To seek which the joy-hunger forces us:
> That, stung by straitness of our life, made strait
> On purpose to make prized the life at large—
> Freed by the throbbing impulse we call death,
> We burst there as the worm into the fly,
> Who, while a worm still, wants his wings. But no!
> Zeus has not yet revealed it; and alas,
> He must have done so, were it possible!

This is one only of Browning's statements of what he held to be the fierce necessity for another life. Without it, nothing is left for humanity, having arrived at full culture, knowledge, at educated love of beauty, at finished morality and unselfishness—nothing in the end but Cleon's cry —sorrowful, somewhat stern, yet gentle—to Protus,

> Live long and happy, and in that thought die,
> Glad for what was. Farewell.

But for those who are not Cleon and Protus, not kings in comfort or poets in luxury, who have had no gladness, what end—what is to be said of them?

I will not stay to speak of *A Death in the Desert*, which is another of these poems, because the most part of it is concerned with questions of modern theology. St. John awakes into clear consciousness just before his death in the cave where he lies tended by a few disciples. He foresees some of the doubts of this century and meets them as he can. The bulk of this poem, very interesting in its way, is Browning's exposition of his own belief, not an imaginative representation of what St. John actually would have said. It does not therefore come into my subject. What does come into it is the extraordinary naturalness and vitality of the description given by John's disciple of the place where they were, and the fate of his companions. This is invented in Browning's most excellent way. It could not be better done.

The next poem is the *Epistle of Karshish, the Arab Physician*, to his master, concerning his strange medical experience. The time is just before the last siege of Jerusalem, and Karshish, journeying through Jericho, and up the pass, stays for a few days at Bethany and meets Lazarus. His case amazes him, and though he thinks his interest in it unworthy of a man of science in comparison with the new herbs and new diseases he has discovered, yet he is carried away by it and gives a full account of it to his master.

I do not think that Browning ever wrote a poem the writing of which he more enjoyed. The creation of Karshish suited his humour and his quaint play with recondite knowledge. He describes the physician till we see him alive and thinking, in body and soul. The creation of Lazarus is even a higher example of the imaginative power of Browning; and that it is shaped for us through the mind of Karshish, and in tune with it, makes the imaginative effort the more remarkable. Then the problem—how to express the condition of a man's body and soul, who, having for three days according to the story as Browning conceives it lived consciously in the eternal and perfect world, has come back to dwell in this world—was so difficult and so involved in metaphysical strangenesses, that it delighted him.

Of course, he carefully prepares his scenery to give a true semblance to the whole. Karshish comes up the flinty pass from Jericho; he is attacked by thieves twice and beaten, and the wild beasts endanger his path;

> A black lynx snarled and pricked a tufted ear,
> Lust of my blood inflamed his yellow balls;
> I cried and threw my staff and he was gone,

and then, at the end of the pass, he met Lazarus. See how vividly the scenery is realised—

> I crossed a ridge of short, sharp, broken hills
> Like an old lion's cheek-teeth. Out there came
> A moon made like a face with certain spots,
> Multiform, manifold and menacing:
> Then a wind rose behind me. So we met
> In this old sleepy town at unaware
> The man and I.

And the weird evening, Karshish thinks, had something to do with the strange impression the man has made on him. Then we are placed in the dreamy village of Bethany. We hear of its elders, its diseases, its flowers, its herbs and gums, of the insects which may help medicine—

> There is a spider here
> Weaves no web, watches on the ledge of tombs,
> Sprinkled with mottles on an ash-grey back;

and then, how the countryside is all on fire with news of Vespasian marching into Judæa. So we have the place, the village, the hills, the animals, and the time, all clear, and half of the character of Karshish. The inner character of the man emerges as clearly when he comes to deal with Lazarus. This is not a case of the body, he thinks, but of the soul. "The Syrian," he tells his master, "has had catalepsy, and a learned leech of his nation, slain soon afterwards, healed him and brought him back to life after three days. He says he was dead, and made alive again, but that is his madness; though the man seems sane enough. At any rate, his disease has disappeared, he is as well as you and I. But the mind and soul of the man, that is the strange matter, and in that he is entirely unlike other men. Whatever he has gone through has rebathed him as in clear water of another life, and penetrated his whole being. He views the world like a child, he scarcely listens to what goes on about him, yet he is no fool. If one could fancy a man endowed with perfect knowledge beyond the fleshly faculty, and while he has this heaven in him forced to live on earth, such a man is he. His heart and brain move there, his feet stay here. He has lost all sense of our values of things. Vespasian besieging Jerusalem and a mule passing with gourds awaken the same interest. But speak of some little fact, little as we think, and he stands astonished with its prodigious import. If his child sicken to death it does not seem to matter to him, but a gesture, a glance from the child, starts him into an agony of fear and anger, as if the child were undoing the universe. He lives like one between two regions, one of distracting glory, of which he is conscious but must not enter yet; and the other into which he has been exiled back again—and between this region where his soul moves and the earth where his body is, there is so little harmony of thought or feeling that he cannot undertake any human activity, nor unite the demands of the two worlds. He knows that what ought to be cannot be in the world he has returned to, so that his life is perplexed; but in this incessant perplexity he falls back on prone submission to the heavenly will. The time will come when death will restore his being to equilibrium; but now he is out of harmony, for the soul knows more than the body and the body clouds the soul."

"I probed this seeming indifference. 'Beast, to be so still and careless when Rome is at the gates of thy town.' He merely looked with his large eyes at me. Yet the man is not apathetic, but loves old and young, the very brutes and birds and flowers of the field. His only impatience is with wrongdoing, but he curbs that impatience."

At last Karshish tells, with many apologies for his foolishness, the strangest thing of all. Lazarus thinks that his curer was God himself who came and dwelt in flesh among those he had made, and went in and out among them healing and teaching, and then died. "It is strange, but why write of trivial matters when things of price call every moment for remark? Forget it, my master, pardon me and farewell."

Then comes the postscript, that impression which, in spite of all his knowledge, is left in Karshish's mind—

> The very God! think, Abib; dost thou think?
> So, the All-Great were the All-Loving too—
> So, through the thunder comes a human voice
> Saying: " O heart I made, a heart beats here!
> Face, my hands fashioned, see it in myself!
> Thou hast no power, nor may'st conceive of mine,
> But love I gave thee, with myself to love,
> And thou must love me who have died for thee!"—
> The madman saith He said so; it is strange.

CHAPTER XII

IMAGINATIVE REPRESENTATIONS
RENAISSANCE

THE Imaginative Representations to be discussed in this chapter are those which belong to the time of the Renaissance. We take a great leap when we pass from Karshish and Cleon to Fra Lippo Lippi, from early Christian times to the early manhood of the Renaissance. But these leaps are easy to a poet, and Browning is even more at his ease and in his strength in the fifteenth century than in the first.

We have seen with what force in *Sordello* he realised the life and tumult of the thirteenth century. The fourteenth century does not seem to have attracted him much, though he frequently refers to its work in Florence; but when the Renaissance in the fifteenth century took its turn with decision towards a more open freedom of life and thought, abandoning one after another the conventions of the past; when the moral limits, which the Church still faintly insisted on, were more and more withdrawn and finally blotted out; when, as the century passed into the next, the Church led the revolt against decency, order, and morality; when scepticism took the place of faith, even of duty, and criticism the place of authority, then Browning became interested, not of course in the want of faith and in immorality, but in the swift variety and intensity of the movement of intellectual and social life, and in the interlacing changes of the movement. This was an enchanting world for him, and as he was naturally most interested in the arts, he represented the way in which the main elements of the Renaissance appeared to him in poems which were concerned with music, poetry, painting and the rest of the arts, but chiefly with painting. Of course, when the Renaissance began to die down into senile pride and decay, Browning, who never ceased to choose and claim companionship with vigorous life, who abhorred decay either in Nature or nations, in societies or in cliques of culture, who would have preferred a blood-red pirate to the daintiest of decadents—did not care for it, and in only one poem, touched with contemptuous pity and humour, represented its disease and its disintegrating elements, with so much power, however, with such grasping mastery, that it is like a painting by Velasquez. Ruskin said justly that the *Bishop orders his Tomb at St. Praxed's Church* concentrated into a few lines all the evil elements of the Renaissance. But this want of care for the decaying Renaissance was contrasted by the extreme pleasure with which he treated its early manhood in *Fra Lippo Lippi*.

The Renaissance had a life and seasons, like those of a human being. It went through its childhood and youth like a boy of genius under the care of parents from whose opinions and mode of life he is sure to sever himself in the end; but who, having made a deep impression on his nature, retain power over, and give direction to, his first efforts at creation. The first art of the Renaissance, awakened by the discovery of the classic remnants, retained a great deal of the faith and superstition, the philosophy, theology, and childlike *naïveté* of the middle ages. Its painting and sculpture, but chiefly the first of these, gave themselves chiefly to the representation of the soul upon the face, and of the untutored and unconscious movements of the body under the influence of religious passion; that is, such movements as expressed devotion, fervent love of Christ, horror of sin, were chosen, and harmonised with the expression of the face. Painting dedicated its work to the representation of the heavenly life, either on earth in the story of the gospels and in the lives of the saints, or in its glory in the circles of heaven. Then, too, it represented the thought, philosophy, and knowledge of its own time and of the past in symbolic series of quiet figures, in symbolic pictures of the struggle of good with evil, of the Church with the world, of the virtues with their opposites. Naturally, then, the expression on the face of secular passions, the movement of figures in war and trade and social life and the whole vast field of human life in the ordinary world, were neglected as unworthy of representation; and the free, full life of the body, its beauty, power and charm, the objects which pleased its senses, the frank representation of its movement under the influence of the natural as contrasted with the spiritual passions, were looked upon with religious dismay. Such, but less in sculpture than in painting, was the art of the Renaissance in its childhood and youth, and Browning has scarcely touched that time. He had no sympathy with a neglect of the body, a contempt of the senses or of the beauty they perceived. He claimed the physical as well as the intellectual and spiritual life of man as by origin and of right divine. When, then, in harmony with a great change in social and literary life, the art of the Renaissance began to turn, in its early manhood, from the representation of the soul to the representation of the body in natural movement and beauty; from the representation of saints, angels and virtues to the representation of actual men and women in the streets and rooms of Florence; from symbolism to reality—Browning thought, "This suits me; this is what I love; I will put this mighty change into a poem." And he wrote *Fra Lippo Lippi.*

As long as this vivid representation of actual human life lasted, the art of the Renaissance was active, original, and interesting; and as it moved on, developing into higher and finer forms, and producing continually new varieties in its development, it reached its strong and eager manhood. In its art then, as well as in other matters, the Renaissance completed its new and clear theory of life; it remade the grounds of life, of its action and passion; and it reconstituted its aims. Browning loved this summer time of the Renaissance, which began with the midst of the fifteenth century. But he loved its beginnings even more than its fulness. That was characteristic. I have said that even when he was eighty years old, his keenest sympathies were with spring rather than summer, with those times of vital change when fresh excitements disturbed the world, when its eyes were smiling with hope, and its feet eager with the joy of pursuit. He rejoiced to analyse and embody a period which was shaking off the past, living intensely in the present, and prophesying the future. It charms us, as we read him, to see his intellect and his soul like two hunting dogs, and with all their eagerness, questing, roving, quartering, with the greatest joy and in incessant movement, over a time like this, where so many diverse, clashing, and productive elements mingled themselves into an enchanting confusion and glory of life. Out of that pleasure of hunting in a morning-tide of humanity, was born *Fra Lippo Lippi*; and there is scarcely an element of the time, except the political elements, which it does not represent; not dwelt on, but touched for the moment and left; unconsciously produced as two men of the time would produce them in conversation. The poem seems as easy as a chat in Pall Mall last night between some intelligent men, which, read two hundred years hence, would inform the reader of the trend of thought and feeling in this present day. But in reality to do this kind of thing well is to do a very difficult thing. It needs a full knowledge, a full imagination and a masterly execution. Yet when we read the poem, it seems as natural as the breaking out of blossoms. This is that divine thing, the ease of genius.

The scenery of the poem is as usual clear. We are in fifteenth-century Florence at night. There is no set description, but the slight touches are enough to make us see the silent lonely streets, the churches, the high walls of the monastic gardens, the fortress-palaces. The sound of the fountains is in our ears; the little crowds of revelling men and girls appear and disappear like ghosts; the surly watch with their weapons and torches bustle round the corner. Nor does Browning neglect to paint by slight enlivening touches, introduced into Lippo Lippi's account of himself as a starving boy, the aspect by day and the character of the Florence of the fifteenth century. This painting of his, slight as it is, is more alive than all the elaborate descriptions in *Romola*.

As to the poem itself, Browning plunges at once into his matter; no long approaches, no elaborate porches belong to his work. The man and his character are before us in a moment—

> I am poor brother Lippo, by your leave!
> You need not clap your torches to my face.
> Zooks, what's to blame? You think you see a monk!
> What, 'tis past midnight, and you go the rounds,
> And here you catch me at an alley's end
> Where sportive ladies leave their doors ajar?

For three weeks he has painted saints, and saints, and saints again, for Cosimo in the Medici Palace; but now the time of blossoms has come. Florence is now awake at nights; the secret of the spring moves in his blood; the man leaps up, the monk retires.

> Ouf! I leaned out of window for fresh air.
> There came a hurry of feet and little feet,
> A sweep of lute-strings, laughs and whifts of song,—
> *Flower o' the broom,*
> *Take away love, and our earth is a tomb!*
> *Flower of the quince,*
> *I let Lisa go, and what good in life since?*
> *Flower of the thyme*—and so on. Round they went.

Scarce had they turned the corner when a titter,
Like the skipping of rabbits by moonlight,—three slim shapes,
And a face that looked up . . . zooks, sir, flesh and blood,
That's all I'm made of! Into shreds it went,
Curtain and counterpane and coverlet,
All the bed-furniture—a dozen knots,
There was a ladder! Down I let myself,
Hands and feet, scrambling somehow, and so dropped,
And after them. I came up with the fun
Hard by St. Laurence, hail fellow, well met,—
   Flower o' the rose,
   If I've been merry, what matter who knows?

It is a picture, not only of the man, but of the time and its temper, when religion and morality, as well as that simplicity of life which Dante describes, had lost their ancient power over society in Florence; when the claim to give to human nature all it desired had stolen into the Church itself. Even in the monasteries, the long seclusion from natural human life had produced a reaction, which soon, indulging itself as Fra Lippo Lippi did, ran into an extremity of licence. Nevertheless, something of the old religious life lasted at the time of this poem. It stretched one hand back to the piety of the past, and retained, though faith and devotion had left them, its observances and conventions; so that, at first, when Lippo was painting, the new only peeped out of the old, like the saucy face of a nymph from the ilexes of a sacred grove. This is the historical moment Browning illustrates. Lippo Lippi was forced to paint the worn religious subjects: Jerome knocking his breast, the choirs of angels and martyrs, the scenes of the Gospel; but out of all he did the eager modern life began to glance! Natural, quaint, original faces and attitudes appeared; the angels smiled like Florentine women; the saints wore the air of Bohemians. There is a picture by Lippo Lippi in the National Gallery of some nine of them sitting on a bench under a hedge of roses, and it is no paradox to say that they might fairly represent the Florentines who tell the tales of the *Decameron.*

The transition as it appeared in art is drawn in this poem. Lippo Lippi became a monk by chance; it was not his vocation. A starving boy, he roamed the streets of Florence; and the widespread intelligence of the city is marked by Browning's account of the way in which the boy observed all the life of the streets for eight years. Then the coming change of the aims of art is indicated by the way in which, when he was allowed to paint, he covered the walls of the Carmine, not with saints, virgins, and angels, but with the daily life of the streets—the boy patting the dog, the murderer taking refuge at the altar, the white wrath of the avenger coming up the aisle, the girl going to market, the crowd round the stalls in the market, the monks, white, grey, and black—things as they were, as like as two peas to the reality; flesh and blood now painted, not skin and bone; not the expression on the face alone, but the whole body in speaking movement; nothing conventional, nothing imitative of old models, but actual life as it lay before the painter's eyes. Into this fresh æra of art Lippo Lippi led the way with the joy of youth. But he was too soon. The Prior, all the representatives of the conservative elements in the convent, were sorely troubled. "Why, this will never do: faces, arms, legs, and bodies like the true; life as it is; nature as she is; quite impossible. And Browning, in

Lippo's defence of himself, paints the conflict of the past with the coming art in a passage too long to quote, too admirable to shorten.

The new art conquered the old. The whole life of Florence was soon painted as it was: the face of the town, the streets, the churches, the towers, the winding river, the mountains round about it; the country, the fields and hills and hamlets, the peasants at work, ploughing, sowing, and gathering fruit, the cattle feeding, the birds among the trees and in the sky; nobles and rich burghers hunting, hawking; the magistrates, the citizens, the street-boys, the fine ladies, the tradesmen's wives, the heads of the guilds; the women visiting their friends; the interior of the houses. We may see this art of human life in the apse of Santa Maria Novella, painted by the hand of Ghirlandajo: in the Riccardi Palace, painted by Benozzo Gozzoli; in more than half the pictures of the painters who succeeded Fra Lippo Lippi. Only, so much of the old clings that all this actual Florentine life is painted into the ancient religious subjects—the life of the Baptist and the Virgin, the embassage of the Wise Men, the life of Christ, the legends of the saints, the lives of the virgins and martyrs, Jerusalem and its life painted as if it were Florence and its life—all the spiritual religion gone out of it, it is true, but yet, another kind of religion budding in it—the religion, not of the monastery, but of daily common life.

>   the world
> —The beauty and the wonder and the power,
> The shapes of things, their colours, lights, and shades,
> Changes, surprises—and God made it all!

Who paints these things as if they were alive, and loves them while he paints, paints the garment of God; and men not only understand their own life better because they see, through the painting, what they did not see before; but also the movement of God's spirit in the beauty of the world and in the life of men. Art interprets to man all that is, and God in it.

> Oh, oh,
> It makes me mad to think what men shall do
> And we in our graves! This world's no blot for us,
> No blank; it means intensely, and means good:
> To find its meaning is my meat and drink.

He could not do it; the time was not ripe enough. But he began it. And the spirit of its coming breaks out in all he did.

We take a leap of more than half a century when we pass from *Fra Lippo Lippi* to *Andrea del Sarto*. That advance in art to which Lippo Lippi looked forward with a kind of rage at his own powerlessness had been made. In its making, the art of the Renaissance had painted men and women, both body and soul, in every kind of life, both of war and peace; and better than they had ever been painted before. Having fulfilled that, the painters asked, "What more? What new thing shall we do? What new aim shall we pursue?" And there arose among them a desire to paint all that was paintable, and especially the human body, with scientific perfection. "In our desire to paint the whole of life, we have produced so much that we were forced to paint carelessly or inaccurately. In our desire to be original, we have neglected technique. In our desire to paint the passions on the face and in the movements of men, we have lost the calm and harmony of the ancient classic work, which made its ethical impression of the perfect balance of the divine nature by the ideal arrangement, in accord with a finished science, of the various members of the body to form a finished whole. Let the face no longer then try to represent the individual soul. One type of face for each class of art-representation is enough. Let our effort be to represent beauty by the perfect drawing of the body in repose and in action, and by chosen attitudes and types. Let our composition follow certain guiding lines and rules, in accordance with whose harmonies all pictures shall be made. We will follow the Greek; compose as he did, and by his principles; and for that purpose make a scientific study of the body of man; observing in all painting, sculpture, and architecture the general forms and proportions that ancient art, after many experiments, selected as the best. And, to match that, we must have perfect drawing in all we do.

This great change, which, as art's adulterous connection with science deepened, led to such unhappy results, Browning represents, when its aim had been reached, in his poem, *Andrea del Sarto;* and he tells us—through Andrea's talk with his wife Lucretia—what he thought of it; and what Andrea himself, whose broken life may have opened his eyes to the truth of things, may himself have thought of it. On that element in the poem I have already dwelt, and shall only touch on the scenery and tragedy, of the piece:

We sit with Andrea, looking out to Fiesole.

> sober, pleasant Fiesole.
> There's the bell clinking from the chapel top:
> That length of convent-wall across the way
> Holds the trees safer, huddled more inside;
> The last monk leaves the garden; days decrease,
> And autumn grows, autumn in everything.

As the poem goes on, the night falls, falls with the deepening of the painter's depression; the owls cry from the hill, Florence wears the grey hue of the heart of Andrea; and Browning weaves the autumn and the night into the tragedy of the painter's life.

That tragedy was pitiful. Andrea del Sarto was a faultless painter and a weak character; and it fell to his lot to love with passion a faithless woman. His natural weakness was doubled by the weakness engendered by unconquerable passion; and he ruined his life, his art, and his honour, to please his wife. He wearied her, as women are wearied, by passion unaccompanied by power; and she endured him only while he could give her money and pleasures. She despised him for that endurance, and all the more that he knew she was guilty, but said nothing lest she should leave him. Browning fills his main subject—his theory of the true aim of art—with this tragedy; and his treatment of it is a fine example of his passionate humanity; and the passion of it is knitted up with close reasoning and illuminated by his intellectual play.

It is worth a reader's while to read, along with this poem, Alfred de Musset's short play, *André del Sarto*. The tragedy of the situation is deepened by the French poet, and the end is told. Unlike Browning, only a few lines sketch the time, its temper, and its art. It is the depth of the tragedy which De Musset paints, and that alone;

and in order to deepen it, Andrea is made a much nobler character than he is in Browning's poem. The betrayal is also made more complete, more overwhelming. Lucretia is false to Andrea with his favourite pupil, with Cordiani, to whom he had given all he had, whom he loved almost as much as he loved his wife. Terrible, inevitable Fate broods over this brief and masterly little play.

The next of these imaginative representations of the Renaissance is, *The Bishop orders his Tomb at St. Praxed's Church.* We are placed in the full decadence of the Renaissance. Its total loss of religion, even in the Church; its immorality—the bishop's death-bed is surrounded by his natural sons and the wealth he leaves has been purchased by every kind of iniquity—its pride of life; its luxury; its semi-Paganism; its imitative classicism; its inconsistency; its love of jewels, and fine stones, and rich marbles; its jealousy and envy; its pleasure in the adornment of death; its delight in the outsides of things, in mere workmanship; its loss of originality; its love of scholarship for scholarship's sake alone; its contempt of the common people; its exhaustion—are one and all revealed or suggested in this astonishing poem.

These are the three greater poems dedicated to this period; but there are some minor poems which represent different phases of its life. One of these is the *Pictor Ignotus*. There must have been many men, during the vital time of the Renaissance, who, born, as it were, into the art-ability of the period, reached without trouble a certain level in painting, but who had no genius, who could not create; or who, if they had some touch of genius, had no boldness to strike it into fresh forms of beauty; shy, retiring men, to whom the criticism of the world was a pain they knew they could not bear. These men are common at a period when life is racing rapidly through the veins of a vivid city like Florence. The general intensity of the life lifts them to a height they would never reach in a dull and sleepy age. The life they have is not their own, but the life of the whole town. And this keen perception of life outside of them persuades them that they can do all that men of real power can do. In reality, they can do nothing and make nothing worth a people's honour. Browning, who himself was compact of boldness, who loved experiment in what was new, and who shaped what he conceived without caring for criticism, felt for these men, of whom he must have met many; and, asking himself "How they would think; what they would do; and how life would seem to them," wrote this poem. In what way will poor human nature excuse itself for failure? How will the weakness in the man try to prove that it was power? How, having lost the joy of life, will he attempt to show that his loss is gain, his failure a success; and, being rejected of the world, approve himself within?

This was a subject to please Browning; meat such as his soul loved: a nice, involved, Dædalian, labyrinthine sort of thing, a mixture of real sentiment and self-deceit; and he surrounded it with his pity for its human weakness.

"I could have painted any picture that I pleased," cries this painter; "represented on the face any passion, any virtue." If he could he would have done it, or tried it. Genius cannot hold itself in.

"I have dreamed of sending forth some picture which should enchant the world (and he alludes to Cimabue's picture)—

> "Bound for some great state,
>   Or glad aspiring little burgh, it went—
>   Flowers cast upon the car which bore the freight,
>   Through old streets named afresh from the event.

"That would have been, had I willed it. But mixed with the praisers there would have been cold, critical faces; judges who would press on me and mock. And I—I could not bear it." Alas! had he had genius, no fear would have stayed his hand, no judgment of the world delayed his work. What stays a river breaking from its fountain-head?

So he sank back, saying the world was not worthy of his labours. "What? Expose my noble work (things he had conceived but not done) to the prate and pettiness of the common buyers who hang it on their walls! No, I will rather paint the same monotonous round of Virgin, Child, and Saints in the quiet church, in the sanctuary's gloom. No merchant then will traffic in my heart. My pictures will moulder and die. Let them die. I have not vulgarised myself or them." Brilliant and nobly wrought as the first three poems are of which I have written, this quiet little piece needed and received a finer workmanship, and was more difficult than they.

Then there is *How it strikes a Contemporary*—the story of the gossip of a Spanish town about a poor poet, who, because he wanders everywhere about the streets observing all things, is mistaken for a spy of the king. The long pages he writes are said to be letters to the king; the misfortunes of this or that man are caused by his information. The world thinks him a wonder of cleverness; he is but an inferior poet. It imagines that he lives in Assyrian luxury; he lives and dies in a naked garret. This imaginative representation might be of any time in a provincial town of an ignorant country like Spain. It is a slight study of what superstitious imagination and gossip will work up round any man whose nature and manners, like those of a poet, isolate him from the common herd. Force is added to this study by its scenery. The Moorish windows, the shops, the gorgeous magistrates pacing down the promenade, are touched in with a flying pencil; and then, moving through the crowd, the lean, black-coated figure, with his cane and dog and his peaked hat, clear flint eyes and beaked nose, is seen, as if alive, in the vivid sunshine of Valladolid. But what Browning wished most to describe in this poem was one of the first marks of a poet, even of a poor one like this gentleman—the power of seeing and observing everything. Nothing was too small, nothing uninteresting in this man's eyes. His very hat was scrutinising.

> He stood and watched the cobbler at his trade,
> The man who slices lemons into drink,
> The coffee-roaster's brazier, and the boys
> That volunteer to help him turn its winch.
> He glanced o'er books on stalls with half an eye,
> And fly-leaf ballads on the vendor's string,
> And broad-edged bold-print posters by the wall.
> He took such cognisance of man and things,
> If any beat a horse you felt he saw;
> If any cursed a woman, he took note;
> Yet stared at nobody, you stared at him,
> And found, less to your pleasure than surprise,
> He seemed to know you and expect as much.

That is the artist's way. It was Browning's way. He is describing himself. In that fashion he roamed through Venice or Florence, stopping every moment, attracted by the smallest thing, finding a poem in everything, lost in himself yet seeing all that surrounded him, isolated in thinking, different from and yet like the rest of the world.

Another poem—*My Last Duchess*—must be mentioned. It is plainly placed in the midst of the period of the Renaissance by the word *Ferrara*, which is added to its title. But it is rather a picture of two temperaments which may exist in any cultivated society, and at any modern time. There are numbers of such men as the Duke and such women as the Duchess in our midst. Both are, however, drawn with mastery. Browning has rarely done his work with more insight, with greater keenness of portraiture, with happier brevity and selection. As in *The Flight of the Duchess*, untoward fate has bound together two temperaments sure to clash with each other—and no gipsy comes to deliver the woman in this case. The man's nature kills her. It happens every day. The Renaissance society may have built up more men of this type than ours, but they are not peculiar to it.

Germany, not Italy, is, I think, the country in which Browning intended to place two other poems which belong to the time of the Renaissance—*Johannes Agricola in Meditation* and *A Grammarian's Funeral*. Their note is as different from that of the Italian poems as the national temper of Germany is from that of Italy. They have no sense of beauty for beauty's sake alone. Their atmosphere is not soft or gay but somewhat stern. The logical arrangement of them is less one of feeling than of thought. There is a stronger manhood in them, a grimmer view of life. The sense of duty to God and Man, but little represented in the Italian poems of the Renaissance, does exist in these two German poems. Moreover, there is in them a full representation of aspiration to the world beyond. But the Italian Renaissance lived for the earth alone, and its loveliness; too close to earth to care for heaven.

It pleased Browning to throw himself fully into the soul of Johannes Agricola; and he does it with so much personal fervour that it seems as if, in one of his incarnations, he had been the man, and, for the moment of his writing, was dominated by him. The mystic-passion fills the poetry with keen and dazzling light, and it is worth while, from this point of view, to compare the poem with Tennyson's *Sir Galahad*, and on another side, with *St. Simeon Stylites*.

Johannes Agricola was one of the products of the reforming spirit of the sixteenth century in Germany, one of its wild extremes. He believes that God had chosen him among a few to be his for ever and for his own glory from the foundation of the world. He did not say that all sin was permitted to the saints, that what the flesh did was no matter, like those wild fanatics, one of whom Scott draws in *Woodstock;* but he did say, that if he sinned it made no matter to his election by God. Nay, the immanence of God in him turned the poison to health, the filth to jewels. Goodness and badness make no matter; God's choice is all. The martyr for truth, the righteous man whose life has saved the world, but who is not elected, is damned for ever in burning hell. "I am eternally chosen; for that I praise God. I do not understand it. If I did, could I praise Him? But I know my settled place in the divine decrees." I quote the beginning. It is pregnant with superb spiritual audacity, and kindled with imaginative pride.

> There's heaven above, and night by night
>   I look right through its gorgeous roof;
> No suns and moons though e'er so bright
>   Avail to stop me; splendour-proof
>   Keep the broods of stars aloof:
> For I intend to get to God,
>   For 'tis to God I speed so fast,
> For in God's breast, my own abode,
>   Those shoals of dazzling glory, passed,
>   I lay my spirit down at last.
> I lie where I have always lain,
>   God smiles as he has always smiled;
> Ere suns and moons could wax and wane,
>   Ere stars were thunder-girt, or piled
>   The heavens, God thought on me his child;
> Ordained a life for me, arrayed
>   Its circumstances every one
> To the minutest; ay, God said
>   This head this hand should rest upon
>   Thus, ere he fashioned star or sun.
> And having thus created me,
>   Thus rooted me, he bade me grow,
> Guiltless for ever, like a tree
>   That buds and blooms, nor seeks to know
>   The law by which it prospers so:
> But sure that thought and word and deed
>   All go to swell his love for me,
> Me, made because that love had need
>   Of something irreversibly
>   Pledged solely its content to be.

As to *A Grammarian's Funeral*, that poem also belongs to the German rather than to the Italian spirit. The Renaissance in Italy lost its religion; at the same time, in Germany, it added a reformation of religion to the New Learning. The Renaissance in Italy desired the fulness of knowledge in this world, and did not look for its infinities in the world beyond. In Germany the same desire made men call for the infinities of knowledge beyond the earth. A few Italians, like Savonarola, like M. Angelo, did the same, and failed to redeem their world; but eternal aspiration dwelt in the soul of every German who had gained a religion. In Italy, as the Renaissance rose to its luxury and trended to its decay, the pull towards personal righteousness made by belief in an omnipotent goodness who demands the subjection of our will to his, ceased to be felt by artists, scholars and cultivated society. A man's will was his only law. On the other hand, the life of the New Learning in Germany and England was weighted with a sense of duty to an eternal Righteousness. The love of knowledge or beauty was modified into seriousness of life, carried beyond this life in thought, kept clean, and, though filled with incessant labour on the earth, aspired to reach its fruition only in the life to come.

This is the spirit and the atmosphere of the *Grammarian's Funeral*, and Browning's little note at the beginning says that its time "was shortly after the revival of learning in Europe." I have really no proof that Browning laid the scene of his poem in Germany, save perhaps the use of such words as "thorp" and "croft," but there is a clean, pure morning light playing through the verse, a fresh, health-breathing northern air, which does not fit in with Italy; a joyous, buoyant youthfulness in the song and march of the students who carry their master with gay strength up the mountain to the very top, all of them filled with his aspiring spirit, all of them looking forward with gladness and vigour to life—which has no relation whatever to the temper of Florentine or Roman life during the age of the Medici. The bold brightness, moral earnestness, pursuit of the ideal, spiritual intensity, reverence for good work and for the man who did it, which breathe in the poem, differ by a whole world from the atmosphere of life in *Andrea del Sarto*. This is a crowd of men who are moving upwards, who, seizing the Renaissance elements, knitted them through and through with reformation of life, faith in God, and hope for man. They had a future and knew it. The semi-paganism of the Renaissance had not, and did not know it had not.

We may close this series of Renaissance representations by *A Toccata of Galuppi's*. It cannot take rank with the others as a representative poem. It is of a different class; a changeful dream of images and thoughts which came to Browning as he was playing a piece of eighteenth-century Venetian music. But in the dream there is a sketch of that miserable life of fruitless pleasure, the other side of which was dishonourable poverty, into which Venetian society had fallen in the eighteenth century. To this the pride, the irreligion, the immorality, the desire of knowledge and beauty for their own sake alone, had brought the noblest, wisest, and most useful city in Italy. That part of the poem is representative. It is the end of such a society as is drawn in *The Bishop orders his Tomb at St. Praxed's Church*. That tomb is placed in Rome, but it is in Venice that this class of tombs reached their greatest splendour of pride, opulence, folly, debasement and irreligion.

Finally, there are a few poems which paint the thoughts, the sorrows, the pleasures, and the political passions of modern Italy. There is the *Italian in England*, full of love for the Italian peasant and of pity for the patriot forced to live and die far from his motherland. Mazzini used to read it to his fellow-exiles to show them how fully an English poet could enter into the temper of their soul. So far it may be said to represent a type. But it scarcely comes under the range of this chapter. But *Up in a Villa, down in the City*, is so vivid a representation of all that pleased a whole type of the city-bred and poor nobles of Italy at the time when Browning wrote the *Dramatic Lyrics* that I cannot omit it. It is an admirable piece of work, crowded with keen descriptions of nature in the Casentino, and of life in the streets of Florence. And every piece of description is so filled with the character of the " Italian person of quality " who describes them—a petulant, humorous, easily angered, happy, observant, ignorant, poor gentleman —that Browning entirely disappears. The poem retains for us in its verse, and indeed in its light rhythm, the childlikeness, the *naïveté*, the simple pleasures, the ignorance, and the honest boredom with the solitudes of nature—of a whole class of Italians, not only of the time when it was written, but of the present day. It is a delightful, inventive piece of gay and pictorial humour.

CHAPTER XIII

WOMANHOOD IN BROWNING

THE first woman we meet in Browning's poetry is Pauline; a twofold person, exceedingly unlike the woman usually made by a young poet. She is not only the Pauline idealised and also materialised by the selfish passion of her lover, but also the real woman whom Browning has conceived underneath the lover's image of her. This doubling of his personages, as seen under two diverse aspects or by two different onlookers, in the same poem, is not unfrequent in his poetry, and it pleased his intellect to make these efforts. When the thing was well done, its cleverness was amazing, even imaginative; when it was ill done, it was confusing. Tennyson never did this; he had not analytic power enough. What he sees of his personages is all one, quite clearly drawn and easy to understand. But we miss in them, and especially in his women, the intellectual play, versatility and variety of Browning. Tennyson's women sometimes border on dulness, are without that movement, change and surprises, which in women disturb mankind for evil or for good. If Tennyson had had a little more of Browning's imaginative analysis, and Browning a little less of it, both would have been better artists.

The Pauline of the lover is the commonplace woman whom a young man so often invents out of a woman for his use and pleasure. She is to be his salvation, to sympathise with his ideals, joys and pains, to give him everything, with herself, and to live for him and him alone. Nothing can be more *naif* and simple than this common selfishness which forgets that a woman has her own life, her own claim on the man, and her own individuality to develop; and this element in the poem, which never occurs again in Browning's poetry, may be the record of an early experience. If so, he had escaped from this youthful error before he had finished the poem, and despised it, perhaps too much. It is excusable and natural in the young. His contempt for this kind of love is embodied in the second Pauline. She is not the woman her lover imagines her to be, but far older and more experienced than her lover; who has known long ago what love was; who always liked to be loved, who therefore suffers her lover to expatiate as wildly as he pleases; but whose life is quite apart from him, enduring him with pleasurable patience, criticising him, wondering how he can be so excited. There is a dim perception in the lover's phrases of these elements in his mistress' character; and that they are in her character is quite plain from the patronising piece of criticism in French which Browning has put into her mouth. The first touch of his humour appears in the contrast of the gentle and lofty boredom of the letter with the torrents of love in the poem. And if we may imagine that the lover is partly an image of what Browning once felt in a youthful love, we may also think that the making of the second and critical Pauline was his record, when his love had passed, of what he thought about it all.

This mode of treatment, so much more analytic than imaginative, belongs to Browning as an artist. He seems, while he wrote, as if half of him sat apart from the personages he was making, contemplating them in his observant fashion, discussing them coolly in his mind while the other half of him wrote about them with emotion; placing them in different situations and imagining what they would then do; inventing trials for them and recombining, through these trials, the elements of their characters; arguing about and around them, till he sometimes loses the unity of their personality. This is a weakness in his work when he has to create characters in a drama who may be said, like Shakespeare's, to have, once he has created them, a life of their own independent of the poet. His spinning of his own thoughts about their characters makes us often realise, in his dramas, the individuality of Browning more than the individuality of the characters. We follow him at this work with keen intellectual pleasure, but we do not always follow him with a passionate humanity.

On the contrary, this habit, which was one cause of his weakness as an artist in the drama, increased his strength as an artist when he made single pictures of men and women at isolated crises in their lives; or when he pictured them as they seemed at the moment to one, two, or three differently tempered persons—pictorial sketches and studies which we may hang up in the chambers of the mind for meditation or discussion. Their intellectual power and the emotional interest they awaken, the vivid imaginative lightning which illuminates them in flashes, arise out of that part of his nature which made him a weak dramatist.

Had he chosen, for example, to paint Lady Carlisle as he conceived her, in an isolated portrait, and in the same circumstances as in his drama of *Strafford*, we should have had a clear and intimate picture of her moving, alive at every point, amidst the decay and shipwreck of the Court. But in the play she is a shade who comes and goes, unoutlined, confused and confusing, scarcely a woman at all. The only clear hints of what Browning meant her to be are given in the *asides* of Strafford.

Browning may have been content with *Strafford* as a whole, but, with his passion for vitality, he could not have been content with either Lady Carlisle or the Queen as representatives of women. Indeed, up to this point, when he had written *Pauline*, *Paracelsus* and *Strafford*, he must have felt that he had left out of his poetry one half of the human race; and his ambition was to represent both men and women. Pauline's chief appearance is in French prose. Michel, in *Paracelsus*, is a mere silhouette of the sentimental German Frau, a soft sympathiser with her husband and with the young eagle Paracelsus, who longs to leave the home she would not leave for the world—an excellent and fruitful mother. She is set in a pleasant garden landscape. Twice Browning tries to get more out of her and to lift her into reality. But the men carry him away from her, and she remains undrawn. These mere images, with the exception of the woman in *Porphyria's Lover*, who, with a boldness which might have astonished even Byron but is characteristic of Browning in his audacious youth, leaves the ball to visit her lover in the cottage in the garden—are all that he had made of womanhood in 1837, four years after he had begun to publish poetry.

It was high time he should do something better, and he had now begun to know more of the variousness of women and of their resolute grip on life and affairs. So, in *Sordello*, he created Palma. She runs through the poem, and her appearances mark turning points in Sordello's development; but thrice she appears in full colour and set in striking circumstances—first, in the secret room of the palace at Verona with Sordello when she expounds her policy, and afterwards leans with him amid a gush of torch-fire over the balcony, whence the grey-haired councillors spoke to the people surging in the square and shouting for the battle. The second time is in the streets of Ferrara, full of camping men and fires; and the third is when she waits with Taurello in the vaulted room below the chamber where Sordello has been left to decide what side he shall take, for the Emperor or the Pope. He dies while they wait, but there is no finer passage in the poem than this of Palma and Taurello talking in the dim corridor of the new world they would make for North Italy with Sordello. It is not dramatic characterisation, but magnificent individualisation of the woman and the man.

We see Palma first as a girl at Goito, where she fills Sordello with dreams, and Browning gives her the beauty of the Venetians Titian painted.

> How the tresses curled
> Into a sumptuous swell of gold and wound
> About her like a glory! even the ground
> Was bright as with spilt sunbeams:

Full consciousness of her beauty is with her, frank triumph in it; but she is still a child. At the Court of Love she is a woman, not only conscious of her loveliness, but able to use it to bind and loose, having sensuous witchery and intellectual power, that terrible combination. She lays her magic on Sordello.

But she is not only the woman of personal magic and beauty. Being of high rank and mixed with great events, she naturally becomes the political woman, a common type in the thirteenth century. And Browning gives her the mental power to mould and direct affairs. She uses her personal charm to lure Sordello into politics.

> Her wise
> And lulling words are yet about the room,
> Her presence wholly poured upon the gloom
> Down even to her vesture's creeping stir.
> And so reclines he, saturate with her.
> * * * * *
> But when she felt she held her friend indeed
> Safe, she threw back her curls, began implant
> Her lessons;

Her long discourse on the state of parties, and how Sordello may, in mastering them, complete his being, fascinates him and us by the charm of her intelligence.

But the political woman has often left love behind. Politics, like devotion, are a woman's reaction from the weariness of loving and being loved. But Palma is young, and in the midst of her politics she retains passion, sentiment, tenderness and charm. She dreams of some soul beyond her own, who, coming, should call on all the force in her character; enable her, in loving him, to give consummation to her work for Italy; and be himself the hand and sword of her mind. Therefore she held herself in leash till the right man came, till she loved. "Waits he not," her heart cries, and mixes him with coming Spring:

> Waits he not the waking year?
> His almond blossoms must be honey-ripe
> By this; to welcome him, fresh runnels stripe
> The thawed ravines; because of him, the wind
> Walks like a herald. I shall surely find
> Him now.

She finds him in Sordello, and summons him, when the time is ripe, to Verona. Love and ambition march together in her now. In and out of all her schemes Sordello moves. The glory of her vision of North Italian rule is like a halo round his brow. Not one political purpose is lost, but all are transfigured in her by love. Softness and strength, intellect and feeling meet in her. This is a woman nobly carved, and the step from Michel, Pauline and Lady Carlisle to her is an immense one.

By exercise of his powers Browning's genius had swiftly developed. There comes a time, sooner or later, to a great poet when, after many experiments, the doors of his intellect and soul fly open, and his genius is flooded with the action and thought of what seems a universe. And with this revelation of Man and Nature, a tidal wave of creative power, new and impelling, carries the poet far beyond the station where last he rested. It came to Browning now. The creation of Palma would be enough to prove it, but there is not a character or scene in *Sordello* which does not also prove it.

In this new outrush of his genius he created a very different woman from Palma. He created Pippa, the Asolan girl, at the other end of society from Palma, at the other end of feminine character. Owing to the host of new thoughts which in this early summer of genius came pouring into his soul —all of which he tried to express, rejecting none, choosing none out of the rest, expressing only half of a great number of them; so delighted with them all that he could leave none out—he became obscure in *Sordello*. Owing also to the great complexity of the historical *mise-en-scène* in which he placed his characters in that poem, he also became obscure. Had he been an experienced artist he would have left out at least a third of the thoughts and scenes he inserted. As it was, he threw all his thoughts and all the matters he had learnt about the politics, cities, architecture, customs, war, gardens, religion and poetry of North Italy in the thirteenth century, pell-mell into this poem, and left them, as it were, to find their own places. This was very characteristic of a young man when the pot of his genius was boiling over. Nothing bolder, more incalculable, was ever done by a poet in the period of his storm and stress. The boundless and to express it, was never sought with more audacity. It was impossible, in this effort, for him to be clear, and we need not be vexed with him. The daring, the rush, the unconsciousness and the youth of it all, are his excuse, but not his praise. And when the public comes to understand that the dimness and complexity of *Sordello* arise from plenteousness not scarcity of thought, and that they were not a pose of the poet's but the natural leaping of a full fountain just let loose from its mountain chamber, it will have a personal liking, not perhaps for the poem but for Browning. "I will not read the book," it will say, "but I am glad he had it in him."

Still it was an artistic failure, and when Browning understood that the public could not comprehend him—and we must remember that he desired to be comprehended, for he loved mankind—he thought he would use his powers in a simpler fashion, and please the honest folk. So, in the joy of having got rid in *Sordello* of so many of his thoughts by expression and of mastering the rest; and determined, since he had been found difficult, to be the very opposite—loving contrast like a poet—he wrote *Pippa Passes*. I need not describe its plan. Our business is with the women in it.

Ottima, alive with carnal passion, in the fire of which the murder of her husband seems a mere incident, is an audacious sketch, done in splashes of ungradated colour. Had Browning been more in the woman's body and soul he would not have done her in jerks as he has done. Her trick of talking of the landscape, as if she were on a holiday like Pippa, is not as subtly conceived or executed as it should be, and is too far away from her dominant carnality to be natural. And her sensualism is too coarse for her position. A certain success is attained, but the imagination is frequently jarred. The very outburst of unsensual love at the end, when her love passes from the flesh into the spirit, when self-sacrifice dawns upon her and she begins to suffer the first agonies of redemption, is plainly more due to the poet's pity than to the woman's spirit. Again, Sebald is the first to feel remorse after the murder. Ottima only begins to feel it when she thinks her lover is ceasing to love her. I am not sure that to reverse the whole situation would not be nearer to the truth of things; but that is matter of discussion. Then the subject-matter is sordid. Nothing relieves the coarseness of Sebald, Ottima and Luca and their relations to one another but the few descriptions of nature and the happy flash of innocence when Pippa passes by. Nor are there any large fates behind the tale or large effects to follow which might lift the crime into dignity. This mean, commonplace, ugly kind of subject had a strange attraction for Browning, as we see in *The Inn Album*, in *Red Cotton Night-Cap Country*, and elsewhere. I may add that it is curious to find him, in 1841, writing exactly like a modern realist, nearly fifty years before realism of this kind had begun. And this illustrates what I have said of the way in which he anticipated by so many years the kind of work to which the literary world should come. The whole scene between Sebald and Ottima might have been written by a powerful, relentless modern novelist.

We have more of this realism, but done with great skill, humanity, even tenderness, in the meeting and talk of the young harlotry on the steps of the Duomo near the fountain. When we think of this piece of bold, clear, impressionist reality cast into the midst of the proprieties of literature in

1841, it is impossible not to wonder and smile. The girls are excellently drawn and varied from each other. Browning's pity gathers round them, and something of underlying purity, of natural grace of soul, of tenderness in memory of their youth emerges in them; and the charm of their land is round their ways. There was also in his mind, I think, a sense of picturesqueness in their class when they were young, which, mingling with his pity for them, attracted his imagination, or touched into momentary life that roving element in a poet which resents the barriers made by social and domestic purity. *Fifine at the Fair* is partly a study of that temper which comes and goes, goes and comes in the life not only of poets but of ordinary men and women.

Then, to illustrate this further, there is in *Sordello* a brilliant sketch of girls of this kind at Venice, full of sunlight, colour and sparkling water, in which he has seen these butterflies of women as a painter would see them, or as a poet who, not thinking then of moral questions or feeling pity for their fate, is satisfied for the flying moment with the picture they make, with the natural freedom of their life.

But he does not leave that picture without a representation of the other side of this class of womanhood. It was a daring thing, when he wished to say that he would devote his whole work to the love and representation of humanity to symbolise it by a sorrowful street-girl in Venice who wistfully asks an alms; worn and broken with sorrow and wrong; whose eyes appeal for pity, for comprehension of her good and for his love; and whose fascination and beauty are more to him than those of her unsuffering companions. The other side of that class of women is here given with clear truth and just compassion, and the representation is lifted into imaginative strength, range and dignity of thought and feeling by her being made the image of the whole of humanity. "This woman," he thought, "is humanity, whom I love, who asks the poet in me to reveal her as she is, a divine seed of God to find some day its flowering—the broken harlot of the universe, who will be, far off, the Magdalen redeemed by her ineradicable love. That, and with every power I have, I will, as poet, love and represent."

This is the imagination working at its best, with its most penetrative and passionate power, and Browning is far greater as a poet in this Thing of his, where thought and love are knit into union to give birth to moral, intellectual and spiritual beauty, than he is in those lighter and cleverer poems in which he sketches with a facile but too discursive a pencil, the transient moments, grave or light, of the lives of women. Yet this and they show his range, his variety, the embracing of his sympathy.

Over against these girls in the market-place, against Ottima in her guilt, and Phene who is as yet a nonentity (her speech to the sculptor is too plainly Browning's analysis of the moment, not her own thinking—no girl of fourteen brought up by Natalia would talk in that fashion) is set Pippa, the light, life and love of the day, the town, the people and the poem. She passes like an angel by and touches with her wing events and persons and changes them to good. She has some natural genius, and is as unconscious of her genius as she is of the good she does. In her unconsciousness is the fountain of her charm. She lives like a flower of the field that knows not it has blest and comforted with its beauty the travellers who have passed it by. She has only one day in the whole year for her own, and for that day she creates a fresh personality for herself. She clothes her soul, intellect, imagination, and spiritual aspiration in holiday garments for the day, becoming for the time a new poetic self, and able to choose any other personality in Asolo from hour to hour—the queen and spirit of the town; not wishing to be, actually, the folk she passes by, but only, since she is so isolated, to be something in their lives, to touch them for help and company.

The world of nature speaks to her and loves her. She sees all that is beautiful, feeds on it, and grasps the matter of thought that underlies the beauty. And so much is she at home with nature that she is able to describe with ease in words almost as noble as the thing itself the advent of the sun. When she leaps out of her bed to meet the leap of the sun, the hymn of description she sings might be sung by the Hours themselves as they dance round the car of the god. She can even play with the great Mother as with an equal, or like her child. The charming gaiety with which she speaks to the sunlights that dance in her room, and to the flowers which are her sisters, prove, however isolated her life may be, that she is never alone. Along with this brightness she has seriousness, the sister of her gaiety; the deep seriousness of imagination, the seriousness also of the evening when meditation broods over the day and its doings before sleep. These, with her sweet humanity, natural piety, instinctive purity, compose her of soft sunshine and soft shadow. Nor does her sadness at the close, which is overcome by her trust in God, make her less but more dear to us. She is a beautiful creation. There are hosts of happy women like her. They are the salt of the earth. But few poets have made so much of them and so happily, or sung about these birds of God so well as Browning has in *Pippa Passes*.

That was in 1841. Pleased with his success in this half-lyrical, half-dramatic piece, he was lured towards the drama again, and also to try his hand at those short lyrics—records of transient emotion on fanciful subjects—or records of short but intense moments of thought or feeling. It is a pity that he did not give to dramatic lyrics (in which species of poetry he is quite our first master) the time he gave to dramas, in which he is not much better than an amateur. Nevertheless, we cannot omit the women in the dramas. I have already written of Lady Carlisle. Polyxena, in *King Victor and King Charles*, is partly the political woman and partly the sensible and loving wife of a strangely tempered man. She is fairly done, but is not interesting. Good womanly intelligence in affairs, good womanly support of her man; clear womanly insight into men and into intrigue—a woman of whom there are hundreds of thousands in every rank of life. In her, as in so much of Browning's work, the intellect of the woman is of a higher quality than the intellect of the man.

Next, among his women, is Anael in the *Return*

of the Druses. She is placed in too unnatural a situation to allow her nature to have fair play. In the preternatural world her superstition creates, she adores Djabal, murders the Prefect, and dies by her own hand. She is, in that world, a study of a young girl's enthusiasm for her faith and her country, and for the man she thinks divine; and were the subject, so far as it relates to her character, well or clearly wrought, she might be made remarkable. As it is wrought, it is so intertwisted with complex threads of thought and passion that any clear outline of her character is lost. Both Djabal and she are like clouds illuminated by flashes of sheet lightning which show an infinity of folds and shapes of vapour in each cloud, but show them only for an instant; and then, when the flashes come again, show new folds, new involutions. The characters are not allowed by Browning to develop themselves.

Anael, when she is in the preternatural world, loves Djabal as an incarnation of the divine, but in the natural world of her girlhood her heart goes out to the Knight of Malta who loves her. The in-and-out of these two emotional states—one in the world of religious enthusiasm, and one in her own womanhood, as they cross and re-cross one another—is elaborated with merciless analysis; and Anael's womanhood appears, not as a whole, but in bits and scraps. How will this young girl, divided by two contemporaneous emotions, one in the supernatural and one in the natural world, act in a crisis of her life? Well, the first, conquering the second, brings about her death the moment she tries to transfer the second into the world of the

Y

first—her dim, half-conscious love for Lois into her conscious adoration of Djabal.

Mildred and Guendolen are the two women in *A Blot in the 'Scutcheon*. Guendolen is the incarnation of high-hearted feminine commonsense, of clear insight into the truth of things, born of the power of love in her. Amid all the weaknesses of the personages and the plot; in the wildered situation made by a confused clashing of pride and innocence and remorse, in which Browning, as it were on purpose to make a display of his intellectual ability, involves those poor folk —Guendolen is the rock on which we can rest in peace; the woman of the world, yet not worldly; full of experience, yet having gained by every experience more of love; just and strong yet pitiful, and with a healthy but compassionate contempt for the intelligence of the men who belong to her.

Contrasted with her, and the quality of her love contrasted also, is Mildred, the innocent child girl who loves for love's sake, and continues to be lost in her love. But Browning's presentation of her innocence, her love, is spoiled by the over-remorse, shame and fear under whose power he makes her so helpless. They are in the circumstances so unnaturally great that they lower her innocence and love, and the natural courage of innocence and love. These rise again to their first level, but it is only the passion of her lover's death which restores them. And when they recur, she is outside of girlhood. One touch of the courage she shows in the last scene would have saved in the previous scene herself, her lover, and her brother. The lie she lets her brother infer when she allows him to think that the lover she has confessed to is not the Earl, yet that she will marry the Earl, degrades her altogether and justly in her brother's eyes, and is so terribly out of tune with her character that I repeat I cannot understand how Browning could invent that situation. It spoils the whole presentation of the girl. It is not only out of her character, it is out of nature. Indeed, in spite of the poetry, in spite of the pathetic beauty of the last scene, Mildred and Tresham are always over-heightened, over-strained beyond the concert-pitch of nature. But the drawing of the woman's character suffers more from this than the man's, even though Tresham, in the last scene, is half turned into a woman. Sex seems to disappear in that scene.

A different person is Colombe, the Duchess in *Colombe's Birthday*. That play, as I have said, gets on, but it gets on because Colombe moves every one in the play by her own motion. From beginning to end of the action she is the fire and the soul of it. Innocent, frank and brave, simple and constant among a group of false and worldly courtiers, among whom she moves like the white Truth, untouched as yet by love or by the fates of her position, she is suddenly thrown into a whirlpool of affairs and of love; and her simplicity, clearness of intelligence, unconscious rightness of momentary feeling, which comes of her not thinking about her feelings—that rare and precious element in character—above all, her belief in love as the one worthy thing in the world, bring her out of the whirlpool, unshipwrecked, unstained by a single wave of ill-feeling or mean thinking, into a quiet harbour of affection and of power. For she will influence Berthold all his life long.

She is herself lovely. Valence loves her at sight. Her love for Valence is born before she knows it, and the touch of jealousy, which half reveals it to her, is happily wrought by Browning. When she finds out that Valence did for love of her what she thought was done for loyalty alone to her, she is a little revolted; her single-heartedness is disappointed. She puts aside her growing love, which she does not know as yet is love, and says she will find out if Berthold wishes to marry her because he loves her, or for policy. Berthold is as honest as she is, and tells her love has nothing to do with the matter. The thought of an untrue life with Berthold then sends her heart with a rush back to Valence, and she chooses love and obscurity with Valence. It is the portrait of incarnate truth, in vivid contrast to Constance, who is a liar in grain.

Constance is the heroine of the fragment of a drama called *In a Balcony*. Norbert, a young diplomat, has served the Queen, who is fifty years old, for a year, all for the love of Constance, a cousin and dependent of the Queen. He tells Constance he will now, as his reward, ask the Queen for her hand. Constance says, "No; that will ruin us both; temporise; tell the Queen, who is hungry for love, that you love her; and that, as she cannot marry a subject, you will be content with me, whom the Queen loves." Norbert objects, and no wonder, to this lying business, but he does it; and the Queen runs to Constance, crying, "I am loved, thank God! I will throw everything aside and marry him. I thought he loved you, but he loves me." Then Constance, wavering from truth again, says that the Queen is right. Norbert does love her. And this is supposed by some to be a noble self-sacrifice, done in pity for the Queen. It is much more like jealousy.

Then, finding that all Norbert's future depends on the Queen, she is supposed to sacrifice herself again, this time for Norbert's sake. She will give him up to the Queen, for the sake of his career; and she tells the Queen, before Norbert, that he has confessed to her his love for the Queen—another lie! Norbert is indignant—he may well be—and throws down all this edifice of falsehood. The Queen knows then the truth, and leaves them in a fury. Constance and Norbert fly into each other's arms, and the tramp of the soldiers who come to arrest them is heard as the curtain falls.

I do not believe that Browning meant to make self-sacrifice the root of Constance's doings. If he did, he has made a terrible mess of the whole thing. He was much too clear-headed a moralist to link self-sacrifice to systematic lying. Self-sacrifice is not self-sacrifice at all when it sacrifices truth. It may wear the clothes of Love, but, in injuring righteousness, it injures the essence of love. It has a surface beauty, for it imitates love, but if mankind is allured by this beauty, mankind is injured. It is the false Florimel of self-sacrifice. Browning, who had studied self-sacrifice, did not exhibit it in Constance. There is something else at the root of her actions, and I believe he meant it to be jealousy. The very first lie she urges her lover to tell (that is, to let the Queen imagine he loves her) is just the thing a jealous woman would invent to try her lover and the Queen, if she suspected the Queen of loving him, and him of being seduced from her by the worldly advantage of marrying the Queen. And all the other lies are best explained on the supposition of jealous experiments. At the last she is satisfied; the crowning test had been tried. Through a sea of lying she had made herself sure of Norbert's love, and she falls into his arms. Had Browning meant Constance to be an image of self-sacrifice, he would scarcely have written that line when Norbert, having told the truth of the matter to the Queen, looks at both women, and cries out, "You two glare, each at each, like panthers now." A woman, filled with the joy and sadness of pure self-sacrifice, would not have felt at this moment like a panther towards the woman for whom she had sacrificed herself.

Even as a study of jealousy, Constance is too subtle. Jealousy has none of these labyrinthine methods; it goes straight with fiery passion to its end. It may be said, then, that Constance is not a study of jealousy. But it may be a study by Browning of what he thought in his intellect jealousy would be. At any rate, Constance, as a study of self-sacrifice, is a miserable failure. Moreover, it does not make much matter whether she is a study of this or that, because she is eminently wrong-natured. Her lying is unendurable, only to be explained or excused by the madness of jealousy, and she, though jealous, is not maddened enough by jealousy to excuse her lies. The situations she causes are almost too ugly. Whenever the truth is told, either by the Queen or Norbert, the situations break up in disgrace for her. It is difficult to imagine how Norbert could go on loving her. His love would have departed if they had come to live together. He is radically true, and she is radically false. A fatal split would have been inevitable. Nothing could be better for them both—after their momentary outburst of love at the end—than death.

From the point of view of art, Constance is interesting. It is more than we can say of Domizia in *Luria*. She is nothing more than a passing study whom Browning uses to voice his theories. Eulalia in *A Soul's Tragedy* is also a transient thing, only she is more colourless, more a phantom than Domizia.

By this time, by the year 1846, Browning had found out that he could not write dramas well, or even such dramatic proverbs as *In a Balcony*. And he gave himself up to another species of his art. The women he now draws (some of which belong to the years during which he wrote dramas) are done separately, in dramatic lyrics as he called them, and in narrative and philosophical poems. Some are touched only at moments of their lives, and we are to infer from the momentary action and feeling the whole of the woman. Others are carefully and lovingly drawn from point to point in a variety of action, passion and circumstance. In these we find Browning at his best in the drawing of women. I know no women among the second-rate poets so sweetly, nobly, tenderly and wisely drawn as Pompilia and Balaustion.

CHAPTER XIV

WOMANHOOD IN BROWNING
(THE DRAMATIC LYRICS AND POMPILIA)

NO modern poet has written of women with such variety as Browning. Coleridge, except in a few love-poems, scarcely touched them. Wordsworth did not get beyond the womanhood of the home affections, except in a few lovely and spiritual sketches of girlhood which are unique in our literature, in which maidenhood and the soul of nature so interchange their beauty that the girl seems born of the lonely loveliness of nature and lives with her mother like a child.

What motherhood in its deep grief and joy, what sisterhood and wifehood may be, have never been sung with more penetration and exquisiteness than Wordsworth sang them. But of the immense range, beyond, of womanhood he could not sing. Byron's women are mostly in love with Byron under various names, and he rarely strays beyond the woman who is loved or in love. The woman who is most vital, true and tender is Haidée in *Don Juan*. Shelley's women melt into philosophic mist, or are used to build up a political or social theory, as if they were "properties" of literature. Cythna, Rosalind, Asia, Emilia are ideas, not realities. Beatrice is alive, but she was drawn for him in the records of her trial. Even the woman of his later lyrics soon ceases to be flesh and blood. Keats let women alone, save in Isabella, and all that is of womanhood in her is derived from Boccaccio. Madeline is nothing but a picture. It is curious that his remarkable want of interest in the time in which he lived should be combined with as great a want of interest in women, as if the vivid life of any period in the history of a people were bound up with the vivid life of women in that period. When women awake no full emotion in a poet, the life of the time, as in the case of Keats, awakes little emotion in him. He will fly to the past for his subjects. Moreover, it is perhaps worth saying that when the poets cease to write well about women, the phase of poetry they represent, however beautiful it be, is beginning to decay. When poetry is born into a new life, women are as living in it as men. Womanhood became at once one of its dominant subjects in Tennyson and Browning. Among the new political, social, religious, philosophic and artistic ideas which were then borne like torches through England, the idea of the free development of women was also born; and it carried with it a strong emotion. They claimed the acknowledgment of their separate individuality, of their distinct use and power in the progress of the world. This was embodied with extraordinary fulness in *Aurora Leigh*, and its emotion drove itself into the work of Tennyson and Browning. How Tennyson treated the subject in the *Princess* is well known. His representation of women in his other poems does not pass beyond a few simple, well-known types both of good and bad women. But the particular types into which the variety of womanhood continually throws itself, the quick individualities, the fantastic simplicities and subtleties, the resolute extremes, the unconsidered impulses, the obstinate good and evil, the bold cruelties and the bold self-sacrifices, the fears and audacities, the hidden work of the thoughts and passions of women in the far-off worlds within them where their soul claims and possesses its own desires —these were beyond the power of Tennyson to describe, even, I think, to conceive. But they were in the power of Browning, and he made them, at least in lyric poetry, a chief part of his work.

In women he touched great variety and great individuality; two things each of which includes the other, and both of which were dear to his imagination. With his longing for variety of representation, he was not content to pile womanhood up into a few classes, or to dwell on her universal qualities. He took each woman separately, marking out the points which differentiated her from, not those which she shared with, the rest of her sex. He felt that if he dwelt only on the deep-seated roots of the tree of womanhood, he would miss the endless play, fancy, movement, interaction and variety of its branches, foliage and flowers. Therefore, in his lyrical work, he leaves out for the most part the simpler elements of womanhood and draws the complex, the particular, the impulsive and the momentary. Each of his women is distinct from the rest. That is a great comfort in a world which, through laziness, wishes to busy itself with classes rather than with personalities. I do not believe that Browning ever met man or woman without saying to himself—Here is a new world; it may be classed, but it also stands alone. What distinguishes it from the rest—that I will know and that describe.

When women are not enslaved to conventions—and the new movement towards their freedom of development which began shortly after 1840 had enfranchised and has continued ever since to enfranchise a great number from this slavery—they are more individual and various than men are allowed to be. They carry their personal desires, aspirations and impulses into act, speech, and into extremes with much greater licence than is possible to men. One touches with them much more easily the original stuff of humanity. It was this original, individual and various Thing in women on which Browning seized with delight. He did not write half as much as other poets had done of woman as being loved by man or as loving him. I have said that the mere love-poem is no main element in his work. He wrote of the original stuff of womanhood, of its good and bad alike, sometimes of it as all good, as in Pompilia; but for the most part as mingled of good and ill, and of the good as destined to conquer the ill.

He did not exalt her above man. He thought her as vital, interesting and important for progress as man, but not more interesting, vital, or important. He neither lowered her nor idealised her beyond natural humanity. She stands in his poetry side by side with man on an equality of value to the present and future of mankind. And he has wrought this out not by elaborate statement of it in a theory, as Tennyson did in the *Princess* with a conscious patronage of womanhood, but by unconscious representation of it in the multitude of women whom he invented.

But though the wholes were equal, the particulars of which the wholes were composed differed in their values; and women in his view were more keenly alive than men, at least more various in their manifestation of life. It was their intensity of life which most attracted him. He loved nothing so much as life—in plant or animal or man. His longer poems are records of the larger movement of human life, the steadfast record in quiet verse as in *Paracelsus*, or the clashing together in abrupt verse as in *Sordello*, of the turmoil and meditation, the trouble and joy of the living soul of humanity. When he, this archangel of reality, got into touch with pure fact of the human soul, beating with life, he was enchanted. And this was his vast happiness in his longest poem, the *Ring and the Book*—

> Do you see this square old yellow book I toss
> I' the air, and catch again, and twirl about
> By the crumpled vellum covers—pure crude fact
> Secreted from man's life when hearts beat hard
> And brains, high blooded, ticked two centuries hence?
> Give it me back. The thing's restorative
> I' the touch and sight.

But in his lyrics, it was not the steady development of life on which he loved to write, but the unexpected, original movement of life under the push of quick thought and sudden passion into some new form of action which broke through the commonplace of existence. Men and women, and chiefly women, when they spoke and acted on a keen edge of life with a precipice below them or on the summit of the moment, with straight and clear intensity, and out of the original stuff of their nature—were his darling lyric subjects. And he did this work in lyrics, because the lyric is the poem of the moment.

There was one of these critical moments which attracted him greatly—that in which all after-life is contained and decided; when a step to the right or left settles, in an instant, the spiritual basis of the soul. I have already mentioned some of these poems—those concerned with love, such as *By the Fireside* or *Cristina*—and the woman is more prominent in them than the man. One of the best of them, so far as the drawing of a woman is concerned, is *Dîs aliter visum*. We see the innocent girl, and ten years after what the world has made of her. But the heart of the girl lies beneath the woman of the world. And she recalls to the man the hour when they lingered near the church on the cliff; when he loved her, when he might have claimed her, and did not. He feared they might repent of it; sacrificing to the present their chance of the eternities of love. "Fool! who ruined four lives—mine and your opera-dancer's, your own and my husband's!" Whether her outburst now be quite true to her whole self or not Browning does not let us know; but it is true to that moment of her, and it is full of the poetry of the moment she recalls. Moreover, these thirty short verses paint as no other man could have done the secret soul of a woman in society. I quote her outburst. It is full of Browning's keen poetry; and the first verse of it may well be compared with a similar moment in *By the Fireside*, where nature is made to play the same part, but succeeds as here she fails:

> Now I may speak: you fool, for all
>   Your lore! Who made things plain in vain?
>   What was the sea for? What, the grey
>   Sad church, that solitary day,
> Crosses and graves and swallows' call?
>
> Was there nought better than to enjoy?
>   No feat which, done, would make time break,
>   And let us pent-up creatures through
>   Into eternity, our due?
> No forcing earth teach heaven's employ?
>
> No wise beginning, here and now,
>   What cannot grow complete (earth's feat)
>   And heaven must finish, there and then?
>   No tasting earth's true food for men,
> Its sweet in sad, its sad in sweet?
>
> No grasping at love, gaining a share
>   O' the sole spark from God's life at strife
>   With death, so, sure of range above
>   The limits here? For us and love,
> Failure; but, when God fails, despair.
>
> This you call wisdom? Thus you add
>   Good unto good again, in vain?
>   You loved, with body worn and weak;
>   I loved, with faculties to seek:
> Were both loves worthless since ill-clad?
>
> Let the mere star-fish in his vault
>   Crawl in a wash of weed, indeed,
>   Rose-jacynth to the finger tips:
>   He, whole in body and soul, outstrips
> Man, found with either in default.
>
> But what's whole, can increase no more,
>   Is dwarfed and dies, since here's its sphere.
>   The devil laughed at you in his sleeve!
>   You knew not? That I well believe;
> Or you had saved two souls: nay, four.

> For Stephanie sprained last night her wrist,
>   Ankle or something. "Pooh," cry you?
> At any rate she danced, all say,
>   Vilely; her vogue has had its day.
> Here comes my husband from his whist.

Here the woman speaks for herself. It is characteristic of Browning's boldness that there are a whole set of poems in which he imagines the unexpressed thoughts which a woman revolves in self-communion under the questionings and troubles of the passions, and chiefly of the passion of love. The most elaborate of these is *James Lee's Wife*, which tells what she thinks of when after long years she has been unable to retain her husband's love. Finally, she leaves him. The analysis of her thinking is interesting, but the woman is not. She is not the quick, natural woman Browning was able to paint so well when he chose. His own analytic excitement, which increases in mere intellectuality as the poem moves on, enters into her, and she thinks more through Browning the man than through her womanhood. Women are complex enough, more complex than men, but they are not complex in the fashion of this poem. Under the circumstances Browning has made, her thought would have been quite clear at its root, and indeed in its branches. She is represented as in love with her husband. Were she really in love, she would not have been so involved, or able to argue out her life so anxiously. Love or love's sorrow knows itself at once and altogether, and its cause and aim are simple. But Browning has unconsciously made the woman clear enough for us to guess the real cause of her departure. That departure is believed by some to be a self-sacrifice. There are folk who see self-sacrifice in everything Browning wrote about women. Browning may have originally intended her action to be one of self-sacrifice, but the thing, as he went on, was taken out of his hands, and turns out to be quite a different matter. The woman really leaves her husband because her love for him was tired out. She talks of leaving her husband free, and perhaps, in women's way, persuades herself that she is sacrificing herself; but she desires in reality to set herself free from an unavailing struggle to keep his love. There comes a time when the striving for love wearies out love itself. And James Lee's wife had reached that moment. Her departure, thus explained, is the most womanly thing in the poem, and I should not wonder if Browning meant it so. He knew what self-sacrifice really was, and this departure of the woman was not a true self-sacrifice.

Another of these poems in which a woman speaks out her heart is *Any Wife to any Husband*. She is dying, and she would fain claim his undying fidelity to his love of her; but though she believes in his love, she thinks, when her presence is not with him, that his nature will be drawn towards other women. Then what he brings her, when he meets her again, will not be perfect. Womanly to the core, and her nature is a beautiful nature, she says nothing which is not kind and true, and the picture she draws of faithfulness, without one stain of wavering, is natural and lovely. But, for all that, it is jealousy that speaks, the desire to claim all for one's self. " Thou art mine, and mine only "—that fine selfishness which injures love so deeply in the end, because it forbids its expansion, that is, forbids the essential nature of love to act. That may be pardoned, unless in its extremes, during life, if the pardon does not increase it; but this is in the hour of death, and it is unworthy of the higher world. To carry jealousy beyond the grave is a phase of that selfish passion over which this hour, touched by the larger thought of the infinite world, should have uplifted the woman. Still, what she says is in nature, and Browning's imagination has closed passionately round his subject. But he has left us with pity for the woman rather than with admiration of her.

Perhaps the subtlest part of the poem is the impression left on us that the woman knows all her pleading will be in vain, that she has fathomed the weakness of her husband's character. He will not like to remember that knowledge of hers; and her letting him feel it is a kind of vengeance which will not help him to be faithful. It is also her worst bitterness, but if her womanhood were perfect, she would not have had that bitterness.

In these two poems, and in others, there is to be detected the deep-seated and quiet half-contempt—contempt which does not damage love, contempt which is half pity—which a woman who loves a man has for his weakness under passion or weariness. Both the wives in these poems feel that their husbands are inferior to themselves in strength of character and of intellect. To feel this is common enough in women, but is rarely confessed by them. A man scarcely ever finds it out from his own observation; he is too vain for that. But

Browning knew it. A poet sees many things, and perhaps his wife told him this secret. It was like his audacity to express it.

This increased knowledge of womanhood was probably due to the fact that Browning possessed in his wife a woman of genius who had studied her own sex in herself and in other women. It is owing to her, I think, that in so many poems the women are represented as of a finer, even a stronger intellect than the men. Many poets have given them a finer intuition; that is a common representation. But greater intellectual power allotted to women is only to be found in Browning. The instances of it are few, but they are remarkable.

It was owing also to his wife, whose relation to him was frank on all points, that Browning saw so much more clearly than other poets into the deep, curious or remote phases of the passions, thoughts and vagaries of womanhood. I sometimes wonder what women themselves think of the things Browning, speaking through their mouth, makes them say; but that is a revelation of which I have no hope, and for which, indeed, I have no desire.

Moreover, he moved a great deal in the society where women, not having any real work to do, or if they have it, not doing it, permit a greater freedom to their thoughts and impulses than those of their sex who sit at the loom of duty. Tennyson withdrew from this society, and his women are those of a retired poet—a few real types tenderly and sincerely drawn, and a few more worked out by thinking about what he imagined they would be, not by knowing them. Browning, roving through his class and other classes of society, and observing while he seemed unobservant, drew into his inner self the lives of a number of women, saw them living and feeling in a great diversity of circumstances; and, always on the watch, seized the moment into which he thought the woman entered with the greatest intensity, and smote that into a poem. Such poems, naturally lyrics, came into his head at the opera, at a ball, at a supper after the theatre, while he talked at dinner, when he walked in the park; and they record, not the whole of a woman's character, but the vision of one part of her nature which flashed before him and vanished in an instant. Among these poems are *A Light Woman, A Pretty Woman, Solomon and Balkis, Gold Hair,* and, as a fine instance of this sheet-lightning poem about women—*Adam, Lilith and Eve. Too Late* and *The Worst of It* do not belong to these slighter poems; they are on a much higher level. But they are poems of society and its secret lives. The men are foremost in them, but in each of them a different woman is sketched, through the love of the men, with a masterly decision.

Among all these women he did not hesitate to paint the types farthest removed from goodness and love. The lowest woman in the poems is she who is described in *Time's Revenges*—

> So is my spirit, as flesh with sin,
> Filled full, eaten out and in
> With the face of her, the eyes of her,
> The lips, the little chin, the stir
> Of shadow round her mouth; and she
> —I'll tell you—calmly would decree
> That I should roast at a slow fire,
> If that would compass her desire
> And make her one whom they invite
> To the famous ball to-morrow night

Contrasted with this woman, from whose brutal nature civilisation has stripped away the honour and passion of the savage, the woman of *In a Laboratory* shines like a fallen angel. She at least is natural, and though the passions she feels are the worst, yet she is capable of feeling strongly. Neither have any conscience, but we can conceive that one of these women might attain it, but the other not. Both are examples of a thing I have said is exceedingly rare in Browning's poetry—men or women left without some pity of his own touched into their circumstances or character.

In a Laboratory is a full-coloured sketch of what womanhood could become in a court like that of Francis I.; in which every shred of decency, gentlehood and honour had disappeared. Browning's description, vivid as it is, is less than the reality. Had he deepened the colours of iniquity and indecency instead of introducing so much detailed description of the laboratory, detail which weakens a little our impression of the woman, he had done better, but all the same there is no poet in England, living or dead, who could have done it so well. One of the best things in the poem is the impression made on us that it is not jealousy, but the hatred of envy which is the motive of the woman. Jealousy supposes love or the image of love, but among those who surrounded Francis, love did not exist at all, only lust, luxury and greed of power; and in the absence of love and in the scorn of it, hate and envy reign unchallenged. This is what Browning has realised in this poem, and, in this differentiation, he has given us not only historical but moral truth.

Apart from these lighter and momentary poems about women there are those written out of his own ideal of womanhood, built up not only from all he knew and loved in his wife, but also out of the dreams of his heart. They are the imaginings of the high honour and affection which a man feels for noble, natural and honest womanhood. They are touched here and there by complex thinking, but for the most part are of a beloved simplicity and tenderness, and they will always be beautiful. There is the sketch of the woman in *The Italian in England*, a never to be forgotten thing. It is no wonder the exile remembered her till he died. There is the image we form of the woman in *The Flower's Name*. He does not describe her; she is far away, but her imagined character and presence fill the garden with an incense sweeter than all the flowers, and her beauty irradiates all beauty, so delicately and so plenteously does the lover's passion make her visible. There is *Evelyn Hope*, and surely no high and pure love ever created a more beautiful soul in a woman than hers who waits her lover in the spiritual world. There are those on whom we have already dwelt—Pippa, Colombe, Mildred, Guendolen. There is the woman in the *Flight of the Duchess*; not a sketch, but a completed picture. We see her, just emerged from her convent, thrilling with eagerness to see the world, believing in its beauty, interested in everything, in the movement of the leaves on the trees, of the birds in the heaven, ready to speak to every one high or low, desirous to get at the soul of all things in Nature and Humanity, herself almost a creature of the element, akin to air and fire.

She is beaten into silence, but not crushed; overwhelmed by dry old people, by imitation of dead things, but the life in her is not slain. When the wandering gipsy claims her for a natural life, her whole nature blossoms into beauty and joy. She will have troubles great and deep, but every hour will make her conscious of more and more of life. And when she dies, it will be the beginning of an intenser life.

Finally, there is his wife. She is painted in these lyric poems with a simplicity of tenderness, with a reticence of worship as sacred as it is fair and delicate, with so intense a mingling of the ideal and the real that we never separate them, and with so much passion in remembrance of the past and in longing for the future, that no comment can enhance the picture Browning draws of her charm, her intellect and her spirit.

These pictures of womanhood were set forth before 1868, when a collected edition of his poems was published in six volumes. They were chiefly short, even impressionist studies, save those in the dramas, and Palma in *Sordello*. Those in the dramas were troubled by his want of power to shape them in that vehicle. It would have then been a pity if, in his matured strength, he had not drawn into clear existence, with full and careful, not impressionist work, and with unity of conception, some women who should, standing alone, become permanent personages in poetry; whom men and women in the future, needing friends, should love, honour and obey, and in whom, when help and sympathy and wisdom were wanted, these healing powers should be found. Browning did this for us in *Pompilia* and *Balaustion*, an Italian and a Greek girl—not an English girl. It is strange how to the very end he lived as a poet outside of his own land.

In 1868, Pompilia appeared before the world, and she has captured ever since the imagination, the conscience and the sentiment of all who love womanhood and poetry. Her character has ennobled and healed mankind. Born of a harlot, she is a star of purity; brought up by characters who love her, but who do not rise above the ordinary meanness and small commercial honesty of their class, she is always noble, generous, careless of wealth, and of a high sense of honour. It is as if Browning disdained for the time all the philosophy of heredity and environment; and indeed it was characteristic of him to believe in the sudden creation of beauty, purity and nobility out of their contraries and in spite of them. The miracle of the unrelated birth of genius—that out of the dunghill might spring the lily, and out of the stratum of crime the saint—was an article of faith with him. Nature's or God's surprises were dear to him; and nothing purer, tenderer, sweeter, more natural, womanly and saintly was ever made than Pompilia, the daughter of a vagrant impurity, the child of crime, the girl who grew to womanhood in mean and vulgar circumstances.

The only hatred she earns is the hatred of Count Guido her husband, the devil who has tortured and murdered her—the hatred of evil for good. When Count Guido, condemned to death, bursts into the unrestrained expression of his own nature, he cannot say one word about Pompilia which is not set on fire by a hell of hatred. Nothing in Browning's writing is more vivid, more intense, than these sudden outbursts of tiger fierceness against his wife. They lift and enhance the image of Pompilia.

When she comes into contact with other characters such as the Archbishop and the Governor, men overlaid with long-deposited crusts of convention, she wins a vague pity from them, but her simplicity, naturalness and saintliness are nearly as repugnant to social convention as her goodness is to villany; and Browning has, all through the poem, individualised in Pompilia the natural simplicity of goodness in opposition to the artificial moralities of conservative society. But when Pompilia touches characters who have any good, however hidden, in them, she draws forth that good. Her so-called parents pass before they die out of meanness into nobility of temper. Conti, her husband's cousin, a fat, waggish man of the world, changes into seriousness, pity and affection under her silent influence. The careless folk she meets on her flight to Rome recognise, even in most suspicious circumstances, her innocence and nobleness; and change at a touch their ordinary nature for a higher. And when she meets a fine character like Caponsacchi, who has been led into a worldly, immoral and indifferent life, he is swept in a moment out of it by the sight alone of this star of innocence and spiritual beauty, and becomes her true mate, daily self-excelled. The monk who receives her dying confession, the Pope, far set by his age above the noise of popular Rome, almost at one with the world beyond death and feeling what the divine judgment would be, both recognise with a fervour which carries them beyond the prejudices of age and of their society the loveliness of Heaven in the spirit of this girl of seventeen years, and claim her as higher than themselves.

It is fitting that to so enskied and saintly a child, when she rests before her death, the cruel life she had led for four years should seem a dream; and the working out of that thought, and of the two checks of reality it received in the coming of her child and the coming of Caponsacchi, is one of the fairest and most delicate pieces of work that Browning ever accomplished. She was so innocent and so simple-hearted—and the development of that part of her character in the stories told of her childhood is exquisitely touched into life—so loving, so born to be happy in being loved, that when she was forced into a maze of villany, bound up with hatred, cruelty, baseness and guilt, she seemed to live in a mist of unreality. When the pain became too deep to be dreamlike she was mercifully led back into the dream by the approach of death. As she lay dying there, all she had suffered passed again into unreality. Nothing remained but love and purity, the thrill when first she felt her child, the prayer to God which brought Caponsacchi to her rescue so that her child might be born, and lastly the vision of perfect union hereafter with her kindred soul, who, not her lover on earth, would be her lover in eternity. Even her boy, who had brought her, while she lived, her keenest sense of reality (and Browning's whole treatment of her motherhood, from the moment she knew she was in child, till the hour when the boy lay in her arms, is as true and tender as if his wife had filled his soul while he wrote), even her boy fades away into the dream. It is true she was dying, and there is no dream so deep as dying. Yet it was bold of Browning, and profoundly imagined by him, to make the child disappear, and to leave the woman at last alone with the thought and the spiritual passion of her union with Caponsacchi—

> O lover of my life, O soldier saint,
> No work begun shall ever pause for death.

It is the love of Percival's sister for Galahad.

It is not that she is naturally a dreamer, that she would not have felt and enjoyed the realities of earth. Her perceptions are keen, her nature expansive. Browning, otherwise, would not have cared for her. It was only when she was involved in evil, like an angel in hell (a wolf's arm round her throat and a snake curled over her feet), that she seemed to be dreaming, not living. It was incredible to her that such things should be reality. Yet even the dream called the hidden powers of her soul into action. In realising these as against evil she is not the dreamer. Her fortitude is unbroken; her moral courage never fails, though she is familiar with fear; her action, when the babe has leaped in her womb, is prompt, decisive and immediate; her physical courage, when her husband overtakes her and befouls her honour, is like a man's. She seizes his sword and would have slain the villain. Then, her natural goodness, the genius of her goodness, gives her a spiritual penetration which is more than an equivalent in her for an educated intelligence. Her intuition is so keen that she sees through the false worldliness of Caponsacchi to the real man beneath, and her few words call it into goodness and honour for ever. Her clear sense of truth sees all the threads of the net of villany in which she has been caught, and the only means to break through it, to reveal and bring it into condemnation. Fortitude, courage, intuition and intelligence are all made to arise out of her natural saintliness and love. She is always the immortal child.

For a time she has passed on earth through the realms of pain; and now, stabbed to her death, she looks back on the passage, and on all who have been kind and unkind to her—on the whole of the falsehood and villany. And the royal love in her nature is the master of the moment. She makes excuses for Violante's lie. "She meant well, and she did, as I feel now, little harm." "I am right now, quite happy; dying has purified me of the evil which touched me, and I colour ugly things with my own peace and joy. Every one that leaves life sees all things softened and bettered." As to her husband, she finds that she has little to forgive him at the last. Step by step she goes over all he did, and even finds excuses for him, and, at the end, this is how she speaks, a noble utterance of serene love, lofty intelligence, of spiritual power and of the forgiveness of eternity.

> For that most woeful man my husband once,
> Who, needing respite, still draws vital breath,
> I—pardon him? So far as lies in me,
> I give him for his good the life he takes,
> Praying the world will therefore acquiesce.
> Let him make God amends,—none, none to me
> Who thank him rather that, whereas strange fate
> Mockingly styled him husband and me wife,
> Himself this way at least pronounced divorce,
> Blotted the marriage bond: this blood of mine

> Flies forth exultingly at any door,
> Washes the parchment white, and thanks the blow
> We shall not meet in this world nor the next,
> But where will God be absent? In His face
> Is light, but in His shadow healing too:
> Let Guido touch the shadow and be healed!
> And as my presence was importunate,—
> My earthly good, temptation and a snare,—
> Nothing about me but drew somehow down
> His hate upon me,—somewhat so excused
> Therefore, since hate was thus the truth of him,—
> May my evanishment for evermore
> Help further to relieve the heart that cast
> Such object of its natural loathing forth!
> So he was made; he nowise made himself:
> I could not love him, but his mother did.
> His soul has never lain beside my soul:
> But for the unresisting body,—thanks!
> He burned that garment spotted by the flesh.
> Whatever he touched is rightly ruined: plague
> It caught, and disinfection it had craved
> Still but for Guido; I am saved through him
> So as by fire; to him—thanks and farewell!

Thus, pure at heart and sound of head, a natural, true woman in her childhood, in her girlhood, and when she is tried in the fire—by nature gay, yet steady in suffering; brave in a hell of fears and shame; clear-sighted in entanglements of villany; resolute in self-rescue; seeing and claiming the right help and directing it rightly; rejoicing in her motherhood and knowing it as her crown of glory, though the child is from her infamous husband; happy in her motherhood for one fortnight; slain like a martyr; loving the true man with immortal love; forgiving all who had injured her, even her murderer; dying in full faith and love of God, though her life had been a crucifixion; Pompilia passes away, and England's men and women will be **always** grateful to Browning for her creation.

CHAPTER XV

BALAUSTION

AMONG the women whom Browning made, Balaustion is the crown. So vivid is her presentation that she seems with us in our daily life. And she also fills the historical imagination.

One would easily fall in love with her, like those sensitive princes in the *Arabian Nights*, who, hearing only of the charms of a princess, set forth to find her over the world. Of all Browning's women, she is the most luminous, the most at unity with herself. She has the Greek gladness and life, the Greek intelligence and passion, and the Greek harmony. All that was common, prattling, coarse, sensual and spluttering in the Greek, (and we know from Aristophanes how strong these lower elements were in the Athenian people), never shows a trace of its influence in Balaustion. Made of the finest clay, exquisite and delicate in grain, she is yet strong, when the days of trouble come, to meet them nobly and to change their sorrows into spiritual powers.

And the *mise-en-scène* in which she is placed exalts her into a heroine, and adds to her the light, colour and humanity of Greek romance. Born at Rhodes, but of an Athenian mother, she is fourteen when the news arrives that the Athenian fleet under Nikias, sent to subdue Syracuse, has been destroyed, and the captive Athenians driven to labour in the quarries. All Rhodes, then in alliance with Athens, now cries, "Desert Athens, side with Sparta against Athens." Balaustion alone resists the traitorous cry. "What, throw off Athens, be disloyal to the source of art and intelligence—

> to the life and light
> Of the whole world worth calling world at all!"

And she spoke so well that her kinsfolk and others joined her and took ship for Athens. Now, a wind drove them off their course, and behind them came a pirate ship, and in front of them loomed the land. "Is it Crete?" they thought; "Crete, perhaps, and safety." But the oars flagged in the hands of the weary men, and the pirate gained. Then Balaustion, springing to the altar by the mast, white, rosy, and uplifted, sang on high that song of Æschylus which saved at Salamis—

> 'O sons of Greeks, go, set your country free,
> Free your wives, free your children, free the fanes
> O' the Gods, your fathers founded,—sepulchres
> They sleep in! Or save all, or all be lost.'

The crew, impassioned by the girl, answered the song, and drove the boat on, "churning the black water white," till the land shone clear, and the wide town and the harbour, and lo, 'twas not Crete, but Syracuse, luckless fate! Out came a galley from the port. "Who are you; Sparta's friend or foe?" "Of Rhodes are we, Rhodes that has forsaken Athens!"

"How, then, that song we heard? All Athens

was in that Æschylus. Your boat is full of Athenians—back to the pirate; we want no Athenians here.... Yet, stay, that song was Æschylus; every one knows it—how about Euripides? Might you know any of his verses?" For nothing helped the poor Athenians so much if any of them had his mouth stored with

> Old glory, great plays that had long ago
> Made themselves wings to fly about the world,—

But most of all those were cherished who could recite Euripides to Syracuse, so mighty was poetry in the ancient days to make enemies into friends, to build, beyond the wars and jealousies of the world, a land where all nations are one.

At this the captain cried: "Praise the God, we have here the very girl who will fill you with Euripides," and the passage brings Balaustion into full light.

> Therefore, at mention of Euripides,
> The Captain crowed out, "Euoi, praise the God!
> Oöp, boys, bring our owl-shield to the fore!
> Out with our Sacred Anchor! Here she stands,
> Balaustion! Strangers, greet the lyric girl!
> Euripides? Babai! what a word there 'scaped
> Your teeth's enclosure, quoth my grandsire's song
> Why, fast as snow in Thrace, the voyage through,
> Has she been falling thick in flakes of him!
> Frequent as figs at Kaunos, Kaunians said.
> Balaustion, stand forth and confirm my speech!
> Now it was some whole passion of a play;
> Now, peradventure, but a honey-drop
> That slipt its comb i' the chorus. If there rose
> A star, before I could determine steer
> Southward or northward—if a cloud surprised
> Heaven, ere I fairly hollaed 'Furl the sail!'—
> She had at fingers' end both cloud and star
> Some thought that perched there, tame and tuneable,

>   Fitted with wings, and still, as off it flew,
>   ' So sang Euripides,' she said, ' so sang
>   The meteoric poet of air and sea,
>   Planets and the pale populace of heaven,
>   The mind of man, and all that's made to soar ! '
>   And so, although she has some other name,
>   We only call her Wild-pomegranate-flower,
>   Balaustion ; since, where'er the red bloom burns
>   I' the dull dark verdure of the bounteous tree,
>   Dethroning, in the Rosy Isle, the rose,
>   You shall find food, drink, odour, all at once ;
>   Cool leaves to bind about an aching brow,
>   And, never much away, the nightingale,
>   Sing them a strophe, with the turn-again,
>   Down to the verse that ends all, proverb like,
>   And save us, thou Balaustion, bless the name "

And she answered : "I will recite the last play he wrote from first to last—*Alkestis*—his strangest, saddest, sweetest song."

>   Then because Greeks are Greeks, and hearts are hearts,
>   And poetry is power,—they all outbroke
>   In a great joyous laughter with much love :
>   " Thank Herakles for the good holiday !
>   Make for the harbour !   Row, and let voice ring,
>   In we row, bringing more Euripides ! ' "
>   All the crowd, as they lined the harbour now,
>   More of Euripides ! "—took up the cry.
>   We landed ; the whole city, soon astir,
>   Came rushing out of gates in common joy
>   To the suburb temple ; there they stationed me
>   O' the topmost step ; and plain I told the play,
>   Just as I saw it ; what the actors said,
>   And what I saw, or thought I saw the while,
>   At our Kameiros theatre, clean scooped
>   Out of a hill side, with the sky above
>   And sea before our seats in marble row :
>   Told it, and, two days more, repeated it
>   Until they sent us on our way again
>   With good words and great wishes.

So, we see Balaustion's slight figure under the

blue sky, and the white temple of Herakles from the steps of which she spoke; and among the crowd, looking up to her with rapture, the wise and young Sicilian who took ship with her when she was sent back to Athens, wooed her, and found answer before they reached Piræus. And there in Athens she and her lover saw Euripides, and told the Master how his play had redeemed her from captivity. Then they were married; and one day, with four of her girl friends, under the grape-vines by the streamlet side, close to the temple, Baccheion, in the cool afternoon, she tells the tale; interweaving with the play (herself another chorus) what she thinks, how she feels concerning its personages and their doings, and in the comment discloses her character. The woman is built up in this way for us. The very excuse she makes for her inserted words reveals one side of her delightful nature—her love of poetry, her love of beauty, her seeing eye, her delicate distinction, her mingled humility and self-knowledge.

> Look at Baccheion's beauty opposite,
> The temple with the pillars at the porch!
> See you not something beside masonry?
> What if my words wind in and out the stone
> As yonder ivy, the God's parasite?
> Though they leap all the way the pillar leads,
> Festoon about the marble, foot to frieze,
> And serpentiningly enrich the roof,
> Toy with some few bees and a bird or two,—
> What then? The column holds the cornice up.

As the ivy is to the pillar that supports the cornice, so are her words to the *Alkestis* on which she comments.

That is her charming way. She also is, like

Pompilia, young. But no contrast can be greater than that between Pompilia at seventeen years of age and Balaustion at fifteen. In Greece, as in Italy, women mature quickly. Balaustion is born with that genius which has the experience of age in youth and the fire of youth in age. Pompilia has the genius of pure goodness, but she is uneducated, her intelligence is untrained, and her character is only developed when she has suffered. Balaustion, on the contrary, has all the Greek capacity, a thorough education, and that education also which came in the air of that time to those of the Athenian temper. She is born into beauty and the knowledge of it, into high thinking and keen feeling; and she knows well why she thought and how she felt. So finely wrought is she by passion and intelligence alike, with natural genius to make her powers tenfold, that she sweeps her kinsfolk into agreement with her, subdues the sailors to her will, enchants the captain, sings the whole crew into energy, would have, I believe, awed and enthralled the pirate, conquers the Syracusans, delights the whole city, draws a talent out of the rich man which she leaves behind her for the prisoners, is a dear friend of sombre Euripides, lures Aristophanes, the mocker, into seriousness, mates herself with him in a whole night's conversation, and wrings praise and honour from the nimblest, the most cynical, and the most world-wise intellect in Athens.

Thus, over against Pompilia, she is the image of fine culture, held back from the foolishness and vanity of culture by the steadying power of genius. Then her judgment is always balanced. Each thing to her has many sides. She decides moral and intellectual questions and action with justice, but with mercy to the wrong opinion and the wrong thing, because her intellect is clear, tolerant and forgiving through intellectual breadth and power. Pompilia is the image of natural goodness and of its power. A spotless soul, though she is passed through hell, enables her, without a trained intellect, with ignorance of all knowledge, and with as little vanity as Balaustion, to give as clear and firm a judgment of right and wrong. She is as tolerant, as full of excuses for the wrong thing, as forgiving, as Balaustion, but it is by the power of goodness and love in her, not by that of intellect. Browning never proved his strength more than when he made these two, in vivid contrast, yet in their depths in harmony; both equal, though so far apart, in noble womanhood. Both are beyond convention; both have a touch of impulsive passion, of natural wildness, of flower-beauty. Both are, in hours of crisis, borne beyond themselves, and mistress of the hour. Both mould men, for their good, like wax in their fingers. But Pompilia is the white rose, touched with faint and innocent colour; and Balaustion is the wild pomegranate flower, burning in a crimson of love among the dark green leaves of steady and sure thought, her powers latent till needed, but when called on and brought to light, flaming with decision and revelation.

In this book we see her in her youth, her powers as yet untouched by heavy sorrow. In the next, in *Aristophanes' Apology*, we first find her in matured strength, almost mastering Aristophanes; and afterwards in the depth of grief, as she flies with her husband over the seas to Rhodes, leaving behind her Athens, the city of her heart, ruined and enslaved. The deepest passion in her, the patriotism of the soul, is all but broken-hearted. Yet, she is the life and support of all who are with her; even a certain gladness breaks forth in her, and she secures for all posterity the intellectual record of Athenian life and the images, wrought to vitality, of some of the greater men of Athens. So we possess her completely. Her life, her soul, its growth and strength, are laid before us. To follow her through these two poems is to follow their poetry. Whenever we touch her we touch imagination. *Aristophanes' Apology* is illuminated by Balaustion's eyes. A glimpse here and there of her enables us to thread our way without too great weariness through a thorny undergrowth of modern and ancient thought mingled together on the subject of the Apology.

In *Balaustion's Adventure* she tells her tale, and recites, as she did at Syracuse, the *Alkestis* to her four friends. But she does more; she comments on it, as she did not at Syracuse. The comments are, of course, Browning's, but he means them to reveal Balaustion. They are touched throughout with a woman's thought and feeling, inflamed by the poetic genius with which Browning has endowed her. Balaustion is his deliberate picture of genius the great miracle.

The story of the *Alkestis* begins before the play. Apollo, in his exile, having served King Admetos as shepherd, conceives a friendship for the king, helps him to his marriage, and knowing that he is doomed to die in early life, descends to hell and begs the Fates to give him longer life. That is a motive, holding in it strange thoughts of life and death and fate, which pleased Browning, and he treats it separately, and with sardonic humour, in the Prologue to one of his later volumes. The Fates refuse to lengthen Admetos' life, unless some one love him well enough to die for him. They must have their due at the allotted time.

The play opens when that time arrives. We see, in a kind of Prologue, Apollo leaving the house of Admetos and Death coming to claim his victim. Admetos has asked his father, mother, relations and servants to die instead of him. None will do it; but his wife, Alkestis, does. Admetos accepts her sacrifice. Her dying, her death, the sorrow of Admetos is described with all the poignant humanity of Euripides. In the meantime Herakles has come on the scene, and Admetos, though steeped in grief, conceals his wife's death and welcomes his friend to his house. As Alkestis is the heroine of self-sacrifice, Admetos is the hero of hospitality. Herakles feasts, but the indignant bearing of an old servant attracts his notice, and he finds out the truth. He is shocked, but resolves to attack Death himself, who is bearing away Alkestis. He meets and conquers Death and brings back Alkestis alive to her husband. So the strong man conquers the Fates, whom even Apollo could not subdue.

This is a fine subject. Every one can see in how many different ways it may be treated, with what different conceptions, how variously the characters may be built up, and what different ethical and emotional situations may be imaginatively treated in it. Racine himself thought it the finest of the

Greek subjects, and began a play upon it. But he died before he finished it, and ordered his manuscript to be destroyed. We may well imagine how the quiet, stately genius of Racine would have conceived and ordered it; with the sincere passion, held under restraint by as sincere a dignity, which characterised his exalted style.

Balaustion treats it with an equal moral force, and also with that modern moral touch which Racine would have given it; which, while it removed the subject at certain points from the Greek morality, would yet have exalted it into a more spiritual world than even the best of the Greeks conceived. The commentary of Balaustion is her own treatment of the subject. It professes to explain Euripides: it is in reality a fresh conception of the characters and their motives, especially of the character of Herakles. Her view of the character of Alkestis, especially in her death, is not, I think, the view which Euripides took. Her condemnation of Admetos is unmodified by those other sides of the question which Euripides suggests. The position Balaustion takes up with regard to self-sacrifice is far more subtle, with its half-Christian touches, than the Greek simplicity would have conceived. Finally, she feels so strongly that the subject has not been adequately conceived that, at the end, she recreates it for herself. Even at the beginning she rebuilds the Euripidean matter. When Apollo and Death meet, Balaustion conceives the meeting for herself. She images the divine Apollo as somewhat daunted, and images the dread meeting of these two with modern, not Greek imagination. It is like the meeting, she thinks, of a ruined eagle, caught as he swooped in a gorge, half heedless, yet terrific, with a lion, the haunter of the gorge, the lord of the ground, who pauses, ere he try the worst with the frightful, unfamiliar creature, known in the shadows and silences of the sky but not known here. It is the first example we have of Balaustion's imaginative power working for itself. There is another, farther on, where she stays her recitation to describe Death's rush in on Alkestis when the dialogue between him and Apollo is over—

>   And, in the fire-flash of the appalling sword,
>   The uprush and the outburst, the onslaught
>   Of Death's portentous passage through the door,
>   Apollon stood a pitying moment-space:
>   I caught one last gold gaze upon the night,
>   Nearing the world now: and the God was gone,
>   And mortals left to deal with misery.

So she speaks, as if she saw more than Euripides, as if to her the invisible were visible—as it was. To see the eternal unseen is the dower of imagination in its loftiest mood.

She is as much at home with the hero of earth, the highest manhood, as she is with the gods. When Herakles comes on the scene she cannot say enough about him; and she conceives him apart from the Herakles of Euripides. She paints in him, and Browning paints through her, the idea of the full, the perfect man; and it is not the ideal of the cultivated, of the sensitive folk. It is more also a woman's than a man's ideal. For, now, suddenly, into the midst of the sorrow of the house, every one wailing, life full of penury and inactivity, there leaps the "gay cheer of a great voice," the full presence of the hero, his "weary happy face, half god, half man, which made the god-part god the more." His very voice, which smiled at sorrow, and his look, which, saying sorrow was to be conquered, proclaimed to all the world " My life is in my hand to give away, to make men glad," seemed to dry up all misery at its source, for his love of man makes him always joyful. When Admetos opened the house to him, and did not tell him of his wife's death, Balaustion comments " The hero, all truth, took him at his word, and then strode off to feast." He takes, she thought, the present rest, the physical food and drink as frankly as he took the mighty labours of his fate. And she rejoices as much in his jovial warmth, his joy in eating and drinking and singing, and festivity, as in his heroic soul. They go together, these things, in a hero.

> Making the most o' the minute, that the soul
> And body, strained to height a minute since,
> Might lie relaxed in joy, this breathing space,
> For man's sake more than ever ;

He slew the pest of the marish, yesterday ; to-day he takes his fill of food, wine, song and flowers ; to-morrow he will slay another plague of mankind.

So she sings, praising aloud the heroic temper, as mighty in the natural joys of natural life, in the strength and honour of the body, as in the saving of the world from pain and evil. But this pleasure of the senses, though in the great nature, is in it under rule, and the moment Herakles hears of Alkestis dead, he casts aside, in " a splendour of resolve," the feast, wine, song, and garlands, and girds himself to fight with Death for her rescue And Balaustion, looking after him as he goes, cries out the judgment of her soul on all heroism. It is Browning's judgment also, one of the deepest things in his heart; a constant motive in his poetry, a master-thought in his life.

> Gladness be with thee, Helper of our world!
> I think this is the authentic sign and seal
> Of Godship, that it ever waxes glad,
> And more glad, until gladness blossoms, bursts
> Into a rage to suffer for mankind,
> And recommence at sorrow: drops like seed
> After the blossom, ultimate of all.
> Say, does the seed scorn earth and seek the sun?
> Surely it has no other end and aim
> Than to drop, once more die into the ground,
> Taste cold and darkness and oblivion there:
> And thence rise, tree-like grow through pain to joy,
> More joy and most joy,—do man good again.

That is the truth Browning makes this woman have the insight to reveal. Gladness of soul, becoming at one with sorrow and death and rising out of them the conqueror, but always rejoicing, in itself, in the joy of the universe and of God, is the root-heroic quality.

Then there is the crux of the play—Alkestis is to die for Admetos, and does it. What of the conduct of Admetos? What does Balaustion, the woman, think of that? She thinks Admetos is a poor creature for having allowed it. When Alkestis is brought dying on the stage, and Admetos follows, mourning over her, Balaustion despises him, and she traces in the speech of Alkestis, which only relates to her children's fate and takes no notice of her husband's protestations, that she has judged her husband, that love is gone in sad contempt, that all

Admetos has given her is now paid for, that her death is a business transaction which has set her free to think no more about him, only of her children. For, what seems most pertinent for him to say, if he loved, " Take, O Fates, your promise back, and take my life, not hers," he does not say. That is not really the thought of Euripides.

Then, and this is subtly but not quite justly wrought into Euripides by Balaustion, she traces through the play the slow awakening of the soul of Admetos to the low-hearted thing he had done. He comes out of the house, having disposed all things duteously and fittingly round the dead, and Balaustion sees in his grave quietude that the truth is dawning on him; when suddenly Pheres, his father, who had refused to die for him, comes to lay his offering on the bier. This, Balaustion thinks, plucks Admetos back out of unselfish thought into that lower atmosphere in which he only sees his own advantage in the death of Alkestis; and in which he now bitterly reproaches his father because he did not die to save Alkestis. And the reproach is the more bitter because—and this Balaustion, with her subtle morality, suggests —an undernote of conscience causes him to see his own baser self, now prominent in his acceptance of Alkestis' sacrifice, finished and hardened in the temper of his father—young Admetos in old Pheres. He sees with dread and pain what he may become when old. This hatred of himself in his father is, Balaustion thinks, the source of his extreme violence with his father. She, with the Greek sense of what was due to nature, seeks to excuse this unfitting scene. Euripides has gone too far for her. She thinks that, if Sophocles had to do with the matter, he would have made the Chorus explain the man.

But the unnatural strife would not have been explained by Sophocles as Balaustion explains it. That fine ethical twist of hers—"that Admetos hates himself in his father," is too modern for a Greek. It has the casuistical subtlety which the over-developed conscience of the Christian Church encouraged. It is intellectual, too, rather than real, metaphysical more than moral, Browning rather than Sophocles. Nor do I believe that a Rhodian girl, even with all Athens at the back of her brain, would have conceived it at all. Then Balaustion makes another comment on the situation, in which there is more of Browning than of herself. "Admetos," she says, "has been kept back by the noisy quarrel from seeing into the truth of his own conduct, as he was on the point of doing, for 'with the low strife comes the little mind.'" But when his father is gone, and Alkestis is borne away, then, in the silence of the house and the awful stillness in his own heart, he sees the truth. His shame, the whole woe and horror of his failure in love, break, like a toppling wave, upon him, and the drowned truth, so long hidden from him by self, rose to the surface, and appalled him by its dead face. His soul in seeing true, is saved, yet so as by fire. At this moment Herakles comes in, leading Alkestis, redeemed from death; and finding, so Balaustion thinks, her husband restored to his right mind.

But, then, we ask, how Alkestis, having found him fail, will live with him again, how she, having topped nobility, will endure the memory of the ignoble in him? That would be the interesting subject, and the explanation Euripides suggests does not satisfy Balaustion. The dramatic situation is unfinished. Balaustion, with her fine instinct, feels that, to save the subject, it ought to be otherwise treated, and she invents a new Admetos, a new Alkestis. She has heard that Sophocles meant to make a new piece of the same matter, and her balanced judgment, on which Browning insists so often, makes her say, "That is well. One thing has many sides; but still, no good supplants a good, no beauty undoes another; still I will love the *Alkestis* which I know. Yet I have so drunk this poem, so satisfied with it my heart and soul, that I feel as if I, too, might make a new poem on the same matter."

> Ah, that brave
> Bounty of poets, the one royal race
> That ever was, or will be, in this world!
> They give no gift that bounds itself and ends
> I' the giving and the taking: theirs so breeds
> I' the heart and soul o' the taker, so transmutes
> The man who only was a man before,
> That he grows godlike in his turn, can give—
> He also: share the poet's privilege,
> Bring forth new good, new beauty, from the old.

And she gives her conception of the subject, and it further unfolds her character.

When Apollo served Admetos, the noble nature of the God so entered into him that all the beast was subdued in the man, and he became the ideal king, living for the ennoblement of his people. Yet, while doing this great work, he is to die, still young, and he breaks out, in a bitter calm, against the fate which takes him from the work of his life.

"Not so," answers Alkestis, "I knew what was

coming, and though Apollo urged me not to disturb the course of things, and not to think that any death prevents the march of good or ends a life, yet he yielded; and I die for you—all happiness."

"It shall never be," replies Admetos; "our two lives are one. But I am the body, thou art the soul; and the body shall go, and not the soul. I claim death."

"No," answered Alkestis; "the active power to rule and weld the people into good is in the man. Thou art the acknowledged power. And as to the power which, thou sayest, I give thee, as to the soul of me—take it, I pour it into thee. Look at me." And as he looks, she dies, and the king is left—still twofold as before, with the soul of Alkestis in him —himself and her. So is Fate cheated, and Alkestis in Admetos is not dead. A passage follows of delicate and simple poetry, written by Browning in a manner in which I would he had oftener written. To read it is to regret that, being able to do this, he chose rather to write, from time to time, as if he were hewing his way through tangled underwood. No lovelier image of Proserpina has been made in poetry, not even in Tennyson's *Demeter*, than this—

> And even while it lay, i' the look of him,
> Dead, the dimmed body, bright Alkestis' soul
> Had penetrated through the populace
> Of ghosts, was got to Koré,—throned and crowned
> The pensive queen o' the twilight, where she dwells
> Forever in a muse, but half away.
> From flowery earth she lost and hankers for,—
> And there demanded to become a ghost
> Before the time.
>   Whereat the softened eyes
> Of the lost maidenhood that lingered still

> Straying among the flowers in Sicily,
> Sudden was startled back to Hades' throne
> By that demand: broke through humanity
> Into the orbed omniscience of a God,
> Searched at a glance Alkestis to the soul
> And said . . .
> "Hence, thou deceiver! This is not to die,
> If, by the very death which mocks me now,
> The life, that's left behind and past my power,
> Is formidably doubled . . ."
> And so, before the embrace relaxed a whit,
> The lost eyes opened, still beneath the look;
> And lo, Alkestis was alive again,
> And of Admetos' rapture who shall speak?

The old conception has more reality. This is in the vague world of modern psychical imagination. Nevertheless it has its own beauty, and it enlarges Browning's picture of the character of Balaustion.

Her character is still further enlarged in *Aristophanes' Apology*. That poem, if we desire intellectual exercise, illuminated by flashings of imagination, is well worth reading, but to comprehend it fully, one must know a great deal of Athenian life and of the history of the Comic Drama. It is the defence by Aristophanes of his idea of the business, the method, and the use of Comedy. How far what he says is Browning speaking for Aristophanes, and how far it is Browning speaking for himself, is hard to tell. And it would please him to leave that purposely obscure. What is alive and intense in the poem is, first, the realisation of Athenian life in several scenes, pictured with all Browning's astonishing force of presentation, as, for instance, the feast after the play, and the grim entrance of Sophocles, black from head to foot, among the glittering and drunken revellers, to announce the death of Euripides.

Secondly, there is the presentation of Aristophanes. Browning has created him for us—

> And no ignoble presence ! On the bulge
> Of the clear baldness,—all his head one brow,—
> True, the veins swelled, blue network, and there surged
> A red from cheek to temple,—then retired
> As if the dark-leaved chaplet damped a flame,—
> Was never nursed by temperance or health.
> But huge the eyeballs rolled back native fire,
> Imperiously triumphant: nostrils wide
> Waited their incense ; while the pursed mouth's pout
> Aggressive, while the beak supreme above,
> While the head, face, nay, pillared throat thrown back,
> Beard whitening under like a vinous foam,
> There made a glory, of such insolence—
> I thought,—such domineering deity
> Hephaistos might have carved to cut the brine
> For his gay brother's prow, imbrue that path
> Which, purpling, recognised the conqueror.
> Impudent and majestic : drunk, perhaps,
> But that's religion ; sense too plainly snuffed :
> Still, sensuality was grown a rite.

We see the man, the natural man, to the life. But as the poem goes on, we company with his intellect and soul, with the struggle of sensualism against his knowledge of a more ideal life ; above all, with one, who indulging the appetites and senses of the natural man, is yet, at a moment, their master. The coarse chambers of his nature are laid bare, his sensuous pleasure in the lower forms of human life, his joy in satirising them, his contempt for the good or the ideal life if it throw the sensual man away. Then, we are made to know the power he has to rise above this —without losing it—into the higher imaginative region where, for the time, he feels the genius of Sophocles, Euripides, the moral power of Balaustion, and the beauty of the natural world. Indeed, in that last we find him in his extant plays. Few of the Greeks could write with greater exquisiteness of natural beauty than this wild poet who loved the dunghill. And Browning does not say this, but records in this *Apology* how when Aristophanes is touched for an instant by Balaustion's reading of the *Herakles*, and seizing the psalterion sings the song of Thamuris marching to his trial with the Muses through a golden autumn morning—it is the glory and loveliness of nature that he sings. This portraiture of the poet is scattered through the whole poem. It is too minute, too full of detail to dwell on here. It has a thousand touches of life and intimacy. And it is perhaps the finest thing Browning has done in portraiture of character. But then there was a certain sympathy in Browning for Aristophanes. The natural man was never altogether put aside by Browning.

Lastly, there is the fresh presentation of Balaustion, of the matured and experienced woman whom we have known as a happy girl. Euthycles and she are married, and one night, as she is sitting alone, he comes in, bringing the grave news that Euripides is dead, but had proved at the court of Archelaos of Macedonia his usefulness as counsellor to King and State, and his power still to sing—

> Clashed thence *Alkaion*, maddened *Pentheus'* up;
> Then music sighed itself away, one moan
> Iphigeneia made by Aulis' strand;
> With her and music died Euripides.

And Athens, hearing, ceased to mock and cried "Bury Euripides in Peiraios, bring his body back." Ah, said Balaustion, Death alters the point of view.

But our tribute is in our hearts; and more, his soul will now for ever teach and bless the world.

> Is not that day come? What if you and I
> Re-sing the song, inaugurate the fame?

For, like Herakles, in his own *Alkestis*, he now strides away (and this is the true end of the *Alkestis*) to surmount all heights of destiny." While she spoke thus, the Chorus of the Comedy, girls, boys, and men, in drunken revel and led by Aristophanes, thundered at the door and claimed admittance. Balaustion is drawn confronting them —tall and superb, like Victory's self; her warm golden eyes flashing under her black hair, "earth flesh with sun fire," statuesque, searching the crowd with her glance. And one and all dissolve before her silent splendour of reproof, all save Aristophanes. She bids him welcome. "Glory to the Poet," she cries. "Light, light, I hail it everywhere; no matter for the murk, that never should have been such orb's associate." Aristophanes changes as he sees her; a new man confronts her.

> "So!" he smiled, "piercing to my thought at once,
> You see myself? Balaustion's fixed regard
> Can strip the proper Aristophanes
> Of what our sophists, in their jargon, style
> His accidents?"

He confesses her power to meet him in discourse, unfolds his views and plans to her, and having contrasted himself with Euripides, bids her use her thrice-refined refinement, her rosy strength, to match his argument. She claims no equality with him, the consummate creator; but only, as a woman, the love of all things lovable with which to meet him who has degraded Comedy. She appeals to the high poet in the man, and finally bids him honour the deep humanity in Euripides. To prove it, and to win his accord, she reads the *Herakles*, the last of Euripides.

It is this long night of talk which Balaustion dictates to Euthycles as she is sailing, day after day, from Athens back to Rhodes. The aspect of sea and sky, as they sail, is kept before us, for Balaustion uses its changes as illustrations, and the clear descriptions tell, even more fully than before, how quick this woman was to observe natural beauty and to correlate it with humanity. Here is one example. In order to describe a change in the temper of Aristophanes from wild license to momentary gravity, Balaustion seizes on a cloud-incident of the voyage—Euthycles, she cries,

> . . . "o'er the boat side, quick, what change,
> Watch—in the water! But a second since,
> It laughed a ripply spread of sun and sea,
> Ray fused with wave, to never disunite.
> Now, sudden, all the surface hard and black,
> Lies a quenched light, dead motion: what the cause?
> Look up, and lo, the menace of a cloud
> Has solemnised the sparkling, spoiled the sport!
> Just so, some overshadow, some new care
> Stopped all the mirth and mocking on his face."

Her feeling for nature is as strong as her feeling for man, and both are woven together.

All her powers have now ripened, and the last touch has been given to them by her ideal sorrow for Athens, the country of her soul, where high intelligence and imagination had created worlds. She leaves it now, ruined and degraded, and the passionate outbreak of her patriotic sorrow with which the poem opens lifts the character and imagination of Balaustion into spiritual splendour. Athens, "hearted in her heart," has perished ignobly. Not so, she thinks, ought this beauty of the world to have died, its sea-walls razed to the ground to the fluting and singing of harlots; but in some vast overwhelming of natural energies —in the embrace of fire to join the gods; or in a sundering of the earth, when the Acropolis should have sunken entire and risen in Hades to console the ghosts with beauty; or in the multitudinous over-swarming of ocean. This she could have borne, but, thinking of what has been, of the misery and disgrace, "Oh," she cries, "bear me away— wind, wave and bark!" But Browning does not leave Balaustion with only this deep emotion in her heart. He gives her the spiritual passion of genius. She is swept beyond her sorrow into that invisible world where the soul lives with the gods, with the pure Ideas of justice, truth and love; where immortal life awaits the disembodied soul and we shall see Euripides. In these high thoughts she will outlive her sorrow.

> Why should despair be? Since, distinct above
> Man's wickedness and folly, flies the wind
> And floats the cloud, free transport for our soul
> Out of its fleshly durance dim and low,—
> Since disembodied soul anticipates
> (Thought-borne as now, in rapturous unrestraint)
> Above all crowding, crystal silentness,
> Above all noise, a silver solitude:—
> Surely, where thought so bears soul, soul in time
> May permanently bide, "assert the wise,"
> There live in peace, there work in hope once more—
> O nothing doubt, Philemon! Greed and strife,
> Hatred and cark and care, what place have they

> In yon blue liberality of heaven?
> How the sea helps! How rose-smit earth will rise
> Breast-high thence, some bright morning, and be Rhodes!
> Heaven, earth and sea, my warrant—in their name,
> Believe—o'er falsehood, truth is surely sphered,
> O'er ugliness beams beauty, o'er this world
> Extends that realm where, " as the wise assert,"
> Philemon, thou shalt see Euripides
> Clearer than mortal sense perceived the man!

We understand that she has drunk deep of Socrates, that her spiritual sense reached onward to the Platonic Socrates. In this supersensuous world of thought she is quieted out of the weakness which made her miserable over the fall of Athens; and in the quiet, Browning, who will lift his favourite into perfectness, adds to her spiritual imagination the dignity of that moral judgment which the intellect of genius gathers from the facts of history. In spite of her sorrow, she grasps the truth that there was justice in the doom of Athens. Let justice have its way. Let the folk die who pulled her glory down. This is her prophetic strain, the strength of the Hebrew in the Greek.

And then the prophet in the woman passes, and the poet in her takes the lyre. She sees the splendid sunset. Why should its extravagance of glory run to waste? Let me build out of it a new Athens, quarry out the golden clouds and raise the Acropolis, and the rock-hewn Place of Assembly, whence new orators may thunder over Greece; and the theatre where Æschylus, Sophocles, Euripides, godlike still, may contend for the prize. Yet—and there is a further change of thought—yet that may not be. To build that poetic vision is to slip away from reality, and the true use of it. The tragedy is there—irrevocable. Let it sink deep in us till we see Rhodes shining over the sea. So great, so terrible, so piteous it is, that, dwelt on in the soul and seen in memory, it will do for us what the great tragedians made their tragic themes do for their hearers. It will purify the heart by pity and terror from the baseness and littleness of life. Our small hatreds, jealousies and prides, our petty passions will be rebuked, seem nothing in its mighty sorrow.

> What else in life seems piteous any more
> After such pity, or proves terrible
> Beside such terror;

This is the woman—the finest creature Browning drew, young and fair and stately, with her dark hair and amber eyes, lovely—the wild pomegranate flower of a girl—as keen, subtle and true of intellect as she is lovely, able to comment on and check Euripides, to conceive a new play out of his subject, to be his dearest friend, to meet on equality Aristophanes; so full of lyric sympathy, so full of eager impulse that she thrills the despairing into action, enslaves a city with her eloquence, charms her girl-friends by the Ilissus, and so sends her spirit into her husband that, when the Spartans advise the razing of Athens to the ground he saves the city by those famous lines of Euripides, of which Milton sang; so at one with natural beauty, with all beauty, that she makes it live in the souls of men; so clear in judgment that she sees the right even when it seems lost in the wrong, that she sees the justice of the gods in the ruin of the city she most loved; so poetic of temper that everything speaks to her of life, that she acknowledges the poetry which rises out of the foulness she hates in Aristophanes, that she loves all humanity, bad or good, and Euripides chiefly because of his humanity; so spiritual, that she can soar out of her most overwhelming sorrow into the stormless world where the gods breathe pure thought and for ever love; and, abiding in its peace, use the griefs of earth for the ennoblement of the life of men, because in all her spiritual apartness, however far it bear her from earth, she never loses her close sympathy with the fortunes of mankind. Nay, from her lofty station she is the teacher of truth and love and justice, in splendid prophecy. It is with an impassioned exaltation, worthy of Sibyl and Pythoness in one, of divine wisdom both Roman and Greek, that she cries to the companions of her voyage words which embody her soul and the soul of all the wise and loving of the earth, when they act for men; bearing their action, thought and feeling beyond man to God in man—

> Speak to the infinite intelligence,
> Sing to the everlasting sympathy!

CHAPTER XVI

THE RING AND THE BOOK

WHEN Browning published *The Ring and the Book*, he was nearly fifty years old. All his powers (except those which create the lyric) are used therein with mastery; and the ease with which he writes is not more remarkable than the exultant pleasure which accompanies the ease. He has, as an artist, a hundred tools in hand, and he uses them with certainty of execution. The wing of his invention does not falter through these twelve books, nor droop below the level at which he began them; and the epilogue is written with as much vigour as the prologue. The various books demand various powers. In each book the powers are proportionate to the subject; but the mental force behind each exercise of power is equal throughout. He writes as well when he has to make the guilty soul of Guido speak, as when the innocence of Pompilia tells her story. The gain-serving lawyers, each distinctly isolated, tell their worldly thoughts as clearly as Caponsacchi reveals his redeemed and spiritualised soul. The parasite of an aristocratic and thoughtless society in *Tertium Quid* is not more vividly drawn than the Pope, who has left in his old age the conventions of society behind him, and speaks in his silent chamber face to face with God. And all the minor characters—of whom there are a great number, ranging from children to old folk, from the peasant to the Cardinal, through every class of society in Italy—are drawn, even when they are slashed out in only three lines, with such force, certainty, colour and life that we know them better than our friends. The variousness of the product would seem to exclude an equality of excellence in drawing and invention. But it does not. It reveals and confirms it. The poem is a miracle of intellectual power.

This great length, elaborate detail, and the repetition so many times of the same story, would naturally suggest to an intending reader that the poem might be wearisome. Browning, suspecting this, and in mercy to a public who does not care for a work of *longue haleine*, published it at first in four volumes, with a month's interval between each volume. He thought that the story told afresh by characters widely different would strike new, if each book were read at intervals of ten days. There were three books in each volume. And if readers desire to realise fully the intellectual *tour de force* contained in telling the same story twelve times over, and making each telling interesting, they cannot do better than read the book as Browning wished it to be read. "Give the poem four months, and let ten days elapse between the reading of each book," is what he meant us to understand. Moreover, to meet this possible weariness, Browning, consciously, or probably unconsciously, since genius does the right thing without asking why, continually used a trick of his own which, at intervals, stings the reader into wakefulness and pleasure, and sends him on to the next page refreshed and happy. After fifty, or it may be a hundred lines of somewhat dry analysis, a vivid illustration, which concentrates all the matter of the previous lines, flashes on the reader as a snake might flash across a traveller's dusty way: or some sudden description of an Italian scene in the country or in the streets of Rome enlivens the well-known tale with fresh humanity. Or a new character leaps up out of the crowd, and calls us to note his ways, his dress, his voice, his very soul in some revealing speech, and then passes away from the stage, while we turn, refreshed (and indeed at times we need refreshment), to the main speaker, the leading character.

But to dwell on the multitude of portraits with which Browning's keen observation, memory and love of human nature have embellished *The Ring and the Book* belongs to another part of this chapter. At present the question rises: "What place does *The Ring and the Book* hold in Browning's development?" It holds a central place. There was always a struggle in Browning between two pleasures; pleasure in the exercise of his intellect—his wit, in the fullest sense of the word; pleasure in the exercise of his poetic imagination. Sometimes one of these had the upper hand in his poems, sometimes the other, and sometimes both happily worked together. When the exercise of his wit had the upper hand, it tended to drive out both imagination and passion. Intellectual play may be without any emotion except its delight in itself. Then its mere cleverness attracts its user, and gives him an easily purchased pleasure. When a poet falls a complete victim to this pleasure, imagination hides her face from him, passion runs away, and what he produces resembles, but is not, poetry. And Browning, who had got perilously near to the absence of poetry in *Bishop Blougram's Apology*, succeeded in *Mr. Sludge, the Medium*, in losing poetry altogether. In *The Ring and the Book* there are whole books, and long passages in its other books in which poetry almost ceases to exist and is replaced by brilliant cleverness, keen analysis, vivid description, and a combination of wit and fancy which is rarely rivalled; but no emotion, no imagination such as poets use inflames the coldness of these qualities into the glow of poetry. The indefinable difference which makes imaginative work into poetry is not there. There is abundance of invention; but that, though a part of imagination, belongs as much to the art of prose as to the art of poetry.

Browning could write thus, out of his intellect alone. None of the greater poets could. Their genius could not work without fusing into their intellectual work intensity of feeling; and that combination secured poetic treatment of their subject. It would have been totally impossible for Milton, Shakespeare, Dante, Vergil, or even the great mass of second-rate poets, to have written some of Browning's so-called poetry—no matter how they tried. There was that in Browning's nature which enabled him to exercise his intellectual powers alone, without passion, and so far he almost ceases to deserve the name of poet. And his pleasure in doing this grew upon him, and having done it with dazzling power in part of *The Ring and the Book*, he was carried away by it and produced a number of so-called poems; terrible examples of what a poet can come to when he has allowed his pleasure in clever analysis to tyrannise over him—*Prince Hohenstiel-Schwangau, The Inn Album, Red Cotton Night-Cap Country*, and a number of shorter poems in the volumes which followed. In these, what Milton meant by passion, simplicity and sensuousness were banished, and imagination existed only as it exists in a prose writer.

This condition was slowly arrived at. It had not been fully reached when he wrote *The Ring and the Book*. His poetic powers resisted their enemies for many years, and had the better in the struggle. If it takes a long time to cast a devil out, it takes a longer time to depose an angel. And the devil may be utterly banished, but the angel never. And though the devil of mere wit and the little devils of analytic exercise—devils when they usurp the throne in a poet's soul and enslave imaginative emotion—did get the better of Browning, it was only for a time. Towards the end of his life he recovered, but never as completely as he had once possessed them, the noble attributes of a poet. The evils of the struggle clung to him; the poisonous pleasure he had pursued still affected him; he was again and again attacked by the old malaria. He was as a brand plucked from the burning.

The Ring and the Book is the central point of this struggle. It is full of emotion and thought concentrated on the subject, and commingled by imagination to produce beauty. And whenever this is the case, as in the books which treat of Caponsacchi and Pompilia, we are rejoiced by poetry. In their lofty matter of thought and feeling, in their simplicity and nobleness of spiritual beauty, poetry is dominant. In them also his intellectual powers, and his imaginative and passionate powers, are fused into one fire. Nor is the presentation of Guido Franceschini under two faces less powerful, or that of the Pope, in his meditative silence. But in these books the poetry is less, and is mingled, as would naturally indeed be the case, with a searching analysis, which intrudes too much into their imaginative work. Over-dissection makes them cold. In fact, in fully a quarter of this long poem, the analysing understanding, that bustling and self-conscious person, who plays only on the surface of things and separates their elements from one another instead of penetrating to their centre; who is incapable of seeing the whole into which the various elements have combined—is too masterful for the poetry. It is not, then, imaginative, but intellectual pleasure which, as we read, we gain.

Then again there is throughout a great part of the poem a dangerous indulgence of his wit; the amusement of remote analogies; the use of far-fetched illustrations; quips and cranks and wanton wiles of the reasoning fancy in deviating self-indulgence; and an allusiveness which sets commentators into note-making effervescence. All these, and more, which belong to wit, are often quite ungoverned, allowed to disport themselves as they please. Such matters delight the unpoetic readers of Browning, and indeed they are excellent entertainment. But let us call them by their true name; let us not call them poetry, nor mistake their art for the art of poetry. Writing them in blank verse does not make them poetry. In *Half-Rome*, in *The Other Half-Rome*, and in *Tertium Quid*, these elements of analysis and wit are exhibited in three-fourths of the verse; but the other fourth—in description of scenes, in vivid portraiture, in transient outbursts out of which passion, in glimpses, breaks—rises into the realm of poetry. In the books which sketch the lawyers and their pleadings, there is wit in its finest brilliancy, analysis in its keenest veracity, but they are scarcely a poet's work. The whole book is then a mixed book, extremely mixed. All that was poetical in Browning's previous work is represented in it, and all the unpoetical elements which had gradually been winning power in him, and which showed themselves previously in *Bishop Blougram* and *Mr. Sludge*, are also there in full blast. It was, as I have said, the central battlefield of two powers in him. And when *The Ring and the Book* was finished, the inferior power had for a time the victory.

To sum up then, There are books in the poem where matter of passion and matter of thought are imaginatively wrought together. There are others where psychological thought and metaphysical reasoning are dominant, but where passionate feeling has also a high place. There are others where analysis and wit far excel the elements of imaginative emotion; and there are others where every kind of imagination is absent, save that which is consistent throughout and which never fails—the power of creating men and women into distinct individualities. That is left, but it is a power which is not special to a poet. A prose writer may possess it with the same fulness as a poet. Carlyle had it as remarkably as Browning, or nearly as remarkably.

He also had wit—a heavier wit than Browning's, less lambent, less piercing, but as forcible.

One thing more may be said. The poem is far too long, and the subject does not bear its length. The long poems of the world (I do not speak of those by inferior poets) have a great subject, are concerned with manifold fates of men, and are naturally full of various events and varied scenery. They interest us with new things from book to book. In *The Ring and the Book* the subject is not great, the fates concerned are not important, and the same event runs through twelve books and is described twelve times. However we may admire the intellectual force which actually makes the work interesting, and the passion which often thrills us in it—this is more than the subject bears, and than we can always endure. Each book is spun out far beyond what is necessary; a great deal is inserted which would be wisely left out. No one could be more concise than Browning when he pleased. His power of flashing a situation or a thought into a few words is well known. But he did not always use this power. And in *The Ring and the Book*, as in some of the poems that followed it, he seems now and then to despise that power.

And now for the poem itself. Browning tells the story eight times by different persons, each from a different point of view, and twice more by the same person before and after his condemnation and, of course, from two points of view. Then he practically tells it twice more in the prologue and the epilogue—twelve times in all—and in spite of what I have said about the too great length of the poem, this is an intellectual victory that no one else but

Browning could have won against its difficulties. Whether it was worth the creation by himself of the difficulty is another question. He chose to do it, and we had better submit to him and get the good of his work. At least we may avoid some of the weariness he himself feared by reading it in the way I have mentioned, as Browning meant it to be read. Poems—being the highest product of the highest genius of which man is capable—ought to be approached with some reverence. And a part of that reverence is to read them in accordance with the intention and desire of the writer.

We ought not to forget the date of the tale when we read the book. It is just two hundred years ago. The murder of Pompilia took place in 1698; and the book completes his studies of the Renaissance in its decay. If *Sordello* is worth our careful reading as a study of the thirteenth century in North Italy, this book is as valuable as a record of the society of its date. It is, in truth, a mine of gold; pure crude ore is secreted from man's life, then moulded into figures of living men and women by the insight and passion of the poet. In it is set down Rome as she was—her customs, opinions, classes of society; her dress, houses, streets, lanes, byeways and squares; her architecture, fountains, statues, courts of law, convents, gardens; her fashion and its drawing-rooms, the various professions and their habits, high life and middle class, tradesmen and beggars, priest, friar, lay-ecclesiastic, cardinal and Pope. Nowhere is this pictorial and individualising part of Browning's genius more delighted with its work. Every description is written by a lover of humanity, and with joy.

Nor is he less vivid in the *mise-en-scène* in which he places this multitude of personages. In *Half-Rome* we mingle with the crowd between Palazzo Fiano and Ruspoli, and pass into the church of Lorenzo in Lucina where the murdered bodies are exposed. The mingled humours of the crowd, the various persons and their characters are combined with and enhanced by the scenery. Then there is the Market Place by the Capucin convent of the Piazza Barberini, with the fountains leaping; then the *Réunion* at a palace, and the fine fashionable folk among the mirrors and the chandeliers, each with their view of the question; then the Courthouse, with all its paraphernalia, where Guido and Caponsacchi plead; then, the sketches, as new matters turn up, of the obscure streets of Rome, of the country round Arezzo, of Arezzo itself, of the post road from Arezzo to Rome and the country inn near Rome, of the garden house in the suburbs, of the households of the two advocates and their different ways of living; of the Pope in his closet and of Guido in the prison cell; and last, the full description of the streets and the Piazza del Popolo on the day of the execution—all with a hundred vivifying, illuminating, minute details attached to them by this keen-eyed, observant, questing poet who remembered everything he saw, and was able to use each detail where it was most wanted. Memories are good, but good usage of them is the fine power. The *mise-en-scène* is then excellent, and Browning was always careful to make it right, fitting and enlivening. Nowhere is this better done than in the Introduction where he finds the book on a stall in the Square of San Lorenzo, and describes modern

Florence in his walk from the Square past the Strozzi, the Pillar and the Bridge to Casa Guidi on the other side of the Arno opposite the little church of San Felice. During the walk he read the book through, yet saw everything he passed by. The description will show how keen were his eyes, how masterly his execution.

> That memorable day,
> (June was the month, Lorenzo named the Square)
> I leaned a little and overlooked my prize
> By the low railing round the fountain-source
> Close to the statue, where a step descends:
> While clinked the cans of copper, as stooped and rose
> Thick-ankled girls who brimmed them, and made place
> For marketmen glad to pitch basket down,
> Dip a broad melon-leaf that holds the wet,
> And whisk their faded fresh. And on I read
> Presently, though my path grew perilous
> Between the outspread straw-work, piles of plait
> Soon to be flapping, each o'er two black eyes
> And swathe of Tuscan hair, on festas fine:
> Through fire-irons, tribes of tongs, shovels in sheaves,
> Skeleton bedsteads, wardrobe-drawers agape,
> Rows of tall slim brass lamps with dangling gear,—
> And worse, cast clothes a-sweetening in the sun:
> None of them took my eye from off my prize.
> Still read I on, from written title page
> To written index, on, through street and street,
> At the Strozzi, at the Pillar, at the Bridge;
> Till, by the time I stood at home again
> In Casa Guidi by Felice Church,
> Under the doorway where the black begins
> With the first stone-slab of the staircase cold,
> I had mastered the contents, knew the whole truth
> Gathered together, bound up in this book,
> Print three-fifths, written supplement the rest.

This power, combined with his power of portraiture, makes this long poem alive. No other man of his century could paint like him the to and fro of a city, the hurly-burly of humanity, the crowd, the movement, the changing passions, the loud or quiet clash of thoughts, the gestures, the dress, the interweaving of expression on the face, the whole play of humanity in war or peace. As we read, we move with men and women; we are pressed everywhere by mankind. We listen to the sound of humanity, sinking sometimes to the murmur we hear at night from some high window in London; swelling sometimes, as in *Sordello*, into a roar of violence, wrath, revenge, and war. And it was all contained in that little body, brain and heart; and given to us, who can feel it, but not give it. This is the power which above all endears him to us as a poet. We feel in each poem not only the waves of the special event of which he writes, but also the large vibration of the ocean of humanity.

He was not unaware of this power of his. We are told in *Sordello* that he dedicated himself to the picturing of humanity; and he came to think that a Power beyond ours had accepted this dedication, and directed his work. He declares in the introduction that he felt a Hand ("always above my shoulder—mark the predestination"), that pushed him to the stall where he found the fated book in whose womb lay his child—*The Ring and the Book*. And he believed that he had certain God-given qualities which fitted him for this work. These he sets forth in this introduction, and the self-criticism is of the greatest interest.

The first passage is, when he describes how, having finished the book and got into him all the gold of its fact, he added from himself that to the gold which made it workable—added to it his live soul, informed, transpierced it through and through with imagination; and then, standing on his balcony over the street, saw the whole story from the beginning shape itself out on the night, alive and clear, not in dead memory but in living movement; saw right away out on the Roman road to Arezzo, and all that there befell; then passed to Rome again with the actors in the tragedy, a presence with them who heard them speak and think and act. The "life in him abolished the death of things—deep calling unto deep." For "a spirit laughed and leaped through his every limb, and lit his eye, and lifted him by the hair, and let him have his will" with Pompilia, Guido, Caponsacchi, the lawyers, the Pope, and the whole of Rome. And they rose from the dead; the old woe stepped on the stage again at the magician's command; and the rough gold of fact was rounded to a ring by art. But the ring should have a posy, and he makes that in a passionate cry to his dead wife—a lovely spell where high thinking and full feeling meet and mingle like two deep rivers. Whoso reads it feels how her spirit, living still for him, brooded over and blest his masterpiece:

> O lyric Love, half angel and half bird
> And all a wonder and a wild desire,—
> Boldest of hearts that ever braved the sun,
> Took sanctuary within the holier blue,
> And sang a kindred soul out to his face,—
> Yet human at the red-ripe of the heart—
> When the first summons from the darkling earth
> Reached thee amid thy chambers, blanched their blue,
> And bared them of the glory—to drop down,
> To toil for man, to suffer or to die,—
> This is the same voice: can thy soul know change
> Hail then, and hearken from the realms of help!
> Never may I commence my song, my due
> To God who best taught song by gift of thee,

> Except with bent head and beseeching hand—
> That still, despite the distance and the dark,
> What was, again may be; some interchange
> Of grace, some splendour once thy very thought,
> Some benediction anciently thy smile:
> —Never conclude, but raising hand and head
> Thither where eyes, that cannot reach, yet yearn
> For all hope, all sustainment, all reward,
> Their utmost up and on,—so blessing back
> In those thy realms of help, that heaven thy home,
> Some whiteness which, I judge, thy face makes proud,
> Some wanness where, I think, thy foot may fall!

The poem begins with the view that one half of Rome took of the events. At the very commencement we touch one of the secondary interests of the book, the incidental characters. Guido, Caponsacchi, Pompilia, the Pope, and, in a lesser degree, Violante and Pietro, are the chief characters, and the main interest contracts around them. But, through all they say and do, as a motley crowd through a street, a great number of minor characters move to and fro; and Browning, whose eye sees every face, and through the face into the soul, draws them one by one, some more fully than others in perhaps a hundred lines, some only in ten. Most of them are types of a class, a profession or a business, yet there is always a touch or two which isolates each of them so that they do not only represent a class but a personal character. He hated, like Morris, the withering of the individual, nor did he believe, nor any man who knows and feels mankind, that by that the world grew more and more. The poem is full of such individualities. It were well, as one example, to read the whole account of the people who come to see the murdered bodies laid out in the Church of Lorenzo. The old, curious, doddering gossip of the Roman street is not less alive than the Cardinal, and the clever pushing Curato; and around them are heard the buzz of talk, the movement of the crowd. The church, the square are humming with humanity.

He does the same clever work at the deathbed of Pompilia. She lies in the House of the dying, and certain folk are allowed to see her. Each one is made alive by this creative pencil; and all are different, one from the other—the Augustinian monk, old mother Baldi chattering like a jay who thought that to touch Pompilia's bedclothes would cure her palsy, Cavalier Carlo who fees the porter to paint her face just because she was murdered and famous, the folk who argue on theology over her wounded body. Elsewhere we possess the life-history of Pietro and Violante, Pompilia's reputed parents; several drawings of the retired tradesmen class, with their gossips and friends, in the street of a poor quarter in Rome; then, the Governor and Archbishop of Arezzo, the friar who is kindly but fears the world and all the busy-bodies of this provincial town. Arezzo, its characters and indwellers, stand in clear light. The most vivid of these sketches is Dominus Hyacinthus, the lawyer who defends Guido. I do not know anything better done, and more amusingly, than this man and his household—a paternal creature, full of his boys and their studies, making us, in his garrulous pleasure, at home with them and his fat wife. Browning was so fond of this sketch that he drew him and his boys over again in the epilogue.

These represent the episodical characters in this drama of life; and Browning has scattered them, as it were, behind the chief characters, whom sometimes they illustrate and sometimes they contrast. Of these the whitest, simplest, loveliest is Pompilia, of whom I have already written. The other chief characters are Count Guido and Giuseppe Caponsacchi; and to the full development of these two characters Browning gives all his powers. They are contrasted types of the spirit of good and the spirit of evil conquering in man. Up to a certain point in life their conduct is much alike. Both belong to the Church—one as a priest, one as a layman affiliated to the Church. The lust of money and self, when the character of Pompilia forces act, turns Guido into a beast of greed and hate. The same character, when it forces act, lifts Caponsacchi into almost a saint. This was a piece of contrasted psychology in which the genius of Browning revelled, and he followed all the windings of it in both these hearts with the zest of an explorer. They were labyrinthine, but the more labyrinthine the better he was pleased. Guido's first speech is made before the court in his defence. We see disclosed the outer skin of the man's soul, all that he would have the world know of him—cynical, mocking, not cruel, not affectionate, a man of the world whom life had disappointed, and who wishing to establish himself in a retired life by marriage had been deceived and betrayed, he pleads, by his wife and her parents—an injured soul who, stung at last into fury at having a son foisted on him, vindicates his honour. And in this vindication his hypocrisy slips at intervals from him, because his hatred of his wife is too much for his hypocrisy.

This is the only touch of the wolf in the man—

his cruel teeth shown momentarily through the smooth surface of his defence. A weaker poet would have left him there, not having capacity for more. But Browning, so rich in thought he was, had only begun to draw him. Guido is not only painted by three others—by Caponsacchi, by Pompilia, by the Pope—but he finally exposes his real self with his own hand. He is condemned to death. Two of his friends visit him the night before his execution, in his cell. Then, exalted into eloquence by the fierce passions of fear of death and hatred of Pompilia, he lays bare as the night his very soul, mean, cruel, cowardly, hungry for revenge, crying for life, black with hate—a revelation such as in literature can best be paralleled by the soliloquies of Iago. Baseness is supreme in his speech, hate was never better given; the words are like the gnashing of teeth; prayers for life at any cost were never meaner, and the outburst of terror and despair at the end is their ultimate expression.

Over against him is set Caponsacchi, of noble birth, of refined manner, one of those polished and cultivated priests of whom Rome makes such excellent use, and of whom Browning had drawn already a different type in Bishop Blougram. He hesitated, being young and gay, to enter the Church. But the archbishop of that easy time, two hundred years ago, told him the Church was strong enough to bear a few light priests, and that he would be set free from many ecclesiastical duties if, by assiduity in society and with women, he strengthened the social weight of the Church. In that way, making his madrigals and confessing fine ladies, he lived for four years. This is an admirable sketch of a type of Church society of that date, indeed, of any date in any Church; it is by no means confined to Rome.

On this worldly, careless, indifferent, pleasure-seeking soul Pompilia, in her trouble and the pity of it, rises like a pure star seen through mist that opens at intervals to show her excelling brightness; and in a moment, at the first glimpse of her in the theatre, the false man drops away; his soul breaks up, stands clear, and claims its divine birth. He is born again, and then transfigured. The life of convention, of indifference, dies before Pompilia's eyes; and on the instant he is true to himself, to her, and to God. The fleeting passions which had absorbed him, and were of the senses, are burned up, and the spiritual love for her purity, and for purity itself —that eternal, infinite desire—is now master of his life. Not as Miranda and Ferdinand changed eyes in youthful love, but as Dante and Beatrice look on one another in Paradise, did Pompilia and Caponsacchi change eyes, and know at once that both were true, and see without speech the central worth of their souls. They trusted one another and they loved for ever. So, when she cried to him in her distress, he did her bidding and bore her away to Rome. He tells the story of their flight, and tells it with extraordinary beauty and vehemence in her defence. So noble is the tale that he convinces the judges who at first had disbelieved him; and the Pope confesses that his imprudence was a higher good than priestly prudence would have been. When he makes his defence he has heard that Pompilia has been murdered. Then we understand that in his conversion to goodness he has not lost but gained passion. Scorn of the judges, who could not see that neither he was guilty nor Pompilia; fiery indignation with the murderer; infinite grief for the lamb slain by the wolf, and irrevocable love for the soul of Pompilia, whom he will dwell with eternally when they meet in Heaven, a love which Pompilia, dying, declares she has for him, and in which, growing and abiding, she will wait for him—burn on his lips. He is fully and nobly a man; yet, at the end—and he is no less a man for it—the wild sorrow at his heart breaks him down into a cry:

> O great, just, good God! Miserable me!

Pompilia ends her words more quietly, in the faith that comes with death. Caponsacchi has to live on, to bear the burden of the world. But Pompilia has borne all she had to bear. All pain and horror are behind her, as she lies in the stillness, dying. And in the fading of this life, she knows she loves Caponsacchi in the spiritual world and will love him for ever. Each speaks according to the circumstance, but she most nobly:

> He is ordained to call and I to come!
> Do not the dead wear flowers when dressed for God?
> Say,—I am all in flowers from head to foot!
> Say,—not one flower of all he said and did,
> Might seem to flit unnoticed, fade unknown,
> But dropped a seed, has grown a balsam-tree
> Whereof the blossoming perfumes the place
> At this supreme of moments! He is a priest;
> He cannot marry therefore, which is right:
> I think he would not marry if he could.
> Marriage on earth seems such a counterfeit,
> Mere imitation of the inimitable:
> In heaven we have the real and true and sure.
> 'Tis there they neither marry nor are given
> In marriage but are as the angels: right,
> Oh how right that is, how like Jesus Christ
> To say that! Marriage-making for the earth,

> With gold so much,—birth, power, repute so much,
> Or beauty, youth so much, in lack of these!
> Be as the angels rather, who, apart,
> Know themselves into one, are found at length
> Married, but marry never, no, nor give
> In marriage; they are man and wife at once
> When the true time is; here we have to wait
> Not so long neither! Could we by a wish
> Have what we will and get the future now,
> Would we wish aught done undone in the past?
> So, let him wait God's instant men call years;
> Meantime hold hard by truth and his great soul,
> Do out the duty! Through such souls alone
> God stooping shows sufficient of His light
> For us i' the dark to rise by. And I rise.

Last of these main characters, the Pope appears. Guido, condemned to death by the law, appeals from the law to the head of the Church, because, being half an ecclesiastic, his death can only finally be decreed by the ecclesiastical arm. An old, old man, with eyes clear of the quarrels, conventions, class prejudices of the world, the Pope has gone over all the case during the day, and now night has fallen. Far from the noise of Rome, removed from the passions of the chief characters, he is sitting in the stillness of his closet, set on his decision. We see the whole case now, through his mind, in absolute quiet. He has been on his terrace to look at the stars, and their solemn peace is with him. He feels that he is now alone with God and his old age. And being alone, he is not concise, but garrulous and discursive. Browning makes him so on purpose. But discursive as his mind is, his judgment is clear, his sentence determined. Only, before he speaks, he will weigh all the characters, and face any doubts that may shoot into his conscience. He passes Guido and the rest before his spiritual tribunal, judging not from the legal point of view, but from that which his Master would take at the Judgment Day. How have they lived; what have they made of life? When circumstances invaded them with temptation, how did they meet temptation? Did they declare by what they did that they were on God's side or the devil's? And on these lines he delivers his sentence on Pompilia, Caponsacchi, Guido, Pietro, Violante, and the rest. He feels he speaks as the Vicegerent of God.

This solemn, silent, lonely, unworldly judgment of the whole case, done in God's presence, is, after the noisy, crowded, worldly judgment of it by Rome, after the rude humours of the law, and the terrible clashing of human passions, most impressive; and it rises into the majesty of old age in the summing up of the characters of Pompilia, Caponsacchi, and Guido. I wish Browning had left it there. But he makes a sudden doubt invade the Pope with a chill. Has he judged rightly in thinking that divine truth is with him? Is there any divine truth on which he may infallibly repose?

And then for many pages we are borne away into a theological discussion, which I take leave to say is wearisome; and which, after all, lands the Pope exactly at the point from which he set out—a conclusion at which, as we could have told him beforehand, he would be certain to arrive. We might have been spared this. It is an instance of Browning's pleasure in intellectual discourse which had, as I have said, such sad results on his imaginative work. However, at the end, the Pope resumes his interest in human life. He determines; and quickly —" Let the murderer die to-morrow."

Then comes the dreadful passion of Guido in the condemned cell, of which I have spoken. And then, one would think the poem would have closed. But no, the epilogue succeeds, in which, after all the tragedy, humour reigns supreme. It brings us into touch with all that happened in this case after the execution of Guido; the letters written by the spectators, the lawyer's view of the deed, the gossip of Rome upon the interesting occasion. No piece of humour in Browning's poetry, and no portrait-sketching, is better than the letter written by a Venetian gentleman in Rome giving an account of the execution. It is high comedy when we are told that the Austrian Ambassador, who had pleaded for Guido's life, was so vexed by the sharp "no" of the Pope (even when he had told the Pope that he had probably dined at the same table with Guido), that he very nearly refused to come to the execution, and would scarcely vouchsafe it more than a glance when he did come—as if this conduct of his were a slight which the Pope would feel acutely. Nor does Browning's invention stop with this inimitable letter. He adds two other letters which he found among the papers; and these give to the characters of the two lawyers, new turns, new images of their steady professional ambition not to find truth, but to gain the world.

One would think, after this, that invention would be weary. Not at all! The Augustinian monk who attended Pompilia has not had attention enough; and this is the place, Browning thinks, to show what he thought of the case, and how he used it in his profession. So, we are given a great part of the sermon he preached on the occasion, and the various judgments of Rome upon it.

It is wonderful, after invention has been actively at work for eleven long books, pouring forth its waters from an unfailing fountain, to find it, at the end, as gay, as fresh, as keen, as youthful as ever. This, I repeat, is the excellence of Browning's genius—fulness of creative power, with imagination in it like a fire. It does not follow that all it produces is poetry; and what it has produced in *The Ring and the Book* is sometimes, save for the metre, nothing better than prose. But this is redeemed by the noble poetry of a great part of it. The book is, as I have said, a mixed book—the central arena of that struggle in Browning between prose and poetry with a discussion of which this chapter began, and with the mention of which I finish it.

CHAPTER XVII

LATER POEMS

A JUST appreciation of the work which Browning published after *The Ring and the Book* is a difficult task. The poems are of various kinds, on widely separated subjects; and with the exception of those which treat of Balaustion, they have no connection with one another. Many of them must belong to the earlier periods of his life, and been introduced into the volumes out of the crowd of unpublished poems every poet seems to possess. These, when we come across them among their middle-aged companions, make a strange impression, as if we found a white-thorn flowering in an autumnal woodland; and in previous chapters of this book I have often fetched them out of their places, and considered them where they ought to be —in the happier air and light in which they were born. I will not discuss them again, but in forming any judgment of the later poems they must be discarded.

The struggle to which I have drawn attention between the imaginative and intellectual elements in Browning, and which was equally balanced in *The Ring and the Book*, continued after its publication, but with a steady lessening of the imaginative and a steady increase of the intellectual elements. One poem, however, written before the publication of *The Ring and the Book*, does not belong to this struggle. This is *Hervé Riel*, a ballad of fire and joy and triumph. It is curiously French in sentiment and expression, and the eager sea-delight in it is plainly French, not English in feeling. Nor is it only French; it is Breton in audacity, in self-forgetfulness, in carelessness of reward, and in loyalty to country, to love and to home. If Browning had been all English, this transference of himself into the soul of another nationality would have been wonderful, nay, impossible. As it is, it is wonderful enough; and this self-transference—one of his finest poetic powers—is nowhere better accomplished than in this poem, full of the salt wind and the leap and joy of the sea-waves; but even more full, as was natural to Browning, of the Breton soul of Hervé Riel.

In *Balaustion's Adventure* (1871) which next appeared, the imaginative elements, as we have seen, are still alive and happy; and though they only emerge at intervals in its continuation, *Aristophanes' Apology* (1875), yet they do emerge. Meanwhile, between *Balaustion's Adventure* and the end of 1875, he produced four poems—*Prince Hohenstiel Schwangau, Saviour of Society; Fifine at the Fair; Red Cotton Nightcap Country, or Turf and Towers;* and *The Inn Album*. They are all long, and were published in four separate volumes. In them the intellectual elements have all but completely conquered the imaginative. They are, however, favourite "exercise-places" for some of his admirers, who think that they derive poetic pleasures from their study. The pleasure these poems give, when they give it, is not altogether a poetic pleasure. It is chiefly the pleasure of the understanding called to solve with excitement a huddle of metaphysical problems. They have the name but not the nature of poetry.

They are the work of my Lord Intelligence—attended by wit and fancy—who sits at the desk of poetry, and with her pen in his hand. He uses the furniture of poetry, but the goddess herself has left the room. Yet something of her influence still fills the air of the chamber. In the midst of the brilliant display that fancy, wit, and intellect are making, a soft steady light of pure song burns briefly at intervals, and then is quenched; like the light of stars seen for a moment of quiet effulgence among the crackling and dazzling of fireworks.

The poems are, it is true, original. We cannot class them with any previous poetry. They cannot be called didactic or satirical. The didactic and satirical poems of England are, for the most part, artificial, concise, clear. These poems are not artificial, clear or concise. Nor do they represent the men and women of a cultured, intellectual and conventional society, such as the poetry of Dryden and Pope addressed. The natural man is in them —the crude, dull, badly-baked man—what the later nineteenth century called the real man. We see his ugly, sordid, contemptible, fettered soul, and long for Salinguerra, or Lippo Lippi, or even Caliban. The representations are then human enough, with this kind of humanity, but they might have been left to prose. Poetry has no business to build its houses on the waste and leprous lands of human nature; and less business to call its work art. Realism of this kind is not art, it is science.

Yet the poems are not scientific, for they have no clarity of argument. Their wanderings of thought are as intertangled as the sheep-walks on league after league of high grasslands. When one has a fancy to follow them, the pursuit is entertaining; but unless one has the fancy, there are livelier employments. Their chief interest is the impression they give us of a certain side of Browning's character. They are his darling debauch of cleverness, of surface-psychology. The analysis follows no conventional lines, does not take or oppose any well-known philosophical side. It is not much more than his own serious or fantastic thinking indulging itself with reckless abandon—amusing itself with itself. And this gives them a humanity—a Browning humanity—outside of their subjects.

The subjects too, though not delightful, are founded on facts of human life. *Bishop Blougram* was conceived from Cardinal Wiseman's career, *Mr. Sludge* from Mr. Home's. *Prince Hohenstiel Schwangau* explains and defends the expediency by which Napoleon III. directed his political action. *The Inn Album, Red Cotton Nightcap Country*, are taken from actual stories that occurred while Browning was alive, and *Fifine at the Fair* analyses a common crisis in the maturer lives of men and women. The poems thus keep close to special cases, yet—and in this the poet appears—they have an extension which carries them beyond the particular subjects into the needs and doings of a wider humanity. Their little rivers run into the great sea. They have then their human interest for a reader who does not wish for beauty, passion, imagination, or the desires of the spirit in his poetry; but who hankers at his solitary desk after realistic psychology, fanciful ethics, curiosities of personal philosophy, cold intellectual play with argument, and honest human ugliness.

Moreover, the method Browning attempts to use in them for the discovery of truth is not the method of poetry, nor of any of the arts. It is almost a commonplace to say that the world of mankind and each individual in it only arrives at the truth on any matter, large or small, by going through and exhausting the false forms of that truth—and a very curious arrangement it seems to be. It is this method Browning pursues in these poems. He represents one after another various false or half-true views of the matter in hand, and hopes in that fashion to clear the way to the truth. But he fails to convince partly because it is impossible to give all or enough of the false or half-true views of any one truth, but chiefly because his method is one fitted for philosophy or science, but not for poetry. Poetry claims to see and feel the truth at once. When the poet does not assert that claim, and act on it, he is becoming faithless to his art.

Browning's method in these poems is the method of a scientific philosopher, not of an artist. He gets his man into a debateable situation; the man debates it from various points of view; persons are introduced who take other aspects of the question, or personified abstractions such as *Sagacity, Reason, Fancy* give their opinions. Not satisfied with this, Browning discusses it again from his own point of view. He is then like the chess-player who himself plays both red and white; who tries to keep both distinct in his mind, but cannot help now and again taking one side more than the other; and who is frequently a third person aware of himself as playing red, and also of himself as playing white; and again of himself as outside both the players and criticising their several games. This is no exaggerated account of what is done in these poems. Three people, even when the poems are monologues, are arguing in them, and Browning plays all their hands, even in *The Inn Album*, which is not a monologue. In *Red Cotton Nightcap Country*, when he has told the story of the man and woman in all its sordid and insane detail, with comments of his own, he brings the victim of mean pleasure and mean superstition to the top of the tower whence he throws himself down, and, inserting his intelligence into the soul of the man, explains his own view of the situation. In *Prince Hohenstiel Schwangau*, we have sometimes what Browning really thinks, as in the beginning of the poem, about the matter in hand, and then what he thinks the Prince would think, and then, to complicate the affair still more, the Prince divides himself, and makes a personage called *Sagacity* argue with him on the whole situation. As to *Fifine at the Fair*—a poem it would not be fair to class altogether with these—its involutions resemble a number of live eels in a tub of water. Don Juan changes his personality and his views like a player on the stage who takes several parts; Elvire is a gliding phantom with gliding opinions; Fifine is real, but she remains outside of this shifting scenery of the mind; and Browning, who continually intrudes, is sometimes Don Juan and sometimes himself and sometimes both together, and sometimes another thinker who strives to bring, as in the visions in the poem, some definition into this changing cloudland of the brain. And after all, not one of the questions posed in any of the poems is settled in the end. I do not say that the leaving of the questions unsettled is not like life. It is very like life, but not like the work of poetry, whose high office it is to decide questions which cannot be solved by the understanding.

Bishop Blongram thinks he has proved his points. Gigadibs is half convinced he has. But the Bishop, on looking back, thinks he has not been quite sincere, that his reasonings were only good for the occasion. He has evaded the centre of the thing. What he has said was no more than intellectual fencing. It certainly is intellectual fencing of the finest kind. Both the Bishop and his companion are drawn to the life; yet, and this is the cleverest thing in the poem, we know that the Bishop is in reality a different man from the picture he makes of himself. And the truth which in his talk underlies its appearance acts on Gigadibs and sends him into a higher life. The discussion—as it may be called though the Bishop only speaks—concerning faith and doubt is full of admirable wisdom, and urges me to modify my statement that Browning took little or no interest in the controversies of his time. Yet, all through the fencing, nothing is decided. The button is always on the Bishop's foil. He never sends the rapier home. And no doubt that is the reason that his companion, with "his sudden healthy vehemence" did drive his weapon home into life—and started for Australia.

Mr. Sludge, the medium, excuses his imposture,

and then thinks "it may not altogether be imposture. For all he knows there may really be spirits at the bottom of it. He never meant to cheat; yet he did cheat. Yet, even if he lied, lies help truth to live; and he must live himself; and God may have made fools for him to live on;" and many other are the twists of his defence. The poem is as lifelike in its insight into the mind of a supple cheat as it is a brilliant bit of literature; but Browning leaves the matter unconcluded, as he would not have done, I hold, had he been writing poetry. Prince Hohenstiel's defence of expediency in politics is made by Browning to seem now right, now wrong, because he assumes at one time what is true as the ground of his argument, and then at another what is plainly false, and in neither case do the assumptions support the arguments. What really is concluded is not the question, but the slipperiness of the man who argues. And at the end of the poem Browning comes in again to say that words cannot be trusted to hit truth. Language is inadequate to express it. Browning was fond of saying this. It does not seem worth saying. In one sense it is a truism; in another it resembles nonsense. Words are the only way by which we can express truth, or our nearest approach to what we think it is. At any rate, silence, in spite of Maeterlinck, does not express it. Moreover, with regard to the matter in hand, Browning knew well enough how a poet would decide the question of expediency he has here brought into debate. He has decided it elsewhere; but here he chooses not to take that view, that he may have the fun of exercising his clever brain. There is no reason why he should not entertain himself and us in this way; but folk need not call this intellectual jumping to and fro a poem, or try to induce us to believe that it is the work of art.

When he had finished these products of a time when he was intoxicated with his intellect, and of course somewhat proud of it, the poet in him began to revive. This resurrection had begun in *Fifine at the Fair*. I have said it would not be just to class this poem with the other three. It has many an oasis of poetry where it is a happiness to rest. But the way between their palms and wells is somewhat dreary walking, except to those who adore minute psychology. The poem is pitilessly long. If throughout its length it were easy to follow we might excuse the length, but it is rendered difficult by the incessant interchange of misty personalities represented by one personality. Elvire, Fifine only exist in the mind of Don Juan; their thoughts are only expressed in his words; their outlines not only continually fade into his, but his thought steals into his presentation of their thought, till it becomes impossible to individualise them. The form in which Browning wrote the poem, by which he made Don Juan speak for them, makes this want of clearness and sharpness inevitable. The work is done with a terrible cleverness, but it is wearisome at the last.

The length also might be excused if the subject were a great one or had important issues for mankind. But, though it has its interest and is human enough, it does not deserve so many thousand lines nor so much elaborate analysis. A few lyrics or a drama of two acts might say all that is worth saying on the matter. What Browning has taken for subject is an every-day occurrence. We are grateful to him for writing on so universal a matter, even though it is unimportant; and he has tried to make it uncommon and important by weaving round it an intricate lace-work of psychology; yet, when we get down to its main lines, it is the ordinary event, especially commonplace in any idle society which clings to outward respectability and is dreadfully wearied of it. Our neighbours across the Channel call it *La Crise* when, after years of a quiet, not unhappy, excellent married existence, day succeeding day in unbroken continuity of easy affection and limited experience, the man or the woman, in full middle life, suddenly wearies of the apparent monotony, the uneventful love, the slow encroaching tide of the commonplace, and looks on these as fetters on their freedom, as walls which shut them in from the vivid interests of the outside world, from the gipsy roving of the passions. The time arrives, when this becomes, they think, too great for endurance, and their impatience shows itself in a daily irritability quite new in the household, apparently causeless, full of sudden, inexplicable turns of thought and act which turn the peaceful into a tempestuous home. It is not that the husband or the wife are inconstant by nature—to call *Fifine at the Fair* a defence of inconstancy is to lose the truth of the matter—but it is the desire of momentary change, of a life set free from conventional barriers, of an outburst into the unknown, of the desire for new experiences, for something which will bring into play those parts of their nature of which they are vaguely conscious but which are as yet unused—new elements in their senses, intellect, imagination, even in their spirit, but not always in their conscience. That, for the time being, as in this poem, is often shut up in the cellar, where its voice cannot be heard.

This is, as I said, a crisis of common occurrence. It may be rightly directed, its evil controlled, and a noble object chosen for the satisfaction of the impulse. Here, that is not the case; and Browning describes its beginning with great freshness and force as Juan walks down to the fair with Elvire. Nor has he omitted to treat other forms of it in his poetry. He knew how usual it was, but he has here made it unusual by putting it into the heart of a man who, before he yielded to it, was pleased to make it the subject of a wandering metaphysical analysis; who sees not only how it appears to himself in three or four moods, but how it looks to the weary, half-jealous wife to whom he is so rude while he strives to be courteous, and to the bold, free, conscienceless child of nature whose favour he buys, and with whom, after all his barren metaphysics, he departs, only to attain, when his brief spell of foolish freedom is over, loneliness and cynic satiety. It may amuse us to circle with him through his arguments, though every one knows he will yield at last and that yielding is more honest than his talk; but what we ask is—Was the matter worth the trouble of more than two thousand lines of long-winded verse? Was it worth an artist's devotion? or, to ask a question I would not ask if the poem were good art, is it of any real importance to mankind? Is it, finally, anything more than an intellectual exercise of Browning on which solitary psychologists may, in their turn, employ their neat intelligence? This poem, with the exceptions of some episodes of noble poetry, is, as well as the three others, a very harlequinade of the intellect.

I may say, though this is hypercritical, that the name of Don Juan is a mistake. Every one knows Don Juan, and to imagine him arguing in the fashion of this poem is absurd. He would instantly, without a word, have left Elvire, and abandoned Fifine in a few days. The connection then of the long discussions in the poem with his name throws an air of unreality over the whole of it. The Don Juan of the poem had much better have stayed with Elvire, who endured him with weary patience. I have no doubt that he bored Fifine to extinction.

The poems that follow these four volumes are mixed work, half imaginative, half intellectual. Sometimes both kinds are found, separated, in the same poem; sometimes in one volume half the poems will be imaginative and the other half not. Could the imaginative and intellectual elements have now been fused as they were in his earlier work, it were well; but they were not. They worked apart. His witful poems are all wit, his analytical poems are all analysis, and his imaginative poems, owing to this want of fusion, have not the same intellectual strength they had in other days. *Numpholeptos*, for instance, an imaginative poem, full too of refined and fanciful emotion, is curiously wanting in intellectual foundation.

The *Numpholeptos* is in the volume entitled *Pacchiarotto, and how he worked in Distemper*. Part of the poems in it are humorous, such as *Pacchiarotto* and *Filippo Baldinucci*, excellent pieces of agreeable wit, containing excellent advice concerning life. One reads them, is amused by them, and rarely desires to read them again. In the same volume there are some severe pieces, sharply ridiculing his critics. In the old days, when he wrote fine imaginative poetry, out of his heart and brain working together, he did not mind what the critics said, and only flashed a scoff or two at them in his creation of Naddo in *Sordello*. But now when he wrote a great deal of his poetry out of his brain alone, he became sensitive to criticism. For that sort of poetry does not rest on the sure foundation which is given by the consciousness the imagination has of its absolute rightness. He expresses his needless soreness with plenty of wit in *Pacchiarotto* and in the *Epilogue*, criticises his critics, and displays his good opinion of his work—no doubt of these later poems, like *The Inn Album* and the rest—with a little too much of self-congratulation. "The poets pour us wine," he says, "and mine is strong—the strong wine of the loves and hates and thoughts of man. But it is not sweet as well, and my critics object. Were it so, it would be more popular than it is. Sweetness and strength do not go together, and I have strength."

But that is not the real question. The question is—Is the strength poetical? Has it imagination? It is rough, powerful, full of humanity, and that is well. But is it half prose, or wholly prose? Or is it poetry, or fit to be called so? He thinks that *Prince Hohenstiel*, or *Red Cotton Nightcap Country*, are poetry. They are, it is true, strong; and they are not sweet. But have they the strength of poetry in them, and not the strength of something else altogether? That is the question he ought to have answered, and it does not occur to him.

Yet, he was, in this very book, half-way out of

this muddle. There are poems in it, just as strong as *The Inn Album*, but with the ineffable spirit of imaginative emotion and thought clasped together in them, so that the strong is stronger, and the humanity deeper than in the pieces he thought, being deceived by the Understanding, were more strong than the poems of old. In *Bifurcation*, in *St. Martin's Summer*, the diviner spirit breathes. There is that other poem called *Forgiveness* of which I have already spoken—one of his masterpieces. *Cenciaja*, which may be classed with *Forgiveness* as a study of the passion of hatred, is not so good as its comrade, but its hatred is shown in a mean character and for a meaner motive. And the *Prologue*, in its rhythm and pleasure, its subtlety of thought, its depth of feeling, and its close union of both, recalls his earlier genius.

The first of the *Pisgah Sights* is a jewel. It is like a poem by Goethe, only Goethe would have seen the "sight" not when he was dying, but when he was alive to his finger-tips. The second is not like Goethe's work, nor Browning's; but it is a true picture of what many feel and are. So is *Fears and Scruples*. As to *Natural Magic*, surely it is the most charming of compliments, most enchantingly expressed.

The next volume of original poems was *La Saisiaz* and the *Two Poets of Croisic*. The *Croisic Poets* are agreeable studies, written with verve and lucidity, of two fantastic events which lifted these commonplace poets suddenly into fame. They do well to amuse an idle hour. The end of both is interesting. That of the first, which begins with stanza lix., discusses the question: "Who cares, how such a mediocrity as René lived after the fame of his prophecy died out?"* And Browning answers—

> Well, I care—intimately care to have
>   Experience how a human creature felt
> In after life, who bore the burthen grave
>   Of certainly believing God had dealt
> For once directly with him: did not rave
>   —A maniac, did not find his reason melt
> —An idiot, but went on, in peace or strife,
> The world's way, lived an ordinary life.

The solution Browning offers is interesting, because it recalls a part of the experiences of Lazarus in the *Epistle to Karshish*. René, like Lazarus, but only for a moment, has lived in the eternal.

Are such revelations possible, is his second question. Yes, he answers; and the form of the answer belongs to the theory of life laid down in *Paracelsus*. Such sudden openings of the greater world are at intervals, as to Abt Vogler, given by God to men.

The end of the second asks what is the true test of the greater poet, when people take on them to weigh the worth of poets—who was better, best, this, that or the other bard? When I read this I trembled, knowing that I had compared him with Tennyson. But when I heard the answer I trembled no more. "The best poet of any two is the one who leads the happier life. The strong and

---

* René Gentilhomme, page to Prince Condé, heir of France since Louis XIII. and his brother Gaston were childless, is surprised, while writing a love poem, by a lightning flash which shatters a marble ducal crown. He thinks this a revelation from God, and he prophecies that a Dauphin will be born to the childless Queen. The Dauphin was born, and René pushed suddenly into fame.

joyful poet is the greater." But this is a test of the greatness of a man, not necessarily of a poet. And, moreover, in this case, Tennyson and Browning both lived equally happy lives. Both were strong to the end, and imaginative joy was their companion. But the verse in which Browning winds up his answer is one of the finest in his poetry.

> So, force is sorrow, and each sorrow, force;
> What then? since Swiftness gives the charioteer
> The palm, his hope be in the vivid horse
> Whose neck God clothed with thunder, not the steer
> Sluggish and safe! Yoke Hatred, Crime, Remorse,
> Despair; but ever mid the whirling fear,
> Let, through the tumult, break the poet's face
> Radiant, assured his wild slaves win the race!

La Saisiaz is a more important poem: it describes the sudden death of his friend, Ann Egerton Smith, and passes from that, and all he felt concerning it, into an argument on the future life of the soul, with the assumption that God is, and the soul. The argument is interesting, but does not concern us here. What does concern us is that Browning has largely recovered his poetical way of treating a subject. He is no longer outside of it, but in it. He does not use it as a means of exercising his brains only. It is steeped in true and vital feeling, and the deep friendship he had for his friend fills even the theological argument with a passionate intensity. Nevertheless, the argument is perilously near the work of the understanding alone—as if a question like that of immortality could receive any solution from the hands of the understanding. Only each man, in the recesses of his own spirit with God, can solve that question for himself, and not for another. That is Browning's position when he writes as a poet, and no one has written more positively on the subject. But when he submits the question to reasoning, he wavers, as he does here, and leaves the question more undecided than anywhere else in his work. This is a pity, but it is the natural penalty of his partial abandonment of the poetic for the prosaic realm, of the imagination for the understanding, of the Reason for reasoning.

CHAPTER XVIII

THE LAST POEMS

TWO Volumes of Dramatic Idyls, one in 1879, the other in 1880, followed *La Saisiaz* and *The Two Poets of Croisic*. These are also mixed books, composed, partly of studies of character written in rhythmical prose, and partly of poems wrought out of the pure imagination. Three of them—if they were written at this time—show how the Greek legends still dwelt with Browning; and they brought with them the ocean-scent, heroic life, and mythical charm of Athenian thought. It would be difficult, if one could write of them at all, not to write of them poetically; and *Pheidippides, Echetlos, Pan and Luna* are alive with force, imaginative joy, and the victorious sense the poet has of having conquered his material. *Pheidippides* is as full of fire, of careless heroism as *Hervé Riel*, and told in as ringing verse. The versing of *Echetlos*, its rugged, rousing sound, its movement, are in most excellent harmony with the image of the rude, giant "Holder of the ploughshare," who at Marathon drove his furrows through the Persians and rooted up the Mede. Browning has gathered into one picture and one sound the whole spirit of the story. *Pan and Luna* is a bold re-rendering of the myth that Vergil enshrines, and the greater part of it is of such poetic freshness that I think it must be a waif from the earlier years of his poetry. Nor is there better imaginative work in his descriptive poetry than the image of the naked moon, in virginal distress, flying for refuge through the gazing heaven to the succourable cloud—fleece on fleece of piled-up snow, drowsily patient—where Pan lay in ambush for her beauty.

Among these more gracious idyls, one of singular rough power tells the ghastly tale of the mother who gave up her little children to the wolves to save herself. Browning liked this poem, and the end he added to the story—how the carpenter, Ivan, when the poor frightened woman confessed, lifted his axe and cut off her head; how he knew that he did right, and was held to have done right by the village and its pope. The sin by which a mother sacrificed the lives of her children to save her own was out of nature: the punishment should be outside of ordinary law. It is a piteous tale, and few things in Browning equal the horror of the mother's vain attempt to hide her crime while she confesses it. Nor does he often show greater imaginative skill in metrical movement than when he describes in galloping and pattering verse the grey pack emerging from the forest, their wild race for the sledge, and their demon leader.

The other idyls in these two volumes are full of interest for those who care for psychological studies expressed in verse. What the vehicle of verse does for them is to secure conciseness and suggestiveness in the rendering of remote, daring, and unexpected turns of thought and feeling, and especially of conscience. Yet the poems themselves cannot be called concise. Their subjects are not large enough, nor indeed agreeable enough, to excuse their length. Goethe would have put them into a short lyrical form. It is impossible not to regret, as we read them, the Browning of the *Dramatic Lyrics*. Moreover, some of them are needlessly ugly. *Halbert and Hob*—and in *Jocoseria*—*Donald*, are hateful subjects, and their treatment does not redeem them; unlike the treatment of *Ivan Ivanovitch* which does lift the pain of the story into the high realms of pity and justice. Death, swift death, was not only the right judgment, but also the most pitiful. Had the mother lived, an hour's memory would have been intolerable torture. Nevertheless, if Browning, in his desire to represent the whole of humanity, chose to treat these lower forms of human nature, I suppose we must accept them as an integral part of his work; and, at least, there can be no doubt of their ability, and of the brilliancy of their psychological surprises. *Ned Bratts* is a monument of cleverness, as well as of fine characterisation of a momentary outburst of conscience in a man who had none before; and who would have lost it in an hour, had he not been hanged on the spot. The quick, agile, unpremeditated turns of wit in this poem, as in some of the others, are admirably easy, and happily expressed. Indeed, in these later poems of character and event, ingenuity or nimbleness of intellect is the chief element, and it is accompanied by a facile power which is sometimes rude, often careless, always inventive, fully fantastical, and rarely imaginative in the highest sense of the word. Moreover, as was not the case of old, they have, beyond the story, a direct teaching aim, which, while it lowers them as art, is very agreeable to the ethical psychologist.

Jocoseria has poems of a higher quality, some of which, like the lovely *Never the Time and Place*, have been already quoted. *Ixion* is too obscurely put to attain its end with the general public. But it may be recommended, though vainly, to those theologians who, hungry for the Divine Right of torture, build their God, like Caliban, out of their own minds; who, foolish enough to believe that the everlasting endurance of evil is a necessary guarantee of the everlasting endurance of good, are still bold and bad enough to proclaim the abominable lie of eternal punishment. They need that spirit of the little child whom Christ placed in the midst of his disciples; and in gaining which, after living the life of the lover, the warrior, the poet, the statesman, *Jochanan Hakkadosh* found absolute peace and joy. Few poems contain more of Browning's matured theory of life than this of the Jewish Rabbi; and its seriousness is happily mingled with imaginative illustrations and with racy wit. The sketch of Tsaddik, who puts us in mind of Wagner in the *Faust*, is done with a sarcastic joy in exposing the Philistine, and with a delight in its own cleverness which is fascinating.

Ferishtah's Fancies and *Parleyings with Certain People* followed *Jocoseria* in 1884 and 1887. The first of these books is much the better of the two. A certain touch of romance is given by the Dervish, by the Fables with which he illustrates his teaching, and by the Eastern surroundings. Some of the stories are well told, and their scenery is truthfully wrought and in good colour. The subjects are partly theological, with always a reference to human life; and partly of the affections and their working. It is natural to a poet, and delightful in Browning, to find him in his old age dwelling from poem to poem on the pre-eminence of love, on love as the ultimate judge of all questions. He asserts this again and again; with the greatest force in *A Pillar at Sebzevar*, and, more lightly, in *Cherries*. Yet, and this is a pity, he is not satisfied with the decision of love, but spends pages in argumentative discussions which lead him away from that poetical treatment of the subjects which love alone, as the master, would have enabled him to give. However, the treatment that love gives we find in the lyrics at the end of each *Fancy*; and some of these lyrics are of such delicate and subtle beauty that I am tempted to think that they were written at an earlier period, and their *Fancies* composed to fit them. If they were written now, it is plain that age had not disenabled him from walking with pleasure and power among those sweet, enamelled meadows of poetry in whose soil he now thought great poetry did not grow. And when we read the lyrics, our regret is all the more deep that he chose the thorn-clad and desert lands, where barren argument goes round and round its subjects without ever finding the true path to their centre.

He lost himself more completely in this error in *Parleyings with Certain People*, in which book, with the exception of the visionary landscapes in *Gerard de Lairesse*, and some few passages in *Francis Furini* and *Charles Avison*, imagination, such as belongs to a poet, has deserted Browning. He feels himself as if this might be said of him; and he asks in *Gerard de Lairesse* if he has lost the poetic touch, the poetic spirit, because he writes of the soul, of facts, of things invisible—not of fancy's feignings, not of the things perceived by the senses? "I can do this," he answers, "if I like, as well as you," and he paints the landscape of a whole day filled with mythological figures. The passage is poetry; we see that he has not lost his poetic genius. But, he calls it "fooling," and then contrasts the spirit of Greek lore with the spirit of immortal hope and cheer which he possesses, with his faith that there is for man a certainty of Spring. But that is not the answer to his question. It only says that the spirit which animates him now is higher than the Greek spirit. It does not answer the question—Whether *Daniel Bartoli* or *Charles Avison* or any of these *Parleyings* even approach as poetry *Paracelsus*, the *Dramatic Lyrics*, or *Men and Women*. They do not. Nor has their intellectual work the same force, unexpectedness and certainty it had of old. Nevertheless, these *Parleyings*, at the close of the poet's life, and with biographical touches which give them vitality, enshrine Browning's convictions with regard to some of the greater and lesser problems of human life. And when his personality is vividly present in them, the argument, being thrilled with passionate feeling, rises, but heavily like a wounded eagle, into an imaginative world.

The sub-consciousness in Browning's mind to which I have alluded—that these later productions of his were not as poetical as his earlier work and needed defence—is the real subject of a remarkable little poem at the end of the second volume of the *Dramatic Idyls*. He is thinking of himself as poet, perhaps of that double nature in him which on one side was quick to see and love beauty; and on the other, to see facts and love their strength. Sometimes the sensitive predominated. He was only the lover of beauty whom everything that touched him urged into song.

> "Touch him ne'er so lightly, into song he broke:
>   Soil so quick-receptive,—not one feather-seed,
> Not one flower-dust fell but straight its fall awoke
>   Vitalising virtue: song would song succeed
>   Sudden as spontaneous—prove a poet-soul!"

This, which Browning puts on the lips of another, is not meant, we are told, to describe himself. But it does describe one side of him very well, and the origin and conduct of a number of his earlier poems. But now, having changed his manner, even the principles of his poetry, he describes himself as different from that—as a sterner, more iron poet, and the work he now does as more likely to endure, and be a power in the world of men. He was curiously mistaken.

Indeed, he cries, is that the soil in which a poet grows?

> "Rock's the song-soil rather, surface hard and bare:
>   Sun and dew their mildness, storm and frost their rage
> Vainly both expend,—few flowers awaken there:
>   Quiet in its cleft broods—what the after-age
>   Knows and names a pine, a nation's heritage."

In this sharp division, as in his *Epilogue* to *Pacchiarotto*, he misses the truth. It is almost needless to say that a poet can be sensitive to beauty, and also to the stern facts of the moral and spiritual struggle of mankind through evil to good. All the great poets have been sensitive to both and mingled them in their work. They were ideal and real in both the flower and the pine. They are never forced to choose one or other of these aims or lives in their poetry. They mingled facts and fancies, the intellectual and the imaginative. They lived in the whole world of the outward and the inward, of the senses and the soul. Truth and beauty were one to them. This division of which Browning speaks was the unfortunate result of that struggle between his intellect and his imagination on which I have dwelt. In old days it was not so with him. His early poetry had sweetness with strength, stern thinking with tender emotion, love of beauty with love of truth, idealism with realism, nature with humanity, fancy with fact. And this is the equipment of the great poet. When he divides these qualities each from the other, and is only æsthetic or only severe in his realism; only the worshipper of Nature or only the worshipper of human nature; only the poet of beauty or only the poet of austere fact; only the idealist or only the realist; only of the senses or only of the soul—he may be a poet, but not a great poet. And as the singular pursuit of the realistic is almost always bound up with pride, because realism does not carry us beyond ourselves into the infinite where we are humbled, the realistic poetry loses imagination; its love of love tends to become self-love, or love of mere cleverness. And then its poetic elements slowly die.

There was that, as I have said, in Browning which resisted this sad conclusion, but the resistance was not enough to prevent a great loss of poetic power. But whatever he lost, there was one poetic temper of mind which never failed him, the heroic temper of the faithful warrior for God and man; there was one ideal view of humanity which dominated all his work; there was one principle which directed all his verse to celebrate the struggle of humanity towards the perfection for which God, he believed, had destined it. These things underlie all the poems in *Ferishtah's Fancies* and the *Parleyings with Certain People*, and give to them the uplifted, noble trumpet note with which at times they are animated. The same temper and principle, the same view of humanity emerge in that fine lyric which is the Epilogue to *Ferishtah's Fancies*, and in the Epilogue to *Asolando*.

The first sees a vision of the present and the future in which all the battle of our life passes into a glorious end; nor does the momentary doubt that occurs at the close of the poem—that his belief in a divine conclusion of our strife may only have been caused by his own happiness in love—really trouble his conviction. That love itself is part of the power which makes the noble conclusion sure. The certainty of this conclusion made his courage in the fight unwavering, despair impossible, joy in battle, duty; and to be "ever a fighter" in the foremost rank the highest privilege of man.

Then the cloud-rift broadens, spanning earth that's under,
  Wide our world displays its worth, man's strife and strife's
      success:
All the good and beauty, wonder crowning wonder,
  Till my heart and soul applaud perfection, nothing less.

And for that reason, because of the perfectness to come, Browning lived every hour of his life for good and against wrong. He said with justice of himself, and with justice he brought the ideal aim and the real effort together:

    I looked beyond the world for truth and beauty:
    Sought, found, and did my duty.

Nor, almost in the very grasp of death, did this faith fail him. He kept, in the midst of a fretful, slothful, wailing world, where prophets like Carlyle and Ruskin were as impatient and bewildered, as lamenting and despondent, as the decadents they despised, the temper of his Herakles in *Balaustion*. He left us that temper as his last legacy, and he could not have left us a better thing. We may hear it in his last poem, and bind it about our hearts in sorrow and joy, in battle and peace, in the hour of death and the days of judgment.

At the midnight in the silence of the sleep-time
    When you set your fancies free,
Will they pass to where—by death, fools think, imprisoned—
Low he lies who once so loved you, whom you loved so
        —Pity me?

Oh to love so, be so loved, yet so mistaken
    What had I on earth to do
With the slothful, with the mawkish, the unmanly?
Like the aimless, helpless, hopeless, did I drivel
        —Being—who?

One who never turned his back, but marched breast forward,
    Never doubted clouds would break,
Never dreamed, though right were worsted, wrong would triumph,
Held we fall to rise, are baffled to fight better,
        Sleep to wake.

No, at noonday in the bustle of man's work-time
    Greet the unseen with a cheer!
Bid him forward, breast and back as either should be,
"Strive and thrive!" cry "Speed,—fight on, fare ever
        There as here!"

With these high words he ended a long life, and his memory still falls upon us, like the dew which fell on Paradise. It was a life lived fully, kindly, lovingly, at its just height from the beginning to the end. No fear, no vanity, no lack of interest, no complaint of the world, no anger at criticism, no villain fancies disturbed his soul. No laziness, no feebleness in effort, injured his work, no desire for money, no faltering of aspiration, no pandering of his gift and genius to please the world, no surrender of art for the sake of fame or filthy lucre, no falseness to his ideal, no base pessimism, no slavery to science yet no boastful ignorance of its good, no morbid naturalism, no devotion to the false forms of beauty, no despair of man, no retreat from men into a world of sickly or vain beauty, no abandonment of the great ideas or disbelief in their mastery, no enfeeblement of reason such as at this time walks hand in hand with the worship of the mere discursive intellect, no lack of joy and healthy vigour and keen inquiry and passionate interest in humanity. Scarcely any special bias can be found running through his work; on the contrary, an incessant change of subject and manner, combined with a strong but not overweening individuality, raced, like blood through the body, through every vein of his labour. Creative and therefore joyful, receptive and therefore thoughtful, at one with humanity and therefore loving; aspiring to God and believing in God, and therefore steeped to the lips in radiant Hope; at one with the past, passionate with the present, and possessing by faith an endless and glorious future—this was a life lived on the top of the wave, and moving with its motion from youth to manhood, from manhood to old age.

There is no need to mourn for his departure. Nothing feeble has been done, nothing which lowers the note of his life, nothing we can regret as less than his native strength. His last poem was like the last look of the Phœnix to the sun before the sunlight lights the odorous pyre from which the new-created Bird will spring. And as if the Muse of Poetry wished to adorn the image of his death, he passed away amid a world of beauty, and in the midst of a world endeared to him by love. Italy was his second country. In Florence lies the wife of his heart. In every city he had friends, friends not only among men and women, but friends in every ancient wall, in every fold of Apennine and Alp, in every breaking of the blue sea, in every forest of pines, in every Church and Palace and Town Hall, in every painting that great art had wrought, in every storied market place, in every great life which had adorned, honoured and made romantic Italy; the great mother of Beauty, at whose breasts have hung and whose milk have sucked all the arts and all the literatures of modern Europe. Venice saw and mourned his death. The sea and sky and mountain glory of the city he loved so well encompassed him with her beauty; and their soft graciousness, their temperate power of joy and life made his departure peaceful. Strong and tender in life, his death added a new fairness to his life. Mankind is fortunate to have so noble a memory, so full and excellent a work to rest upon and love.

INDEX

OF PASSAGES RELATING TO THE POEMS

A

ANDRÉ DEL SARTO (A. de Musset), 312
Animal Studies, 83-85, 277
Arnold, Matthew, 2, 6, 11
Art, Poems dealing with, 20-21, 141-176, 301-317
    Romantic Revival in, 161-164
    During the Renaissance, 302-321
Art, Browning's Poetic,
    Compared with that of Tennyson, 38-56
    Compared with that of Morris and Rossetti, 141-143
    In Abt Vogler, 150-153
    In the Grammarian's Funeral, 153-155
    In the Ring and the Book, 391-393
Art, Browning's Theory of,
    In Andrea del Sarto, 156-159, 310-313
    In Pippa Passes, 164-167
    In Sordello, 167-176, 203-211
Aurora Leigh (E. B. Browning), 345

B

BALAUSTION'S Adventures and Aristophanes' Apology,
    Character of the Heroine, 365, 369-372, 377, 384-390
    Contrast between Balaustion and Pompilia, 370-371
    Balaustion's Prologue, 365-369
    The Story of Alkestis, 372-382
    Representation of Aristophanes, 383-384
Becket (Tennyson), 223, 225
Boccaccio, 181-182
Browning, Elizabeth Barrett, 2, 245
    Poems relating to, 249-251, 403-404

Browning—
    His relation to his Age, 1-3, 5, 6, 9, 11-12, 14-15, 21, 30, 201-202
    His artistic Development, 202-208, 210-211, 244, 329-330, 393-397, 422, 429, 435-438
    His Art Poems, 20-21, 141-176, 301-317
    His Minor Characters, 193-195, 231, 391-392, 404-405
    His Sense of Colour, 80-82, 88
    His Composition, 48
    His Cosmopolitan Sympathies, 26-36, 359, 415
    As a Dramatist, 219-241, 325
    As Poet of Humanity, 44-45, 68-69, 79, 106, 115, 218, 249, 348, 402, 433
    His Imagination, 20-21, 148, 282-286, 289, 297, 305, 334, 403, 413, 415, 432, 438
    The Influence of Shelley, 92
    Intellectual Analysis, 11-14, 42, 45-46, 107, 143, 144, 231, 244-245, 325, 393-398, 411, 414-425, 435, 438
    His Love Poems, 242-263, 403-404
    His Lyrical Poems, 241, 245, 246-249, 253, 336, 348-349, 435
    His Methods, 10, 37-38, 82, 150-153, 187-199, 304-305, 325-326, 332-333, 402-403, 418-420
    His Treatment of Nature, 57-114
    His Obscurity, 50, 94, 198-199, 417
    His Originality, 21-24, 49, 91, 115, 276, 416
    His Treatment of the Renaissance, 301-304, 307, 310-311, 313
    Romantic and Classic Elements in, 212-218, 270-279
    His Spontaneity, 16-17, 92, 413
    His Style, 31-33, 49-55, 94, 121, 210-211, 213, 432
    Compared with Tennyson, 1-56, 58, 60-62, 66, 92, 106, 171, 220-226, 280, 281, 323, 345-346, 348, 354, 428
    His Theory of Life, 12-17, 106, 110-112, 115-140, 150, 203-208, 217, 262-263, 428-429, 436, 438, 439-440
    His Wideness of Range, 6, 16, 44, 284, 346
    His Wit and Humour, 32, 240, 265-266, 296, 324, 373, 396, 405, 412
Byron, 34-35, 68, 93, 221, 223, 344

C

CAIN (Byron), 221
Carlyle, 51, 195, 397

Cenci, The (Shelley), 222
Charles the First (Shelley), 222
Chaucer, 219–220
Clough, 2
Coleridge, 35, 62, 68, 93, 104, 221, 344
Colour-sense in Browning, 80–82, 88
Cup, The (Tennyson), 224, 225

D

DANTE, 43, 50, 181, 182, 217
Decameron (Boccaccio), 181
Dramas, The, 219–241
    Absence of Nature Pictures in, 104
    Defects in Browning's Dramatic Treatment, 219–221, 222, 224, 229, 325
    Dramas separately considered, 225–41
Dramatic Poems, 242
Duchess of Malfi (Webster), 270

E

ENGLISH Scenery in Browning, 27–28, 108

F

FALCON, The (Tennyson), 224
Form in Poetry, 47
French Revolution, its Influence in England, 35–6

H

HAND and Soul (Rossetti), 143
Harold (Tennyson), 220, 223
History, Imaginative Study of, 18–20
Homer, 43, 50, 211
Humanity, Browning's Treatment of, 44, 45, 68–69, 79, 106, 115, 218, 249, 348, 402, 433
Humour, Browning's, 32, 240, 265–266, 296, 373, 396, 405, 412
Hunt, Holman, 163

I

IMAGINATION in Browning, 20–21, 148, 282–286, 289, 297, 305, 334, 413, 415, 432

Imaginative Representations, 280-322
    Definition of Term, 280-284
    Their Inception, 285-286
    Theological Studies, 286-300
    Renaissance Studies, 301-322
    Poems on Modern Italy, 322
In Memoriam (Tennyson), 4, 5, 15, 285

K

KEATS, 26, 35, 68, 90, 345
King Lear, 275

L

LANDSCAPES, Browning's, 74-80, 87
Later Poems, 414-430
    More intellectual than imaginative, 414, 416, 417, 418-422, 425
    Subjects generally founded on Fact, 417
    Show Sensitiveness to Criticism, 426
Last Poems, 431-440
    Psychological Studies in, 432-434
Lotos-Eaters, The (Tennyson), 87
Love Poetry,
    What it is and when produced, 242-244
    Rare in Browning, 245-246, 249, 347
Love Poems, The
    Poems of Passion, 246-247, 261
    Poems to Elizabeth Barrett Browning, 63, 245, 249-251, 403-404
    Impersonal Poems, 252-260
    Poems embodying Phases of Love, 261-262
Lyrical Element in Browning, 241, 245, 246-249, 253, 336, 348-349, 435

M

MALORY, 212
Manfred (Byron), 221
Mariana in the South (Tennyson), 28
Maud (Tennyson), 2
Mazzini, 322

INDEX

Midsummer Night's Dream, A, 63, 68
Millais, 163
Milton, 211
Morris, 2, 8, 11, 142
Musset, Alfred de, 312

N

NATURE, Browning's Treatment of, 57-114
    Separate from and subordinate to Man, 60, 86, 97, 101-102
    Joy in Nature, 66-72, 74, 86
    God and Nature, 62, 72, 99, 111-12, 136
    The Pathetic Fallacy, 60, 66-67, 75, 87
    Illustrations drawn from Nature, 70-72
    Browning's view compared with that of other Poets, 25, 27-28, 57, 58, 62, 65, 66, 68, 75, 94, 104
    His Treatment illustrated in Saul, 85, 87
    Faults in his Treatment, 93, 95, 96, 98, 103
    Nature Pictures, 75, 77, 82, 85-87, 93-96, 107, 108, 190-193, 277, 297, 386
    Later Indifference to Nature, 105-107, 109-114
New Age, The (Arnold), 11
Northern Farmer, The (Tennyson), 280

O

Œnone (Tennyson), 87
Originality, Browning's, 21-24, 49, 91, 115, 276.

P

PALACE of Art, The (Tennyson), 124, 170
Paracelsus, 3, 8, 9, 14, 15, 26, 55, 62, 79, 190, 199, 210, 217, 226, 240, 244, 263, 326, 348, 428
    Nature-description in, 67, 83, 84, 96-101
    Theory of Life in, 115-116, 202
    Sketch of Argument, 127-140
Passions, Poems of the Fiercer, 264-270
    Poems of the Romantic, 270-279
Pathetic Fallacy, The, 60, 66-67, 75, 87
Pauline, 21, 28, 79, 87, 88, 104, 190, 244
    Theory of Life in, 15, 115, 116, 120-121
    Nature-description in, 90-96
    Mental Development of Hero, 120-126

Pauline—*continued*
    Character of Pauline, 323–325
Petrarch, 181, 182
Pippa Passes, 4, 9, 195, 225, 240–241, 268–270
    Nature-description in, 30, 77–78, 80
    Theory of Art in, 164–167
    Lyrics in, 273–274
    Studies of Women in, 331–336
Plato, 216
Poems, Passages relating to,
    Abt Vogler, 21, 55, 119, 141, 149–153, 271
    Adam, Lilith and Eve, 355
    After, 266
    Andrea del Sarto, 21, 141, 155–159, 310–313
    Any Wife to any Husband, 352–353
    Aristophanes' Apology, 20, 73, 371–372, 382–390, 415
    Asolando, 3, 109–112, 115, 245–248, 439–440
    Balaustion's Adventure, 20, 365–390, 415
    Bean Stripe, A, 71
    Before, 266–267
    Bells and Pomegranates, 4, 8, 26
    Bifurcation, 256, 427
    Bishop Blougram, 21, 281, 394, 397, 417, 420
    Bishop orders his Tomb at St. Praxed's Church, The, 20, 302, 313
    Blot in the 'Scutcheon, A, 4, 231–235, 338–339
    By the Fireside, 63, 69, 79, 104, 243–245, 247, 249–250
    Caliban upon Setebos, 21, 83, 280, 283, 284, 286–290
    Cavalier Tunes, 28
    Cenciaja, 427
    Charles Avison, 435, 436
    Cherries, 435
    Childe Ronald, 66, 87, 271, 274–276
    Christmas Eve, 21, 75–76, 214
    Cleon, 20, 280, 284, 290–295
    Colombe's Birthday, 226, 235–236, 339–340
    Confessions, 259
    Count Gismond, 261
    Cristina, 255, 349
    Cristina and Monaldeschi, 270
    Daniel Bartoli, 436
    Death in the Desert, A, 3, 21, 30, 283, 296
    De Gustibus, 26

INDEX

Poems—*continued*
- Dis Aliter Visum, 256, 349–351
- Donald, 433
- Dramas, The, 219–241
    - Strafford, 4, 26, 101, 220, 222, 226–228, 326
    - King Victor and King Charles, 228–230, 336
    - The Return of the Druses, 230–231, 336–338
    - A Blot in the 'Scutcheon, 4, 231–235, 338–339
    - Colombe's Birthday, 226, 235–236, 339–340
    - Luria, 236–238, 343
    - A Soul's Tragedy, 225, 238–240, 243
    - Pippa Passes, 4, 9, 30, 77–78, 80, 164–167, 195, 225, 240–241, 268–270, 273–274, 331–336
- Dramatic Idylls, 109, 431–434, 436–437
- Dramatic Lyrics, 242, 344–359, 433
- Dramatic Romances, 242
- Dramatis Personæ, 5, 242

- Easter Day, 21, 33, 126, 141, 145–148
- Echetlos, 431
- Englishman in Italy, The, 27, 65, 82
- Epilogue to Asolando, 111, 439–40
- Epilogue to Ferishtah's Fancies, 439
- Epilogue to Pacchiarotto, 426, 437
- Epistle of Karshish, An, 55, 85, 280, 285, 296–300, 428
- Evelyn Hope, 255, 357

- Fears and Scruples, 427
- Ferishtah's Fancies, 109, 248, 434–435, 439
- Fifine at the Fair, 60, 77, 106, 107, 240–241, 333, 415–417, 419, 422–425
- Filippo Baldinucci, 34, 425
- Flight of the Duchess, The, 78, 271, 274, 276–279, 357–358
- Flower's Name, The, 258, 357
- Forgiveness, A, 267–268, 427
- Fra Lippo Lippi, 21, 280, 282, 283, 285, 302, 304–310
- Francis Furini, 30, 435

- Gerard de Lairesse, 87–89, 109, 435–436
- Glove, The, 262
- Gold Hair, 355
- Grammarian's Funeral, A, 20, 78, 120, 141, 153–155, 317, 319–321

- Halbert and Hob, 433

Poems—*continued*
  Hervé Riel, 29, 415
  Holy Cross Day, 34
  Home Thoughts from Abroad, 10, 27–28
  Home Thoughts from the Sea, 29–30
  How it strikes a Contemporary, 315–317
  How they Brought the Good News from Ghent to Aix, 28

  In a Balcony, 221, 225, 236, 254, 340–343
  In a Gondola, 257
  Inn Album, The, 107, 108, 332, 395, 417, 415, 419, 427
  Instans Tyrannus, 265
  In Three Days, 253
  Italian in England, The, 322, 357
  Ivan Ivanovitch, 432–433
  Ixion, 434

  James Lee's Wife, 60, 79–81, 256, 351–352
  Jochanan Hakkadosh, 34, 434
  Jocoseria, 109, 433, 434
  Johannes Agricola in Meditation, 317–319

  King Victor and King Charles, 228–230, 336

  Laboratory, The, 10, 20, 265, 356
  Last Ride Together, The, 245
  Light Woman, A, 355
  Lost Mistress, The, 256
  Love Among the Ruins, 77, 252–3
  Lovers' Quarrel, A, 69, 82, 257–8
  Luria, 236–238, 343

  Meeting at Night—Parting at Morning, 258–259
  Men and Women, 5, 242
  Mr. Sludge, the Medium, 281, 394, 417, 420–421
  My Last Duchess, 4, 10, 317

  Natural Magic, 427
  Natural Theology on the Island, 21, 83, 280, 283, 284, 286–290
  Ned Bratts, 433
  Never the Time and the Place, 261, 434
  Now, 246
  Numpholeptos, 425

Poems—*continued*
- Old Pictures in Florence, 76, 141, 159-163
- One Word More, 250
  - Pacchiarotto, 108, 425-427, 437
    - ,,   Prologue to, 108, 427
    - ,,   Epilogue to, 437
  - Pan and Luna, 431-432
  - Paracelsus, 3, 8, 9, 14, 15, 26, 55, 62, 67, 79, 83, 84, 96-101, 115-116, 127-140, 164, 190, 199, 202, 210, 217, 226, 240, 244, 263, 271-272, 326, 348, 428
  - Parleyings with Certain People, 3, 87, 434, 435-436, 439
  - Pauline, 15, 21, 28, 79, 87, 88, 90-96, 104, 115, 116, 120-127, 244, 323-326
  - Pearl—A Girl, A, 246-247
  - Pheidippides, 431
  - Pictor Ignotus, 313-315
  - Pied Piper of Hamelin, The, 4, 262
  - Pillar at Sebzevar, A, 435
  - Pippa Passes, 4, 9, 30, 77-78, 80, 164-167, 195, 225, 240-241, 268-270, 273-274, 331-336
  - Pisgah Sights, 427
  - Porphyria's Lover, 10, 326-327
  - Pretty Woman, A, 355
  - Rabbi Ben Ezra, 34, 148-149
  - Red Cotton Nightcap Country, 332, 395, 415, 417, 419, 426
  - Return of the Druses, The, 230-231, 336-338
  - Rêverie, 111
  - Rudel and the Lady of Tripoli, 274
  - St. Martin's Summer, 260, 427
  - Saislaz, La, 59, 109, 429-430
  - Saul, 4, 85-87
  - Serenade at the Villa, A, 260
  - Soliloquy of the Spanish Cloister, A, 20, 266
  - Solomon and Balkis, 355
  - Sordello, 4, 8, 9, 10, 20, 26, 44, 70-71, 87, 88, 101-106, 122, 167-176, 177-199, 200-218, 240, 282, 301, 327-331, 333, 348, 399
  - Soul's Tragedy, A, 225, 238-240, 343
  - Speculative, 246-247
  - Strafford, 4, 26, 101, 220, 222, 226-228, 326

Poems—*continued*
   Summum Bonum, 246-247
   Time's Revenges, 355-356
   Toccata of Galuppi's, A, 21, 321-322
   Too Late, 256, 355
   Transcendentalism, 144-145
   Two in the Campagna, 77, 254
   Two Poets of Croisic, 427-429
   Up in a Villa—Down in the City, 83, 322
   Waring, 4, 10
   Worst of it, The, 355
   Youth and Art, 256

Poet, Characteristics of a, 316-317, 437-438
Poetry
   Grounds of Judgment on, 39-42
   Characteristics of Best, 41-43, 47, 53
   Form in, 47, 53-56
   Matter in, 47
   Thought and Emotion in, 47
Portraiture, Browning's Power of Minute, 193-195, 383-384, 404-405
Prelude, The (Wordsworth), 124
Princess, The (Tennyson), 2, 3, 348
Promise of May, The (Tennyson), 224
Purgatorio, The (Dante), 217

Q

QUEEN MARY (Tennyson), 223

R

RACINE, 373-374
Realism in Browning, 18-20, 331-333
Religious Phases, Poems dealing with, 21, 284-300
Renaissance, The, 182, 301-304, 307, 310-311, 313, 317-320
Renaissance, Poems dealing with the, 305-322, 399
Renan, 287
Revenge, The (Tennyson), 29
Ring and the Book, The
   Nature-description in, 105-106

INDEX

Ring and the Book, The—*continued*
    Its Position among Browning's Works, 391–392, 395–396
    Its Plan, 392–393, 398–399
    Humour and Wit in, 396, 405, 412
    Partly intellectual, partly imaginative, 393–398, 413
    Study of Renaissance in, 399
    Scenery and human Background, 348, 400–402
    Browning's imaginative Method in, 403
    Minor Characters in, 404–405
    Principal Characters
        Guido, 264, 406–407
        Caponsacchi, 406–409
        Pompilia, 359–364, 369–371, 408–410
        The Pope, 410–411
    The Conclusion, 412–413
Rizpah (Tennyson), 280
Robin Hood (Tennyson), 224
Romantic Spirit in Browning, 212–218, 270–279
Rossetti, 2, 6, 11, 142, 143, 163
Ruskin, 60, 80, 302

S

St. Simeon Stylites (Tennyson), 318
Scott, 80, 221, 223
Shakespeare, 34, 43, 50, 52, 220, 223, 287, 288–289
Shelley, 22, 35, 68, 74, 90, 92, 93, 94, 221–222, 344–345
Sir Galahad (Tennyson), 318
Sordello, 4, 8, 9, 10, 20, 26, 44, 70–71, 87, 88, 122, 167, 213, 240–241, 282, 301, 333, 348, 399
    Landscape in, 101–106
    The Temperament of the Hero, 163–171, 183–187
    His artistic Development, 171–176
    The Argument, 171–179
    Historical Background to the Story, 177, 183, 187–190
    Nature Pictures, 190–193
    Portraiture, 193–195
    Illustrative Episodes, 196–198
    Analogy between Sordello and Browning, 200–205, 208–211
    Theory of Art in, 167–176, 203–211

Sordello—*continued*
    Theory of Life in, 203-208, 216-217
    Character of the Heroine, 327-331
Style in Browning, 31-33, 49-55, 94, 121, 210-211, 213, 432
Swinburne, 2, 11

T

TEMPEST, The (Shakespeare), 63, 284, 287-289
Tennyson, 1-56, 58, 60, 61, 66, 68, 74, 80, 92, 98, 104, 106, 124, 170-171, 211-212, 220-221, 222-225, 280, 318, 323, 345-346, 348
Turner, 104, 162
Theory of Life, Browning's, 109-112, 428, 436
    Its main Features, 116-120, 121, 131, 158-159, 203, 217, 249, 262-263, 438-440
    In Pauline, 120-127
    In Paracelsus, 127-140, 202
    In Easter Day, 145-148
    In Abt Vogler, 149-150
    In Andrea del Sarto, 155, 157-159
    In Old Pictures in Florence, 160-161
    In Sordello, 203-208, 217

V

VERGIL, 43, 211, 216
Vita Nuova, La (Dante), 181

W

WILL WATERPROOF's Monologue (Tennyson), 32
Womanhood, Studies of
    In the Early Poems, 323-327
        Pauline, 323-325
        Lady Carlisle, 326
        Palma, 327-330
    In the Dramas, &c., 327-343
        Ottima, 331-332
        Pippa, 334-336
        Anael, 336-338
        Mildred and Guendolen, 338-339
        Colombe, 339-340
        Constance, 340-343

Womanhood—*continued*
>   In the Dramatic Lyrics, 344-359
>   Characteristics of Browning's Women, 346-349
>   Poems to Mrs. Browning, 249-251, 358, 403-404
>   Pompilia, 359-364, 370-371
>   Balaustion, 365-390

Womanhood in the Modern Poets, 344-346

Wordsworth, 35, 57, 58, 59, 65, 68, 75, 93-94, 124, 162-163, 221, 223, 245, 344

14 DAY USE
RETURN TO DESK FROM WHICH BORROWED
LOAN DEPT.

This book is due on the last date stamped below, or on the date to which renewed.
Renewed books are subject to immediate recall.

MAY 23 1966	
	MAY 17 '66
	REC'D LD
NOV 16 1966 20	
RECEIVED	
NOV 4 '66 -10 AM	
LOAN DEPT.	JUN 14 1970 8 3
REC'D LD JUN 9 70 -11AM 7 6	
DEC 12 1975	

LD 21A–60m-10,'65
(F7763s10)476B

General Library
University of California
Berkeley